The Romantic Sublime

THE ROMANTIC SUBLIME: Studies in the Structure and Psychology of Transcendence

THOMAS WEISKEL

The Johns Hopkins University Press
Baltimore and London

The Johns Hopkins University Press, Baltimore, Maryland 21218
The Johns Hopkins University Press Ltd., London

Library of Congress Catalog Card Number 75–36932
ISBN 0–8018–1770–6

Library of Congress Cataloging in Publication data will be found on the
last printed page of this book.

Contents

Foreword

A Personal Introduction

Let Tom say the first words. Some time in the spring of 1973 my husband made this brief response for appearance in his tenth high school reunion publication:

> Essentially, these last years I've been learning and teaching. Next year [1973–74] I'm off on sabbatical leave to write a book, garden, fool with my daughter, Shelburne Heidi, and get enough sleep for the first time since high school. Met my wife, Portia, right after high school—on a romantic island—married after I'd returned from England and she had finished at Radcliffe. She taught English in high school while I got my Ph.D. and we lived by the ocean near New Haven. Now we live in Leverett, a small town in Western Massachusetts, and work hard on what my father calls our "Three Bears hut in the woods." Our life includes horses, dogs, cats, building roofs and barns, gardening with outrageous zeal, food co-ops, children and friends of all stripes. We find life exhausting, difficult, wonderful. Literature is a close second.

Tom worried some during his Yale sabbatical year about writing what he called a "safe" book. He said he felt himself pulled at times toward a book more likely to be successful but also, he felt, more likely to be derivative. But he would not let that happen. I recall many times his telling me that he was unable to write if he felt compelled only by prospective increase of influence, busyness, or academic success. Rather, he was after transcendence, something that would suddenly project him onto a different stage. However appalled he was at times by its pretensions, he finally could write no other book. He wished to serve both criticism and morality and at the same time he felt deeply original impulses working forth; and he found himself in new and strange areas with technical language and symbols not always made clear. His best writing, he sensed, had to have rigor, honesty, yet naïveté, and a certain risk; it could not commend itself by complexity alone: a clear issue had to be at stake. And he could never stay within the text itself, was always after further meaning, depth. This pulled him to sources outside the

NOTE: Professor Thomas Francis Weiskel of the Department of English at Yale drowned with his daughter Shelburne Heidi while the two were skating and sleighing on the lake below their house in Leverett, Massachusetts, on December 1, 1974.

Romantics and brought him to an ever enlarging focus. He could link profound moments in Wordsworth with contemporary physicists' perplexity and awe in the face of black holes and antimatter. His universe had no edges. But with exhilaration came also the risk.

Thus the book in him was not a safe book, nor can my introduction to it be a conventional one. Although it is a privilege seldom granted a wife to introduce her husband's major work, it is a nightmarish task to do so without him here to laugh with me about my inspired flow. And, although I, too, studied the English Romantics, loved especially Keats and Wordsworth, and continue to have intimations of immortality, I prefer instead to write not primarily an introduction to the book but rather something of the man who wrote it.

I should first like to explain why he was living 100 miles north of New Haven. One reason was that we took a look at our two horses, two dogs, three cats and the children, goats, and chickens we planned soon to add and found nowhere near Yale where they would fit. So we moved to a rural town in the Connecticut Valley near Amherst College, where we had already put down roots.

Tom was also what our astrologically oriented friends called the perfect Gemini—he needed and created a double life. He believed very strongly that he should not center himself in the academic world alone, that in order for him to radiate meaning into scholarship through life and experience, another focus of his life had to be elsewhere. Once out there, fully aware and engaged, everything seemed interrelated, nothing was irrelevant.

So he made once a week on Thursday evening that 100 mile trek home. About 7:30 he would come in the door greeted by Bonnie and Jubilation, the two welcoming dogs, swing his satchel full of books and student papers over the chair, hug Shelburne and me, inquire in what way the wry Dumptruck (a cat) and the lazy Gilly (a horse) had been up to no good in his absence, put on the Rolling Stones, very loud, and sit down to a late dinner.

He brought home so many books, papers, stories, concerns—sometimes even the students themselves. His commitment to them, to learning on a grand scale, to learning made personal, was pervasive and felt by all who knew him. One student wrote to me with gratitude to Tom for handing over to others such an expansive sense of the possible. Others, still full of human concern but reacting against the fiercely and sometimes narrowly held political ideologies of just three or four years earlier, thanked Tom for sharing with them his exploration of the subtleties of moral gesture. Another student wrote of her admiration for his unwillingness to be anything less than a total person; he was clear

in his mind about commitment to the people, activities, and learning he
loved most. It was not a complacent contentment, she felt, rather a constantly active creation and participation. And as his family was inter-
woven with his work, so also were his students and love of learning a
central part of our home. His roots were deep in both places, and there
were some gentle and humorous occasions when the two lives inter-
sected, such as the Hallowe'en Eve before her death when our daughter,
holding a long piece of baling twine pinned to the back of her overalls,
telephoned her father in his Yale office, where he was at that moment
deep in conversation about important things, to tell him she was a mouse.

Perhaps the most remarkable thing about Tom was that he ever
wrote the book at all. I do not mean, of course, that he was not capable
or not interested. The book, I know, was in him for at least as long as I
knew him, but I do not think anyone can tell when Tom had time to
write. He took uncommon joy from life and was so ambitious, imaginatively and morally, that he allowed almost nothing to pass before him
without interest, even absorption. The secret was that the book was
brewing in him all the time. I remember a day in early November of his
sabbatical year when we were cutting wood on our land. He seemed
totally absorbed, as usual, delighted with the assurance that we would
have enough wood for the winter. On the way home he quietly told me
that while cutting he had worked out a central argument for his book.
His journal preserves the moment of his discovery of the sublime un-
folded at length in the present book: "I see now—this will be the working
definition of the sublime—it is that moment when the relation between
the signifier and signified breaks down and is replaced by an indeterminate relation." Although in some passages of the journal he seems to
have demystified the sublime, in other moods in the same journal he
reaffirmed his theological sense of the sublime. "Thus," he records later,
"the problem of my life and the problem of my book are one: to find
either a mode of sublimation which does not attenuate what the sublime
pretends to be or a mode of desublimation that is not merely natural."
The book, itself highly structured, reflects this tension.

Tom was finally a deeply religious person, although unattached to
anything as formal as a congregation. "I want belief," he wrote, "need
a cure, but not by denying the mind's rugged skepticism. I am a skeptic,
yet this makes possible, even as it defines, faith. A theology must not
negate Freud, but must begin where he leaves off." It was in active
nature, most of all, in hard and ordinary work and play in garden, field,
and hillside rather than in contemplative solitude, as was true of most
of his Romantic predecessors, that Tom saw most clearly the essentials,
the interrelatedness of things. These moments were intensely religious:

he was always aware of the Creator's power and mystery and ever grateful for the beautiful things put into our lives. I cannot imagine Tom writing in his penetrating and comprehensive way about Romanticism and its distinctive perception of nature and the self had he not been indelibly influenced by his diverse entries into the realm of nature: in the Maine woods, on Star Island off Portsmouth, New Hampshire, in Wales, on our hill in Shelburne over the Deerfield River, and our family home in Leverett with the animals. And it seems fitting to say here that Tom in his death, following by seconds his daughter's, sudden, unfathomable, and tragic, knew in an instant both the sublime and the terror of the nature he wrote about. Inanimate nature is perhaps indifferent, but some creatures, those most humanized by our love, surely participate with us in grief. The great and little beasts with whom we made our home clearly sensed the awesomeness of what had befallen their household. And our friends and family were moved to learn that the world of nature which we loved so much mourned with us, even though that basic element of our planet which makes life possible also claimed their lives.

To whom would Tom have dedicated his book? We cannot know for sure, but we can assume he would have included his parents, who gave him such a profound, religious sense that something large and grand and sacred informed the world; perhaps also his parents-in-law, with whom he enjoyed rich conversation; surely his first daughter, whose birth he participated in almost as fully as I and with whom he so continually renewed his sense of having fun that it seemed at times almost to take over; and his second daughter, whose arrival he anticipated but never experienced.

I imagine also that Tom would have thought to mention at least two of his former teachers at Amherst College whose musings on life he treasured, and certainly his senior colleagues at Yale, notably Professors Harold Bloom and Geoffrey Hartman, who lovingly helped in the preparation of the typescript for the printer; the Fishels of Leverett, who provided the room in their home for his study during the year he wrote the book on the Morse Fellowship; John Joseph, of the Choate School and Shelburne, Massachusetts, with whom we all spent the most idyllic of summer days, discovering remote back roads, odd inns, and savory valley tales; the Andrew Sparks family, who on cool evenings sat with us around the fire, reading aloud from the Molesworth stories; and finally, each treasured friend who spent a summer evening or more with us up at the hut lighted only with lanterns and sometimes the moon shining off the Deerfield River mist below, who gave each in his or her own distinctive way to the sense that our life was enchanted.

Tom once said he needed at least five lifetimes to do all he envisioned. He was not granted the completion of one. It is a relentless horror for me that he and our daughter are not with us. But he used to the full his twenty-nine years and he died as he lived—brave, loving, vulnerable, and with flourish.

I do not know what Tom would say now, but I can guess it might be something like the last sentences he wrote in his final journal entry of the autumn of 1974. He was speaking of the book's possible reception and what he would be doing with his future. He wrote, "I just have to go my own way, work hard, and not waste time thinking about recognition. . . . This book isn't worth everything. . . . I wouldn't trade my life for anyone's."

Earlier in his journals, which he had kept since high school, Tom recorded his musings about himself, his career, and destiny. He wondered whether he was essentially a poet, a novelist, or a philosopher. In the book he has left us, he was not all three in one, but he was much more than a literary critic of the sublime.

Portia Williams Weiskel
Leverett, Massachusetts
June 5, 1975

The Romantic Sublime

Part One: The Sublime Moment

es ist auch meiner Heimat Aether—Hegel

1. *For, as if instinctively, our soul is uplifted by the true sublime; it takes a proud flight, and is filled with joy and vaunting, as though it had itself produced what it has heard.*
—Longinus, *Peri Hypsous*

Approaching the Romantic Sublime

The essential claim of the sublime is that man can, in feeling and in speech, transcend the human. What, if anything, lies beyond the human —God or the gods, the daemon or Nature—is matter for great disagreement. What, if anything, defines the range of the human is scarcely less sure. For Longinus, the human was the domain of art or *techne*; the sublime, just that which eluded the art in our experience of art, the soul of the rhetorical body. The sublime must be referred to nature (*physis*), for "it is by nature that man is a being gifted with speech," but the sublime is a spiritual principle: "in discourse," he says, "we demand that which transcends the human" (36.3).[1] Without some notion of the beyond, some credible discourse of the superhuman, the sublime founders; or it becomes a "problem." This is as true in Romanticism as in antiquity. "The beautiful," says Schiller, "is valuable only with reference to the *human being*, but the sublime with reference to the *pure daemon*" in man, "the statutes of pure spirit."[2] A humanistic sublime is an oxymoron.

Yet here is a fact, perhaps too obvious and unwieldy to make much of: in the history of literary consciousness the sublime revives as God withdraws from an immediate participation in the experience of men. The secondary or problematic sublime is pervaded by the nostalgia and the uncertainty of minds involuntarily secular—minds whose primary experience is shaped by their knowledge and perception of secondary causes. The Romantic sublime was an attempt to revise the meaning of transcendence precisely when the traditional apparatus of sublimation—spiritual, ontological, and (one gathers) psychological and even perceptional—was failing to be exercised or understood. It was the most spectacular response of the literary mind to the dualisms which cut across post-Renaissance thinking and made so much authoritative doctrine suddenly in need of interpretation. It was not least a hermeneutic, a remarkably successful way to read, offering formulas which preserved the authority of the past within the ramified strictures of dualism. It provided a language for urgent and apparently novel experiences of anxiety and excitement which were in need of legitimation. In largest perspective, it was a major analogy, a massive transposition of transcendence into a naturalistic key; in short, a stunning metaphor.

To the eye of the present, everything in the past looks like a compromise between the still further back and the yet to be or the new. That is not how the past felt or was lived, but it is, perhaps inevitably, the way its significance is structured. A metaphor is a compromise struck between the old and the new, between the overwhelming authority of language and the irrepressible anarchy of wit, or whatever principle of unprincipled association makes wit possible. We cannot conceive of a literal sublime. Already in Longinus, *hypsos*, or height, is metaphor presiding over the illusions endemic to reading: we are uplifted as if instinctively, and our proud flight exalts our soul *as though we had created* what we merely heard (7.2). The affective aggrandizement of the sublime moment supports an illusion, a metaphorical union with the creator which suppresses the inferiority of our status as listeners. (Or is it, as Longinus elsewhere implies [17.1–2], the poor worker of words who is inferior and must avoid at all cost raising by his art the suspicions of an all-powerful auditor?) By some such illusion of joining with the creator, we read and learn to think. *Sublime* is one of those terms like *inspiration, vision, apocalypse, imagination,* the *daemonic*—and, of course, *transcendence*—whose continual sublimation into metaphor makes thought possible by enabling us to grasp experience in terms sanctioned by the past—the essential critical gesture, already sophisticated in antiquity. Merely to invoke such terms is to beg many questions; yet the terms are indispensable, for the data of experience cannot be authenticated or even recognized without implicit acts of metaphor. And it is not a purely rational process, a mere abstraction. Behind each act of intellectual metaphor is an imitation, an identification or *mimesis*.

Longinian mimesis has engendered a good deal of wordy pretension, but it has also nourished a perennial and valid response to great writing.[3] Even in Longinus this response has the look of a defense, for hypsos brings "power and irresistible might to bear" (1.4); it aims at transport (*ekstasis*) and is always cloaked in metaphors of aggression. Discourse, in the *Peri Hypsous (On Great Writing)*, is a power struggle. Vivid imagery, for example, is recommended for the "enthrallment" (*ekpleksis*) of the poor reader (15.2), who is scorched, pierced, inundated, blown down, and generally knocked about by the sublime, if Longinus is any guide. At other times the reader is in the feared position. In the subtlest reading the treatise has received, Neil Hertz has found in the text the sketch of an oedipal confrontation in which the auditor as an authority figure is threatened by the artist in the role of a potential usurper.[4] The reader who is also a poet presents a case to which Longinus is especially alert. The poet is uniquely vulnerable to the hypsos of past masters, but his counteroffensive of identification or mimesis can make the power of hypsos his own. In its Romantic transposition, this identification exhibits the precise features of an oedipal crisis, as we shall see. These shifting confrontations, the turns and reversals of literary power, are what seem to be the timeless elements of the sublime, requiring only some kind of auxiliary idealism for their local support.

Yet the Romantic sublime is not only or even primarily Longinian. The still more delimited terrain of the eighteenth-century sublime has been thoroughly explored by a number of scholars working in the train of S. H. Monk's classic history of the sublime as a critical fashion.[5] By now the field is fairly well carved up into distinct emphases upon the "rhetorical," the "natural," the "religious" sublimes, and others.[6] This has been a valuable scholarship, yet it has left us with no perspective which can really claim priority, still less a point of view for the larger drama of Romantic transcendence. The matter of the proper stance deserves some consideration before we get caught up in the story. The challenge is to find the structure that is immanent in a vast and eclectic theory and practice in the conviction, not here to be disguised or much argued, that the structure still undergirds our imaginative intellection.

It is increasingly a commonplace that twentieth-century literary consciousness is a late variant of Romanticism, though little of Romantic doctrine survives. Certainly, as an ideology—as a constellation of themes—the Romantic sublime, which once achieved such prestige in England and then in Germany, is now pretty much dead. It would be hard to overestimate the presence of the Romantic sublime in the nineteenth century. In one direction the sublime opens out through Kant into the vast and gloomy corridors of German idealism. The "dynamical" sublime, which concerns power and sets man and nature in desperate opposition, became an obsessive structure for the German sensibility. In England we observe finer accommodations, in which nature is not merely thrown over but appears as the medium through which the mind discovers and presents itself, in eddies of separation and reunion. Wordsworth's success, equivocal but profound, in gentling the daemonic, opened the subtlest possibilities. And the themes of the sublime might easily draw us outside the world of discourse, or even of art. In Victorian architecture, for example, the sublime was a constitutive idea in the construction of local environments—jails, railway stations, street edifices, public works—whose aggregate was the swarming imperial city.[7]

But we have long since been too ironic for the capacious gestures of the Romantic sublime. When Nietzsche proposed "heights of the soul from which even tragedy ceases to look tragic," he took Romantic hypsos about as far as it can go.[8] Freud was definitely and remarkably immune to the sublime moment, whose "oceanic" and daemonic guises he brilliantly exposed. To please us, the sublime must now be abridged, reduced, and parodied as the grotesque, somehow hedged with irony to assure us we are not imaginative adolescents. The infinite spaces are no longer astonishing; still less do they terrify. They pique our curiosity, but we have lost the obsession, so fundamental to the Romantic sublime, with natural infinitude. We live once again in a finite natural world whose limits are beginning to press against us and may well crush our children. Like Chaucer's Troilus looking down from the eighth sphere, we see in those pictures taken aboard the Apollo spacecraft "this litel spot of erth, that with the see embraced is,"[9] and we know that the ethos of expansion is doomed. We hear in the background of the Romantic sublime the grand confidence of a heady imperialism, now superannuated as ethic or state of mind—a kind of spiritual capitalism, enjoining a pursuit of the infinitude of the private self. "Is not the sublime felt in an analysis as well as in a creation?" asked Emerson.[10] I don't think many analytic intellectuals could now endorse such a claim. In contemporary criticism and the general development of structuralist thinking we are instructed how little, really, of our creations belongs to individual vision and choice. It is against this sense of an increasingly constricted and structured world that the ideology of the sublime looms up retrospectively, as a moribund aesthetic.

There were, of course, modes of aspiration alternative to the sublime within Romanticism. The aesthetic of the beautiful was and is a humanizing influence; as it developed in idealist thought, it came to subvert the very dualisms—of eye and object, spirit and sense—that the sublime presupposed and reinforced. And there is the odd literalism of the visionary tradition, a persistent atavism which found in Blake a major representative. We are never wholly sure in reading Blake that he did not understand something like imagination quite literally after all. Evidently Blake could still see the immensities of inner space from outside. The natural sublime established inner space by a conceptual metaphor in which the immeasurability of physical space was linked to the infinitude of our supersensible faculty. For Blake, both dimensions of space, outer and inner, were fused in the pernicious totality of "Female Space," which is "Limited to those without but Infinite to those within."[11] "Female Space" stands over and against "the Organs of Life," since it is predicated, as we shall see in Kant, on the defeat of the imagination. Blake hated the indefinite, rejected the numinous, and insisted on the primacy of the imagination. His work makes a profound critique of the natural sublime.

But is it a critique that we can adopt in good faith? Kant, the chief philosopher of the sublime, would have called Blake a victim of fanaticism (*Schwärmerei*), a kind of monomania "deep-seated and brooding," which Kant saw as intellectual sickness. Fanaticism "is a delusion that would insist on SEEING something out beyond all the bounds of sensibility, i.e., would dream according to principles (rave rationally)." What outrages Kant is the visionary's claim that the unconditioned can be (and must be) *seen*, realized through perception: "for the *inscrutability of the idea of freedom* precludes all positive presentation."[12] Blake's enmity to the inscrutability which always attends the numinous could not be more extreme. It is not over the question of rationality that the sublime and the visionary are joined in opposition. *Nach Grundsätzen träumen* could serve loosely as the motto of the radical, visionary tradition in which Blake follows Milton and Spenser. (Here is an incidental burden of our argument, the illumination of the divide between the sublime and the visionary; it is a running theme which tends to present itself when the giant forms of Blake and Wordsworth rise up on opposite sides of our path.) Though the visionary tradition can be focused to a sharp indictment of perceptional sublimation, there are obvious objections to its mere invocation by a writer not in any sense a visionary. Blake must here play an ancillary, critical role.

"What burden then?"

It is not as theme or image, ideology or ethic that the sublime still speaks to us. In the past few years a compelling preoccupation has arisen rather sharply in the more advanced academic criticism of Romantic writing. We always knew it was there, but we are still surprised by its evident importance. I am referring of course to the constellation of concerns deftly articulated in W. Jackson Bate's elegant book *The Burden of the Past and the English Poet* and in the major allied inquiries of Harold Bloom, Geoffrey Hartman, Thomas McFarland, and others.[13] In one sense the Romantic sublime begins with the discovery of an ancient rhetorician who could authorize an escape from the ancients. Longinus's *Peri Hypsous* was translated and publicized in 1674. Milton had known Longinus and made little of him; he had no need to. What created an immediate and growing audience for Longinus was the dilemma or anxiety of modernism.

As a state of mind, modernism is an incurable ambivalence about authority—in the literary case, the authority of priority conferred on past poets by the immensity of their achievement. Experience and authority are ancient adversaries—we think of the Wife of Bath—yet they had never confronted each other in quite the same way before. Conflict is not necessarily ambivalence, and it is perfectly possible for a transitional critic like John Dennis to invoke now authority and now experience with no anxiety about their potential contradiction.[14] (By the middle of the century Burke is simply rejecting the "false lights" of received doctrine in favor of "an easy observation of the most common, sometimes of the meanest things in nature" in his own naturalistic theory of the sublime; "art," he says, "can never give the rules that make an art."[15]) What is new in modernism is an opposition, latent at first, but unavoidable, between authority and authenticity, between imitation, the traditional route to authentic identity, and originality, impossible but necessary. The poet's is a specially intense case of an ambivalence which is ramified throughout the culture of modernism.

In 1674 also appeared the twelve-book edition of *Paradise Lost*, which was to preside with Boileau's Longinus over the fashion of the sublime.[16] Harold Bloom has found in the Satan of the early books the essential predicament of the modern poet.[17] Satan and the fallen angels have been *deidentified*; for some reason inexplicable to themselves if not to Milton, they cannot be themselves and stay in heaven. "For what place" says Mammon, "can be for us / Within heaven's bound, unless heaven's lord supreme / We overpower?" (*PL* 2.235–37).[18] It is less the subjection than the boredom of heaven's "splendid vassalage" that Mammon finds or pretends to find so intolerable. To celebrate the Father with "warbled hymns" and "Forced hallelujahs" is both tedious and humiliating: "how wearisome / Eternity so spent in worship paid / To whom we hate" (2.241–49). Mammon and Belial, two halves of the incipient bourgeois consciousness, are persuasive in their programs for life in hell, though their advice is laced with illusions such as the progressive utopianism which neither can resist (2.210–25, 274–78). Their dilemma is Satan's, but he is made of sterner, more archaic stuff. His ambition, the necessary logic of power, locks him into the sort of competition with the Father that bourgeois resignation, accepting a displaced arena of activity, can largely evade. The result is a genuine ambivalence in which identity must be at once ascribed to the Father and won from him:

> Ah wherefore! He deserved no such return
> From me, whom he created what I was
> In that bright eminence, and with his good
> Upbraided none; nor was his service hard.
> What could be less than to afford him praise,
> The easiest recompense, and pay him thanks,
> How due! Yet all his good proved ill in me,
> And wrought but malice; lifted up so high
> I sdeigned subjection, and though one step higher
> Would set me highest, and in a moment quit
> The debt immense of endless gratitude,
> So burdensome still paying, still to owe;
> Forgetful what from him I still received,
> And understood not that a grateful mind
> By owing owes not, but still pays, at once
> Indebted and discharged; what burden then? [4.42–57]

Satan cannot really answer his own question, except by appealing to an inner necessity for which—the last irony—he has only his Father's terms. At the least, he is thinking in one psycho-logic and feeling in another; that he felt as burden his endless indebtedness cannot be justified or explained, and he knows it.

It is often averred that individualism, with its economic corollary, capitalism, bears the marks of an original sin against authority. Robinson Crusoe, type of economic man, in effect is forced to follow the advice of Mammon, who said that we seek

> Our own good from ourselves, and from our own
> Live to ourselves, though in this vast recess
> Free, and to none accountable, preferring
> Hard liberty before the easy yoke
> Of servile pomp. Our greatness will appear
> Then most conspicuous, when great things of small,
> Useful of hurtful, prosperous of adverse
> We can create, and in what place so e'er
> Thrive under evil, and work ease out of pain
> Through labor and endurance. [2.253–62]

Crusoe's is a choice and yet not a choice, for he is urged by his uneasiness, an "evil influence" he can neither understand nor resist, to
disobey his father and exile himself—an act he names his "original sin."
Milton had encompassed the psychological guilt of modernism with
theological terms, but for whiggish moderns like Defoe, three worlds—
social, psychological, and theological—were becoming estranged, and
the locus of authority was uncertain. The guilt of an original disobedience
remained, but authority no longer ensured correction or disaster. It was
becoming disastrous *not* to leave home, strike out on one's own, try to be
original. The founding gesture of the ego was becoming the requisite for
success. In the end, Crusoe makes much more money than he would
have made staying obediently at home and accepting his father's lot.
Hence guilt, no longer actualized as a nemesis immanent in the world
or in a course of events, becomes in various ways unconscious.

The poet's dilemma was more stringent than that of the secular
individualist if only because the poet could afford less dissociation, less
inner estrangement. In confuting Abdiel, Satan had resorted to denial,
the most primitive of defenses:

> . . . who saw
> When this creation was? Remember'st thou
> Thy making, while the maker gave thee being?
> We know no time when we were not as now;
> Know none before us, self-begot, self-raised
> By our own quickening power. . . .   [5.856–61]

But this illusion is no doubt designed for the comsumption of his rebellious confederates; when Satan is alone he knows better, as we have
seen. Now the sublime offers far more sophisticated defenses—versions
of "family romance"—against the fact of origins, which is always veiled
by amnesia, and against the obscure guilt which is the surest signal of
those origins. The "proud flight" of the soul, "filled with joy and vaunting, as though it had itself produced what it has heard," appears at once
to acknowledge authority and to fulfill identity. How is this possible?
Not, I submit, through any idealism that denies the fact and the burden
of indebtedness, but rather through an amazing and subtle metaphor
whose larger narrative form has been marked indelibly by Freud as the
oedipus complex. Bate ends his book with a moving invocation of the
"vision of greatness" which was, he says, Longinus's prime value to the
eighteenth century and to us:

> The essential message of Longinus is that, in and through the personal
> rediscovery of the great, we find that we need not be the passive

victims of what we deterministically call "circumstances" (social, cultural, or reductively psychological-personal), but that by linking ourselves through what Keats calls an "immortal free-masonry" with the great we can become freer—freer to be ourselves, to be what we most want and value; and that by caring for the kinds of things that they did we are not only "imitating" them, in the best and most fruitful sense of the word, but also "joining them."[19]

Bate knows and has just been measuring the risks of such a faith, but he chooses for final emphasis "the creative and formative essentialism" of the ideal as the ultimate answer to the burden of the past. The essential transcendence of the humanist has not been put more simply or clearly in our time.

The following study seeks to expose the structure implicit in the act of "joining" with the great. An idealism is a metaphor in which one believes, but the question of belief (and its contrary, a deidealizing scepticism) is less compelling and relevant than it seems at first. The matter is too large not to admit the irresistible influence of temperament, but too important to be determined by it. A structure as capacious as the oedipus complex can host enthusiasm and despair. What we wish to isolate and analyze is a moment—call it the sublime or original moment— in which a burden (of the past, but not exclusively) is lifted and there is an influx of power. We might begin with the hypothesis that the encounter with literary greatness—the so-called rhetorical sublime—is structurally cognate with the transcendence, gentle or terrible, excited in the encounter with landscape, the "natural" sublime. This is not so outrageous an idea as it at first appears. In Burke's *Of the Sublime and Beautiful*, for example, the only allusion to Longinus is to just the "proud flight" passage we have been privileging, and it establishes a connection between scenes of terror and the "true sublime" in the poets.[20] In any case, our hypothesis commits us to a search for a structure beneath the vast epiphenomena of the sublime.

It is not, however, possible to write completely exoterically. Philology teaches, or used to teach, that the history of ideas is a history of metaphors made and remade; so, too, the history of criticism. It is difficult to be wholly clear about the logical status of the metaphorical moment we seek. The conflict subsumed in a major metaphor may only be inferred, but to take the metaphor for the lived reality is to neglect the presentness of the past, the fact that it too was once a moment of origin, an instant before the metaphor crystallized. Or was it? The image of thinker or poet standing as a third term in triangular opposition to discourse (language), on the one hand, and experience (sensation and its unconscious derivatives), on the other, has an impossibly abstract look. It may be that the original moment is always just next to us, but it cannot be definitively specified or pinned in a temporal sequence, except hypothetically. For the historian, the moment of macro- or micro-origin is usually a retrospective construction designed both to secure and to assuage a necessary alienation from the past. Throughout the analytical tradition the sublime moment tends to have a typical or fictional status. The dialectic of continuity and originality can only be resolved in a fiction of some kind, and it may be that the origin, like a screen memory, is a compromise between what we cannot fail to know and what we need to believe—the latter usually a mystery to ourselves. We write, in short, about modernism from within some version of it.

The Eighteenth-Century Sublime

The fashion of the sublime had many tributaries, and it is idle to try to arrange a definitive priority of cause and concomitant. Undoubtedly the "vision of greatness" was, as Bate says, Longinus's deepest appeal, but it was the close association of the natural and the transcendent, or superhuman, that made the vision readily assimilable in the changing culture of eighteenth-century England. In Longinus's text, hypsos is a quality immanent in great writing which refers us to eternity (aion); it is not distinction itself, but that which produces distinction; it is immediately communicable between author and reader (hearer) because it transcends the local determinants of culture, language, and technique. Hence it is the resource and the goal of great-souled men, especially in times of cultural degeneracy. Hypsos may be attained through the mimesis and emulation of the masters. Longinus's Platonism is evident, and he was also influenced by the Stoic conception of Nature (physis) as the demiourgos, the "artificer of man" (43.5), who "implants in our souls the unconquerable love of whatever is elevated and more divine than we" (35.2). Nature is beneficent and methodical, and it is thus possible to speak of her art as the ground of that which is beyond human or technical art. Technique, however, is also a necessary condition of the sublime (2), and indeed, rhetorical prescription occupies the bulk of the surviving manuscript. The five "sources" of the sublime mentioned in chapter eight—vigorous mental conception; strong and inspired emotion; the employment of just figures; nobility of diction; and comprehensively, synthesis, or composition that is exceptional—are not homologous and in fact exhibit the confusion of nature and art, author and work, which will become the trademark of the Longinian or affective critic.

Certain passages plucked from the Peri Hypsous seemed tailored to fit the congeries of influences working to realign fundamental relations, to nature and to words, in the eighteenth century. Longinus had made Nature the demiurge responsible not only for man's physical being but also for that which "transcends the human"—thought, imagination, speech (*logos*). This emphasis was congenial to the English mind, for it seemed to authorize an alternative to the more reductive and empirical conception of the natural which was gaining ground. It was a way of having it both ways, a transcendence without any controversial theology, a natural religion. From Addison to Shelley a passage like the following famous one could be approved:

> Wherefore not even the entire universe suffices for the thought and contemplation within the reach of the human mind, but our imaginations often pass beyond the bounds of space, and if we survey our life on every side and see how much more it everywhere abounds in what is striking, and great, and beautiful, we shall soon discern the purpose of our birth. This is why, by a sort of natural impulse, we admire not the small streams, useful and pellucid though they be, but the Nile, the Danube or the Rhine, and still more the Ocean.
>
> [35.3–4]

Longinus was virtually unknown in the Renaissance and rarely read in the seventeenth century. When he was rather suddenly revived by a number of critics following Boileau, it soon appeared that he could be invoked to provide a vocabulary for a powerful experience whose origins are obscure. This was an exciting and apparently novel moment of heightened or intensified consciousness, strangely allied to anxiety and commonly evoked by the spectacular and wild in nature or by a vivid impression of supernatural beings such as the ghosts and demons recently banished from the civilized mind.[21] Around the Longinian "transport" congealed a psychologically correlative vocabulary: "awe-full," "amazement," "astonishment," and so on. Monk was the first to review with precision and sensitivity the mass of speculation that grew up at this intersection of a first-century rhetorician and a modern affect. Reviewing Monk's work, R. S. Crane divided theoretical versions of the sublime into two distinct traditions—a properly rhetorical criticism directly inspired by Longinus and a nascent psychological aesthetics concerned with the pleasures of the imagination.[22] But aesthetic speculation in the eighteenth century was enthusiastically eclectic. The line is not sharp between rhetorical critics like Dennis, the Wartons, the originalist Young, and psychological critics like Addison, Burke, and Reid. No categorical distinction between life and art could be erected on Locke's psychology. Critics tended to fall back on Addison's notion of art as a "secondary" pleasure of the imagination, dependent on the "primary" impressions ever decaying in the memory and limited in its fictions by the exclusively combinatory powers of the imagination.[23] Even Kant is seduced into the view that the sublime in art must always be governed by the conditions of its agreement with nature.[24]

The natural sublime was developing independently of literary influence. In one sense, it was a response to the darker implications of Locke's psychology and what that psychology represented of changes in perception. If the only route to the intellect lies through the senses, belief in a supernatural Being finds itself insecure. God had to be saved, even if He had to marry the world of appearances. And so, in the natural sublime, He did. The first development, in the seventeenth century, was the identification of the Deity's traditional attributes—infinity, immensity, coexistence—with the vastness of space newly discovered by an emergent astronomy.[25] The emotions traditionally religious were displaced from the Deity and became associated first with the immensity of space and secondarily with the natural phenomena (oceans, mountains) which seemed to approach that immensity.[26] Soon a sense of the numinous was diffused through all the grander aspects of nature. The mental result was enormously to enhance the prestige of the sensible imagination as the faculty which mediated the divine presence felt to be immanent in nature, or at least likely to be evoked by nature's grander aspect. Indeed, the imagination became the surest guide and recourse for the moral sense.

There were, however, currents more turbulent and less visible running through the Lockean psychology. Locke had removed the soul from the circuit of analogical relations in which it had been installed, thereby decisively displacing the locus of order. Monk finds in John Baillie's discussion of the sublime (1747) the crucial transitional moment when speculation withdrew from the search for sublimity in the object and began to be centered in the emotions of the subject. We might linger over the passage Monk quotes:

> But as a *Consciousness* of her [the soul's] own *Vastness* is what pleases, so nothing raises this Consciousness but a *Vastness* in the *Objects* about which she is employed. For whatever the *Essence* of the *Soul* may be, it is the *Reflections* arising from *Sensations* only which makes [*sic*] her acquainted with Herself, and know her *Faculties*. Vast objects occasion vast Sensations, and vast sensations give the Mind a higher Idea of her own Powers—small scenes (except from Association . . .) have never this Effect; . . . the *Soul* is never filled by them.[27]

The passage is typical of early associationist psychology, and it is worth remarking the metaphorical structures Baillie assumes, for they undergird the natural sublime in its simplest form. The "essence" of the soul is now unknowable or even hypothetical; Locke had emptied it out. The soul is a vacancy, whose extent is discovered as it is filled. Inner space, the infinitude of the Romantic mind, is born as a massive and more or less unconscious emptiness, an absence. Curiously, the mind receives an idea of its own powers in an event to which it apparently makes no conscious or voluntary contribution. Objects "occasion" sensations, and sensations quite automatically produce reflections, which may in turn be recognized in consciousness. The soul is the space in which these "sublimations" occur, but it has no constitutive effect upon the relation between sensation and reflection. This relation is unmotivated, as the metaphor buried in "reflection" suggests, and it is in fact a metaphorical and semiotic relation between two incommensurable terms: a vast sensation *signifies* (because it is somehow like) a vast faculty. If the semiotic code or "association" were changed, a small sensation could signify a vast faculty. Order in this scheme consists of the constant, though arbitrary, relation between sensation and reflection, a relation certified by language—here the word *vast*. Consciousness is thus set over and against order, as a spectator who plays no role and cannot interfere; yet it has no self-knowledge outside of this order. If the sensations are withdrawn, consciousness knows only a vacancy.

We might infer that a rather crude associationism has supplanted analogy in the structure of reflective perception. *Vast* in one domain or discourse simply equals *vast* in another. What makes this possible is an unexamined convention that the meaning of words lies solely in the way they are used, for in principle an appeal beyond language to Nature has no logical ground. Locke was among the first to see the implications of this point of view, which is, of course, very much alive in contemporary structuralism. What, it may be asked, is to prevent the indefinite extension of words and their illegitimate combination in propositions beyond verification? Locke would like to confine the abuse of words to errors within the domain of order: a sign (sound-sensation) ought to be allied to a clear and distinct idea (reflection) in a strictly observed congruence. Order is thus entirely psychological (a relation within the mind), but stable, because arbitrary. But there is no assurance, in Locke's view, that the "ideas" correspond to the forms of reality: "That everything has a real constitution, whereby it is what it is, and on which its sensible qualities depend, is past doubt; but I think it has been proved that this makes not the distinction of species as *we* rank them, nor the boundaries of their names."[28] Nature or reality is undifferentiated and

stands over and against order. Locke himself fends off the obvious consequence of his view by recommending, rather half-heartedly, a dic-
tionary which would indicate by a picture the idea of every sign.[29] He
fails to see that this scheme merely relates one sign to another. A dic-
tionary, like an Academy, would merely institutionalize the social consensus that is the ground of signification.

Now the sublime plays a critical role in the semiotic economy of the
eighteenth century. In poetry and in theory the sublime becomes associated not with the clear and the distinct but with the vague and the
obscure; hence it wears the aspect of a radical alternative to the visual
emphasis of Lockean psychology and to the decorous precision of neo-
classical diction.[30] Yet, in fact, the sublime merely plays out a logic
implicit in the classical notion of signification. Burke, for example, has
no trouble basing his own evocative theory of diction on Locke's treatment of words, for the premise of such a theory—that words have no
necessary ("natural") connection with things—is already conceded by
Locke. "Nothing," says Burke, "is an imitation further than as it resembles some other thing; and words undoubtedly have no sort of resemblance to the ideas for which they stand." From this it follows that
poetry is not, strictly speaking, an imitative art, and *descriptive* poetry in
particular "operates chiefly by *substitution*; by the means of sounds,
which by custom have the effect of realities."[31] We properly associate
the divorce of *res* and *verba* with the program of the scientific moderns,
to which Locke is responsive, but this divorce lies at the base of the sublime, too. Scientific thinking and the aesthetic of the sublime are correlative expressions of an episteme in which order is arbitrary, a matter
of hypothesis, or as Burke says, of custom.

The theory of diction is intimately tied to the chief philosophical obsession of the age, the relation between ideas (reflections) and sensation.
Could it be that just as the logic of language is essentially independent
of ideas, so the ideas themselves are structurally independent of sensations? Anyone who has read in the period knows the various apparatus
invented to construe and resolve the problem. It is certainly more difficult
to concede the constitutive role of custom in the substitution of ideas for
sensations. For us it has become axiomatic that the data of sensation
cannot be organized into an idea without the mediation of language: we
do not define a mountain out of a perceptual field without the term
"mountain." But the integrity of the ideas was taken for granted in
Lockean psychology, and disturbances among them—obscurity, fantastic
combination, variation in intensity—were referred in general to the effect
of the passions. So Burke argues that obscurity has a greater affective

appeal than clarity, which "is in some sort an enemy to all enthusiasms whatever." In nature, "dark, confused, uncertain images have a greater power on the fancy to form the grander passions than those have which are more clear and determinate." This is so because "it is our ignorance of things that causes all our admiration, and chiefly excites our passions. Knowledge and acquaintance make the most striking causes affect but little."[32] Hence the sublime comes to be associated both with the failure of clear thought and with matters beyond determinate perception. It is not a radical alternative but a necessary complement to a psychology that stressed its own limits.

The true function of the sublime is to legitimate the necessary discontinuities in the classical scheme of signification and to justify the specific affective experience which these discontinuities entailed. Baillie had assumed an equivalence of vast object, vast sensation, and the mind's "higher Idea of her own Powers," but this equivalence could not be naively construed if the mind were to have any autonomy or self-consciousness. Actually, a deeper analysis was to prevail. "It is curious," says Monk, "that Baillie should consider difficulty to be derogatory to the sublime," for a contrary emphasis on "pain and difficulty *overcome* in the apprehension of vast objects" grew to be general.[33] The "difficulty" so central in Burke, Kant, and others is the affective correlative of a semiotic discontinuity in the inexplicable passage between one order or discourse and another. A general semiotic of the sublime would find, I think, the same discontinuity between sensation and idea as between idea and word—this is, at any rate, the substance of my hypothesis in fusing the natural and rhetorical sublimes.

In the alliance of the sublime and the pathetic we can discern the economic importance of the gaps, or lacunae, in the Lockean semiotic. The experience of a discontinuity produces a momentary conflict or anxiety in the mind. The affective life of the eighteenth century is somewhat alien to us, no doubt because our own feeling has largely been educated by Romanticism. Nevertheless we have the impression—it is no more than that—that several experiences, notably boredom and anxiety, assumed their modern, secular quality at this time. The role of one kind of traumatic anxiety or terror is so prominent in Burke's theory of the sublime that we may be distracted from subtler manifestations. What is the state of the soul before it is "filled," as Baillie and others say? If the soul is the locus of order and has no essential substance independent of the ideas it entertains, the moment of discontinuity will reveal a frightening vacancy. The Lockean model subverts the autonomy of mind or soul; the mind is not its own place, but the space in which semiotic sublimations occur. It cannot control the making of meaning, though increasingly the imagination is granted a limited autonomy, a license to compose the ideas in novel combinations.

Locke himself, in the revision of the *Essay concerning Human Understanding*, began to recognize how his evacuation of the soul had undermined the doctrine of the will. He withdrew his concurrence in the received view that the greatest good determines the will and founded his system of motivation on *uneasiness*.[34] All desire is "uneasiness in the want of an absent good." The will arises from the perception of absence. Uneasiness or anxiety is the affective correlative of the inner vacancy, and it accounts for all activity in this homeostatic view. "But so much as there is anywhere of desire, so much there is of uneasiness." Anxiety will always exceed its occasion because the soul can never be entirely filled by the sensations and reflections which arise from an object "out there"—an object whose essential absence is presupposed by perception. On the other hand, the soul has no direct commerce with itself; it is dependent for self-knowledge upon the ideas. "Another reason why it is uneasiness alone determines the will, is this: because that alone is present and, it is against the nature of things, that what is absent should operate where it is not." Anxiety replaces the will as the principle of individuation. These are moving, somewhat melancholy pages, for Locke has discovered a modern form of anxiety. "Life itself, and all its enjoyments, is a burden cannot be borne under the lasting and unremoved pressure of such an uneasiness." In his view that the phenomenology of anxiety must center on absence, Locke directly anticipates Freud, as indeed he does in several other matters.[35]

A history of anxiety is a prime desideratum in humanistic studies, and we shall later explore some episodes of that history in the psychology of the sublime. Clearly, the sublime was an antidote to the boredom that increased so astonishingly throughout the eighteenth century. Addison had celebrated the *Uncommon* along with the *Great* and the *Beautiful* (*Spectator*, no. 412), and Burke began his treatise by laying down a premise that the passions are never engaged by the familiar. Boredom masks uneasiness, and intense boredom exhibits the signs of the most basic of modern anxieties, the anxiety of nothingness, or absence. In its more energetic renditions the sublime is a kind of homeopathic therapy, a cure of uneasiness by means of the stronger, more concentrated—but momentary—anxiety involved in astonishment and terror. Yet the eighteenth-century sublime presents no sustained critique of the dissociated sensibility which generates an alienation from "those things which a daily and vulgar use have brought into a stale unaffecting familiarity," as Burke put it.[36] It was Wordsworth who first attempted to assimilate the perception of everyday reality to the affective structure of the sublime in his great program of defamiliarization.

The dissociation or dualism at the core of the eighteenth-century sublime had profoundly ideological implications, and the various forms of alienation reinforced by the sublime—between the familiar and the novel, the human and the natural, the low and the high—could not be shaken until these ideological correlatives were questioned in the ferment of social revolution. Yet the sublime moment brought the high and the low into dangerous proximity, as the great Augustan reactionaries perceived at the beginning of the century. Connections clear to the Tory satirists have since been obscured by Romanticism, but the peculiar complexes of psychological and social tendencies that coalesced in the pilloried form of Swift's Modern and (still more grotesquely) in Pope's dunces were not conceived eccentrically. In their conceptions of order and of signification, Pope and Swift appealed implicitly to a scheme older than what we have called the classical or Lockean semiotic. In the traditional rhetorical doctrine of the humanists from whom Pope and Swift descended, words did imitate or participate in things; the authority of language, as of social order, was not arbitrary but natural. To confound words was to confound reality and to disturb nature as well as the social order.

There are two ways to tamper with the received "natural" meanings of signs which have constituted the heart of order. The first is to open a gap between word and thing, which was, roughly speaking, the program of the scientific "moderns" and which Pope made the passionate project of dullness in the fourth book of the Dunciad. The second is to use words out of their accustomed, "natural" order, to violate decorum. Decorum might be construed as an ideological version of Longinus's synthesis, "a harmony of that language which is implanted by nature in man and which appeals not to the hearing only but to the soul itself" (39.3). Pope was certainly alive to the discontinuities that pervaded his culture, but he feared that the nascent aesthetic of the sublime was about to embrace them in the wrong way. In Longinus, bathos is more or less an equivalent of hypsos (2.1); Pope persuasively reinvents the word. Bathos is an "anti-natural way of thinking."[37] The aspirant to bathos or "the true Genius for the Profound" is to

> mingle bits of the most various, or discordant kinds, landscape, history, portraits, animals, and connect them with a great deal of flourishing, by heads or tails, as it shall please his imagination. . . . His design ought to be like a labyrinth, out of which nobody can get clear but himself. And since the great Art of all Poetry is to mix

Truth with Fiction, in order to join the *Credible* with the *Surprising*; our author shall produce the Credible, by painting nature in her lowest simplicity; and the Surprising, by contradicting common opinion. In the very Manners he will affect the *Marvellous*; he will draw Achilles with the patience of Job; a Prince talking like a Jackpudding; a Maid of honour selling bargains; a footman speaking like a philosopher; and a fine gentleman like a scholar. Whoever is conversant in modern Plays, may make a most noble collection of this kind, and, at the same time, form a complete body of *modern Ethics and Morality*.[38]

Yet the greatest master of bathos in the language is unquestionably Pope. The mock-heroic is a brilliant, self-conscious exploiting of bathos; all that prevents the worlds of words and things from spinning wildly apart is irony, and the irony becomes, through the *Dunciad*, increasingly violent.[39] The mock-heroic is such a precarious and inimitable achievement because it depends upon the very discontinuities in the structure of signification whose illegitimate confusion it protests. When irony falters, Pope is in danger of lapsing (or rising) to the evocative writing of the true sublime, as in the nightmare of the last lines of the *Dunciad*. Only irony, not any alternative semiotic, separates bathos and the true sublime. Indeed, in the ironic notion of bathos the mock-heroic and the aesthetic of the sublime converge: both are responses to the fission of word and thing, or signifier and signified.

Bathos, or the art of the profound, is at the heart of the Wordsworthian revision of the sublime. The programmatic confusion in Wordsworth's theory of diction has often been remarked, perhaps best by Coleridge, who saw that his colleague had dissolved order and in fact institutionalized bathos. But Coleridge's criticism of Wordsworth, acute and conservative as it is, has a way of remarking just those elements in Wordsworth which appeal to us most radically. He cites, as one of Wordsworth's defects, "thoughts and images too great for the subject . . . a disproportion of thought to the circumstance and occasion." As a first instance:

> For oft, when on my couch I lie
> In vacant or in pensive mood,
> They flash upon that inward eye
> Which is the bliss of solitude.

"In what words," says Coleridge,

> shall we describe the joy of retrospection, when the images and actions of a whole well-spent life, pass before that conscience which is indeed the *inward* eye: which is indeed *"the bliss of solitude?"*

Assuredly we seem to sink most abruptly, not to say burlesquely, and almost as in a *medley*, from this couplet to—
And then my heart with pleasure fills,
And dances with the daffodils.[40]

Coleridge appears to miss cleanly the pathos of the poem, which is inseparable from its bathos. The joys of solitude culminate in an imaginative community with nature at her simplest and humblest, a union impossible in the actual presence of nature ("I gazed—and gazed—but little thought / What wealth the show to me had brought"),[41] a wealth founded on absence. Bathos, in Wordsworth's leveling muse, becomes expressive pathos.

We are no longer too sure about what is high and what is low, not least because of Wordsworth's revolution; certainly we are no longer plunged into bathos by daffodils. Yet our experience remains riddled by discontinuities, and the sublime or something like it, as well as the bathetic or something like it, will always be found in the ill-defined zones of anxiety between discrete orders of meaning. In the sublime moment, we are on the verge of or in passage to a "higher" meaning; in bathos, our laughter is a defense against the anxiety of losing or falling out of what meaning we've got—it is directed at the unfortunate who has fallen out of the great social bond without knowing it. Clearly the opposition of higher and lower, and indeed of meaning and nonsense, is critically determined by ideological presuppositions. But I think there may be a structure to the sublime that transcends its local determinants.

We might begin by inquiring whether it is possible to *de*idealize the Romantic sublime, since transcendent idealism of one kind or another no longer seems as inevitable for aesthetics as it once did. Actually, attempts to *think through* the sublime—as opposed to historical commentary—are surprisingly rare, at least since the idealist tradition of Kant, Hegel, and epigoni like A. C. Bradley. (The bathetic may be assimilated to the comic, and is in better theoretical shape.) We have, however, useful suggestions, such as Paul Goodman's definition of the sublime as "actual experience of a tendency of combinations to break the aesthetic surface"[42]—a formulation which diametrically reverses Longinus's emphasis on organic continuity. Goodman's fragmentary note is rooted in Kant's theory of the sublime, which largely subsumes the eighteenth-century tradition. In the Kantian moment of the sublime the surface is broken, the discourse breaks down, and the faculties are checked or suspended: a discontinuity opens between what can be grasped and what is felt to be meaningful. As we move to the Kantian and other versions of the Romantic sublime proper, our inquiry requires much closer argument. Indeed, anyone with a sense of the literature will have recognized how drastically we were required to foreshorten as we sketched in, somewhat impressionistically, a background for the Romantic sublime. Before, however, we turn to the writers themselves, we need a preliminary analytic.

The Structure of Romantic Transcendence

To separate the original from the revisionist in Romanticism is impossible, for they are often identical. The genius of Romantic thinking lay not least in its energetic appropriation of received doctrine and in its (often unconscious) subversion of received terms through an ingenious reflex of metaphorical transposition. Wordsworth's psychology and affective diction are closely derived from the developed tradition of Lockean thought, but his meanings are not: a range of terms, such as the beauty and the terror of the Burkean aesthetic, are implicitly and persuasively recreated. More than this, however, the Romantics discovered excitement in the *making of meaning*. Romantic transcendence cannot be explained wholly in terms of the particular points of departure and arrival it employed. The sublime dramatized the rhythm of transcendence in its extreme and purest form, for the sublime began where the conventional systems, readings of landscape or text, broke down, and it found in that very collapse the foundation for another order of meaning.

The analytic study of the sublime requires a preliminary simplification, perhaps an operative definition that might at the least provide stable terms for recurring elements. The most comprehensive of Kant's several definitions suggests a point of departure:

> Man kann das Erhabene so beschreiben: as ist ein Gegenstand (der Natur), dessen Vorstellung das Gëmuth bestimmt, sich die Unerreichbarkeit der Natur als Darstellung von Ideen zu denken.

> We can describe the sublime in this way: it is an object (of nature) the representation of which determines the mind to think the unattainability of nature as a presentation of [reason's] ideas.[43]

In Kant's view the "representation" of such an object must collapse, and this failure yields the intuition of "unattainability." But reason's ideas (of the unconditioned, the totality, etc.) are also "unattainable" since they cannot be imagined or presented in sensible form. Hence the Janus-faced mind is confronted with two dimensions of "unattainability," and it simply identifies them in what amounts to a metaphorical intuition. The imagination's inability to comprehend or represent the object comes to signify the imagination's relation to the ideas of reason. In the opposing case of the beautiful, the natural object itself comes to signify. In the sublime, a *relation* to the object—the negative relation of unattainability—becomes the signifier in the aesthetic order of meaning.

If Kant's definition is to be useful to us it must be purged of its idealist metaphysics. Can the sublime be construed at all outside the presuppositions of idealism—whether Platonic or Kantian, theological or simply egotistical? It is possible, I believe, to preserve the dichotomous structure of Kant's formulation in a "realist" or psychological account. The metaphorical moment of the sublime would be understood as an internalization or sublimation of the imagination's relation to the object. The "unattainability" of the object with respect to the mind would be duplicated as an inner structure, so that in the sublime moment the mind would discover or posit an undefinable (ungraspable) domain within. But before we deploy an alternative psychological model, we might try the experiment of extending Kant's terms into a general definition. Kant is concerned exclusively with the natural sublime, holding as he does the rather inadequate and conventional view that the sublime of art is "always restricted by the conditions of an agreement with nature."[44] For Kant's *Gegenstand (der Natur)* we may in the first place substitute *any* object (a line of poetry, for example), which leads us to a formulation something like this: We call an object sublime if the attempt to represent it determines the mind to regard its inability to grasp wholly the object as a symbol of the mind's relation to a transcendent order. It is convenient to unfold this definition in terms of a sublime moment whose temporality is in the last analysis fictional or merely operative. The sublime moment, so understood, seems to consist of three phases or economic states.

In the first phase, the mind is in a determinate relation to the object, and this relation is habitual, more or less unconscious (preconscious in the Freudian sense), and harmonious. This is the state of normal perception or comprehension, the syntagmatic linearity of reading or taking a walk or remembering or whatnot. No discrepancy or dissonance interrupts representation, the smooth correspondence of inner and outer. Boredom signals an incipient disequilibrium which is not yet strong enough to break into consciousness and bring to a halt the automatic, linear rhythm of sensation and reflection.

In the second phase, the habitual relation of mind and object suddenly breaks down. Surprise or astonishment is the affective correlative, and there is an immediate intuition of a disconcerting disproportion between inner and outer. Either mind or object is suddenly in excess—and then both are, since their relation has become radically indeterminate. We are reading along and suddenly occurs a text which exceeds comprehension, which seems to contain a residue of signifier which finds no reflected signified in our minds. Or a natural phenomenon catches us unprepared and unable to grasp its scale. Any excess on the part of the object cancels the representational efficacy of the mind which can only turn, for its new object, to itself. But self-consciousness, too, can be prior and can force the rupture when the object (or memory) represented is too insignificant (fails to signify). We think of prominent examples in Wordsworth, for whom the object (often a memory) is always in danger of precipitant attenuation.

In the third, or reactive, phase of the sublime moment, the mind recovers the balance of outer and inner by constituting a fresh relation between itself and the object such that the very indeterminacy which erupted in phase two is taken as symbolizing the mind's relation to a transcendent order. This new relation has a "meta" character, which distinguishes it from the homologous relation of habitual perception. (In the case of poetic imagery, however, it is notoriously difficult to draw a clear line between the image as perception and as sign standing for the nonsensible or the unimaginable—a fact that accounts for a history of quarrels over what is or is not sublime.) Should there be a reversion to habitual perception, the sublime moment subsides or collapses into something else. For it is precisely the semiotic character of the sublime moment which preserves the sublimation necessary to the sublime.

The idealist, on the face of it, has a decided advantage in performing this sublimation; for him the transcendent exists a priori and may simply be recognized or invoked at the crucial point. Kant states flatly that the sublime is unthinkable without "the moral attitude," i.e., the mind's susceptibility to reason's ideas.[45] But we should like an ampler theory, for many also experience the sublime whose adhesion to the empirical is firm to the point of scepticism toward any particular transcendent schema. In fact, the intuition of *depth* which occurs in the third phase seems to be curiously proportionate to the reluctance of the mind to invoke transcendent categories. Height and depth are of course merely two perspectives within the same dimension of verticality; what is "lofty" for the idealist will be "profound" for the naturalizing mind. Northrop Frye has called attention to the antinomian transvaluation of verticality which is a feature of Romantic imagery,[46] and in our day depth is the unchallenged locus of god or value. The sublime moment establishes depth because the presentation of unattainability is phenomenologically a negation, a falling away from what might be seized, perceived, known, As an image, it is the abyss. When the intervention of the transcendent becomes specific, however, the image is converted into a symbol, and height takes over as the valorizing perspective. Here we see, at the level of theme or imagery, one of several differences between the idealist and naturalized versions of the sublime.

The three-phase model has limitations, but it serves to emphasize two features of the sublime moment without which an analytic is in danger of collapsing into merely another thematic exercise. In the first place, the model renders the sublime moment as an *economic* event, a series of changes in the distribution of energy within a constant field; this presupposes a homeostatic principle in the mind. Lockean and Freudian psychologies converge in the belief that nothing is got for nothing. If we desert an economic principle—at least the theoretical possibility of roughly calculating gain and loss—we have in my judgment no way to keep the sublime closed to "mystical" explanations. We should have to concede, for example, that the energy which powers the "proud flight" of the soul, its "joy and vaunting," may indeed be infused by a daemon or a "collective unconscious" or some suprapersonal reservoir which cannot be refuted or verified. The price of an economic principle is a severe reduction, and here the second feature of the model comes into play. Kant seems at times to be playing word games when he matches the "power" of the mind against the "power" of nature—how are these commensurable? Clearly, an implicit semiotic code authorizes the exchange of outer and inner: the sublimation which achieves homeostasis involves a metaphorical transposition of, say, two orders of "unattainability."

The critical roles of "representation" (*Vorstellung*) and "presentation" (*Darstellung*) in Kant's theory suggest semiotics as a likely direction of further steps away from his metaphysics. But a semiotic of the sublime encounters at once the difficulty that the sublime moment is diachronic. Kant speaks of a "mental *movement* combined with the estimate of the object"; "the mind feels itself *set in motion* in the representation of the sublime."[47] This "characteristic feature" may be isolated but not explained in the course of a synchronic analysis of the phases of the sublime. Kant himself, as we shall see, is led by the three-phase model into a dubious explanation of why comprehension must break down in the estimation of a vast magnitude. A semiotic translation will prove useful, however, as long as we do not fail to note its limits; it restates the difficult dynamic problem in slightly more rigorous fashion but tells us nothing of the mechanism which enables the mind to move all but instantaneously from one phase to another. Moreover, semiotics is an analogical enterprise, even at the elementary and unobjectionable level here in prospect.[48] It employs linguistic terms without exclusive or even primary reference to linguistic entities, and perhaps its fusion of the rhetorical and natural sublimes is too reductive to serve either more than provisionally.

It is the "mind-object" terminology which seems so portentous and vague—a bit antiquated—in the former model. The relation of the first phase can be reduced to the dialectic of signification, which suggests in turn a *signifier* (object) in a determinate relation to a *signified* (mind). It makes no difference whether the form of the signifier is marks on a page, a disposition of colors, shapes, and lines that can be read as a landscape, or—to speak more precisely—the sensible representation of such realities in the primary or preconscious imagination. The "flow" of the signifiers constitutes a "chain" or a syntagmatic progress whose continuity remains undisturbed until it is suddenly disrupted, in phase two, in what might be thought of as a spontaneous commutation test. We have seen that the disruption of the discourse may result from an excess on the plane of either the signifier or the signified.

In the first case (Kant's mathematical sublime), the feeling is one of *on and on*, of being lost. The signifiers cannot be grasped or understood; they overwhelm the possibility of meaning in a massive underdetermination that melts all oppositions or distinctions into a perceptual stream; or there is a sensory overload. Repetition, or any excess of "substance" in the signifier is a technique, familiar in architecture, music, and poetry, for inducing the sense of *on and on*. A good example is contemporary rock music which attempts to induce the sublime reaction by an insistent repetition of beat and by getting louder and louder until something breaks. (Burke: "Excessive loudness alone is sufficient to overpower the soul, to suspend its action, and to fill it with terror."[49]) The imagery appropriate to this variety of the sublime is usually characterized by featureless (meaningless) horizontality or extension: the wasteland. Indeed, the wasteland motif of Romantic and modernist literature presents an abridgment of the sublime moment so that we are confined to the second phase and await futilely the restorative reaction which never comes, except ironically.

In the second case, we may imagine the discourse to be ruptured by an excess of the signified. Here meaning is overwhelmed by an overdetermination which in its extreme threatens a state of absolute metaphor, "a universe in which everything is potentially identical with everything else."[50] Such a state is apocalyptic: it abrogates temporality, which is the necessary dimension of the syntagmatic flow. We are reading and suddenly we are caught up in a word (or any signifying segment) which seems to "contain" so much that there is nothing we cannot "read into" it. The word dissolves into the Word. Or we are suddenly fixated by a spot in the landscape which becomes an omphalos—a recurrent event in Wordsworth, which Geoffrey Hartman has brilliantly isolated as the "spot syndrome."[51] Verticality is the appropriate dimension, and the image is inevitably some variant of the abyss, the "fixed, abysmal, gloomy breathing-place" which is the central image in *The Prelude,* and indeed in most romantic poetry. What threatens here is stasis, a kind of death by plenitude, which Wordsworth elsewhere calls an "abyss of idealism" and which destroys the seeking for a signifier, the "perpetual logic" in which alone the mind can continue to live.[52]

Hartman has informed us so fully about this situation in Wordsworth that our brief exposition can linger instead with the event of reading words rather than landscapes. Longinus inaugurated a great cliché when he found the silence of Ajax in the underworld "more sublime than words" (9.2). The attenuation of the text (signifier) to the zero degree—a significant absence[53]—results in the richly ambivalent affective situation at the core of what Bloom calls the "anxiety of influence." The dissolving of word into Word, or for that matter of face into Human Form, is a moment of "daemonic" influx. It can be isolated only theoretically because in our experience it is penetrated by the reactive third phase in which we break out of the fixation by displacing the abundance of *presence* along the syntagmatic chain, like the young Wordsworth, who "spread [his] thoughts / And spread them with a wider creeping" (*P* 3.117–18). The word is reconstituted in a series of differential oppositions; it becomes opaque again. The residue of signified which had adumbrated the Word in phase two redounds to our own credit (we feel self-enhanced and take our "proud flight") as a latent capability of metaphor or identification. This power includes the lesser word (the one we actually read) as merely the one of a number of possibilities which happened to be actualized. Bloom calls this process or something similar *daemonization,* or a "personalized Counter-Sublime."[54]

We have examined the two ways in which the discourse breaks down. The bipolarity of mode apparent in the disruption naturally extends into the third, or reactive, phase of the sublime moment, which recovers the discourse by righting the balance. This modal dichotomy proves to be far more interesting and useful than a thematic opposition of naturalized versus idealist or other classificatory schemes. We are able to discern two distinct modes of the sublime moment, each with its characteristic anxiety and with opposed strategies of resolution.

In the first case, which threatens an excess on the plane of the signifiers, the syntagmatic flow must be halted, or at least slowed, and the chain broken up if the discourse is to become meaningful again. This can only be done through the insertion of a substituted term into the chain, i.e., through metaphor. The absence of a signified itself assumes the status of a signifier, disposing us to feel that behind this newly significant absence lurks a newly discovered presence, the latent referent, as it were, mediated by the new sign. We recall Kant's terms: "unattainability" (*Unerreichbarkeit*) is regarded as a "presentation" (*Darstellung*): indeterminacy signifies. We merely deidealize Kant's formulation in this semiotic translation by refusing to specify *presence* as a transcendent term. Perhaps *being* and *depth* have no independent ontological status; perhaps they are reifications of the signifying power, spontaneously created by the mind at the zero degree, in the mere reflex of making absence significant.

The discourse newly established in this mode of the sublime is not, evidently, a metalanguage (like literary criticism or aesthetics) but a connotative system. The signifiers of a connoted or second-order system are themselves constituted by the signs or signifying relations of a first-order, denoted system. The second-order system constitutes an independent code that subsumes the first-order system and cannot be derived from it. (Thus in literature, for example, the connotative meanings cannot be derived from the denotative plane of language.) What this comes down to, in this mode of the sublime, is a simple but important principle: the "meaning" of the sublime moment cannot be derived from the signifying relations that occasion it. In this third phase an ideological component necessarily enters the sublime moment. Roland Barthes speculates usefully that "*ideology* is the *form* . . . of the signifides of connotation, while *rhetoric* is the form of the connotators."[55] Anyone who reads into the tradition of speculation about the sublime knows in what a variety of ideologies the sublime moment finds a central place. What happens to you standing at the edge of the infinite spaces can be made, theoretically, to "mean" just about anything. Such agreement as in fact occurs in the tradition is a precise function of a correlative ideological unanimity.

We may call the mode of the sublime in which the absence of determinate meaning becomes significant the *metaphorical* sublime, since it resolves the breakdown of discourse by substitution. This is, properly, the natural or Kantian sublime, and we might think of it as the hermeneutic or "reader's" sublime. It has proved to be especially compatible with associationist psychology. Associationist theories of the sublime generally put the cart before the horse. They take the metaphorical substitutions which resolve the sublime moment as the causes of it. Burke saw this and chose to found his psychology in perception.

He objects, for example, to Locke's view that darkness is terrible only by association, with, say, the ideas of ghosts and goblins.[56] For Burke, all privations—whether of signified (light without source, sound without sense) or of signifier (vacuity, darkness, solitude, and silence)—expose us to terror of themselves. Theological mysteries and allegories without an evident "key" (like Kafka's work—"somehow meaningful but not quite graspable") are examples of the hermeneutic sublime cited in another connection by Goodman.[57] In some sense all works of literature which tease us out of thought will participate momentarily in the "reader's" sublime.

The other mode of the sublime may be called *metonymical*. Overwhelmed by meaning, the mind recovers by displacing its excess of signified into a dimension of contiguity which may be spatial or temporal. We may be tempted to talk of displacement as projection, for a dynamic element is involved, a motion of presence outward and through substance:

> And I have felt
> A presence that disturbs me with the joy
> Of elevated thoughts; a sense sublime
> Of something far more deeply interfused,
> Whose dwelling is the light of setting suns,
> And the round ocean and the living air,
> And the blue sky, and in the mind of man:
> A motion and a spirit, that impels
> All thinking things, all objects of all thought,
> And rolls through all things.[58]

A characteristic of this mode of the sublime is elision, for it is responding to the danger of stasis or fixation. The disruption, or "fall," of what we have marked as the second phase is imminent whenever the objects or signifiers begin to crystallize too distinctly, to stand out in sharp relief from the continuities which normally subdue them. As if warned, the mind begins to "spread its thoughts," to avert the lingering which could deepen into an obsessive fixation. The Wordsworth of "Tintern Abbey" is profoundly threatened by such a disorder of continuity. The poem is always in danger of coming to a dangerous halt, and does so, four times. Each of the paragraphs begins anew, in reaction to a hidden sense of presence which cannot be signified but which is located in those mysterious breaks.

> And now, with gleams of half-extinguished thought,
> With many recognitions dim and faint,

And somewhat of a sad perplexity,
The picture of the mind revives again:
While here I stand, not only with the sense
Of present pleasure, but with pleasing thoughts
That in this moment there is life and food
For future years. And so I dare to hope,
Though changed, no doubt, from what I was when first
I came among these hills. . . .   [58–67]

Here is a mind in recovery, unable to signify what has occupied it
(thought, recognitions of what?) but revived back into time ("And now")
by a "picture." The hope of such a mind is to spread the present into
the future, but here the difficulty is that such a saving continuity seems
to be denied by the cleavage of past and present.

The metonymical mode suggest the *poet*'s as opposed to the *reader*'s
sublime. In an influential article, Roman Jakobson has correlated the two
operational axes of language with two kinds of aphasia.[59] In *similarity
disorder* the subject loses the capacity to substitute associated terms
into the continuous chain of discourse. In the complementary *contiguity
disorder* the subject's speech is discontinuous, and the operations
necessary to the syntagma (grammar, syntax, contiguity, contexture)
are suppressed. Jakobson's discovery is enormously fruitful, and he
himself draws some implications for the analysis of literary style into
the metaphorical (symbolist) and the metonymical (realist). Although he
does not speculate about possible analogues of aphasia, Jakobson does
claim general validity for this bipolarity of mode in any semiotic system.
Now the moment of the sublime appears to involve a kind of temporary
aphasia, which we have characterized as a lapsing out of discourse. Is
this not the germ of truth behind the enduring cliché that such and
such an event, prospect, or text leaves the subject "speechless"?

And, it would seem, in two possible ways. The reader's sublime is a
similarity disorder. Jakobson quotes a clinical description: "patients of
this type 'grasped the words in their literal meaning but could not be
brought to understand the metaphorical character of the same words.' "[60]
This is roughly the situation of the reader confronted by theological
mystery, the dark conceits of allegory, or any text whose ultimate meaning lies in just the fact that it cannot be grasped. So too with the beholder of a natural scene, which can be literally *seen* well enough but
which cannot be wholly *read* and seems instinct with latent significance.
The poet's sublime, on the other hand, is a contiguity disorder, and indeed further inquiry might find here a source of the "agrammatism," the
attenuation of visual and conceptual syntax, which is such a conspicuous

development in modernist poetics as a whole. These disorders refer, of course, to what disrupts the discourse, and we have seen that this second phase of the sublime moment is often available to us only by inference. It seems odd and confusing that the poet who is subject to contiguity disorder will emphasize continuity, as a theme and in his style. But the text we have is a recovered speech, a discourse resumed after the silent break—often, as it were, the moment just before the poem—which defines its value. So too the affective elaborations of the reader's sublime will abound in the metaphorical associations which have rescued the possibility of meaning from the ambivalent excitement of incomprehension.

All readers are poets in some degree, and all poets are also readers, so that the modal opposition here adumbrated has no value whatsoever as a scheme for classifying poets and texts or even for reading events. Later on we shall have to exchange these modes for a related but simpler opposition between the *positive* (metonymical) and *negative* (metaphorical) versions of the sublime. But in general, it is wise to wear loosely such apparatus as we need; in particular, we ought to be wary of the tendency in structuralist thinking to turn a preliminary heuristic into a deduction. The structures elucidated in this book may all be considered instances of *sublimation,* a psychoanalytic concept which evokes both the cultural prestige of the aesthetic sublime and the usual sense of the word in chemistry, i.e., the direct passage from a solid to a gaseous state. But the theory of sublimation is in a very unsatisfactory state, and it is this more than anything which defeats the possibility of a definitive typology of the Romantic sublime. Even outside the popular literature "sublimation" is used loosely of displacement, internalization, substitution, symbolism, and indeed of any deflection of instinct from aim or object—in fact, of any defense against disequilibrium (anxiety) that "works."[61] The crucial questions, left ambiguous by Freud, are economic and moral. We should like to know, first, whether and in what sense sublimation implies a relative attenuation of energy in the transubstantiation of the "lower" into the "higher." Clearly, the economics of sublimation can never be verified precisely because a semiotic transposition is always involved in the deflection of the "lower" energy; yet the concept presupposes an economic exchange: at times the loss *feels* greater, at times the gain. Second, is sublimation always the preferred fate of energy? This is a question of value, and I do not see how a critic can avoid assuming a moral position in the face of it; to invoke the prestige of high culture in defense of sublimation is to enter a circular argument. Actually, there is much writing in the Romantic tradition which abandons the sublime; there is a contrary poetry of *de*sublimation, a poetry intensely sceptical of the fictional ladders which rise out of the rag and bone shop of the heart.

To consider the problem of originality is to find the two kinds of sublimation, poet's and reader's, compounded or superimposed. In the sublime moment the poet will be "daemonized," or possessed by a power which seems to be merely mediated by the text or the scene he reads. So Longinus believed hypsos, a quasi-divine quality of greatness, was transferred along the "inner canals" of the mind. Yet even daemonic possession is already a saving defense founded on a metaphor, and the supererogatory "identification" on which it turns is from a psychological point of view an especially intense variant of the reader's sublime. Its resolution, however, is different. The paradox, at least of the Romantic sublime, is this: the daemonized ego can speak again only through a displacement, a secondary, metonymical sublimation that diffuses the power of the ego and subverts its freedom. This is the cost of recovered speech, of writing the poem. Wordsworth writes of a "bodily eye" that

> Could find no surface where its power might sleep;
> Which spake perpetual logic to my soul,
> And by an unrelenting agency
> Did bind my feelings even as in a chain.   [P 3.166–69]

The "power" of the eye seeks discharge, a state of equilibrium in which it may "sleep," but it can never find an adequate "surface" or signifier into which it can be taken up. Hence an oscillation which the soul understands but which binds the feelings into a compulsive repetition. To entertain such power is oddly to lose a measure of freedom, to become subject to the pressure of an "unrelenting agency." The word can never be finally spoken; like the process as a whole it is a "perpetual logic," and the necessary quest for it binds the feelings into a syntagmatic chain. Sublimation offers motility and answers the daemonic tendency of the power to become fixated to one "surface," but it requires submission to a new control.

One elementary principle requires reaffirmation before we move from preliminary speculation to a closer analysis of the sublime moment. Much criticism of Romantic poetry has as its implicit protagonist not the "I" or ego of the poem, not the poet as man or maker of the poem, but an ill-defined consciousness somewhere in between. It may be that the experience dramatized *within* the poem, and the formal experience for poet and reader (in different ways) *of* the poem, correspond to two phases of the sublime moment. In "Resolution and Independence," for example, the ego is deeply afflicted by contiguity disorder:

The old Man still stood talking by my side;
But now his voice to me was like a stream
Scarce heard; nor word from word could I divide;
And the whole body of the Man did seem
Like one whom I had met with in a dream;
Or like a man from some far region sent,
To give me human strength, by apt admonishment.   [106–12][62]

Speech cannot be kept up; the landscape and the old man by the side of the protagonist slip away, out of context, into a field of associations so troubled that it is never fully brought to light. Yet this sublime aphasia occurs within Spenserian cadences that roll onward as by an unrelenting agency or a saving chain of form—the province of poet and reader, not of the "I." Does the form represent in some sense a recovery of the power of speech and of listening? The question seems to me too difficult for a clear answer, and in consequence I have refrained from using sublimation as a genetic category. The focus of this study is on the various careers of egos within poems; they ought to be accurately described before the questions of form and its makers can be properly addressed. In the meantime, there is much in the moment of the sublime still to consider.

2. *The nature of a Female Space is this: it shrinks the Organs
Of Life till they become Finite & Itself seems Infinite
And Satan vibrated in the immensity of the Space! Limited
To those without but Infinite to those within: it fell down and
Became Canaan: closing Los from Eternity in Albions Cliffs*
—Blake, *Milton*

The Ethos
of Alienation:
Two Versions
of Transcendence

In the economy of the mind at least, you can't get something for
nothing. Semiotics merely draws in firmer outline what we have often
thought and said in other terms. No genuine thesis can remain within
the domain of one heuristic, and semiotics yields no thesis; criticism is
revealed to be necessary by the preliminary effort of clearing its ground.
Our goal is to press beyond the tautology which subverts the value of
most academic renditions of the sublime. We learn something but lose
our chance of a deeper grasp of the sublime moment when we merely
translate its terms or imagery into another set of terms (power, duration, transcendence, etc.) that are in the same order of complexity as the
first and themselves require interpretation. If the critic is to commit
himself momentarily to theory, he must suppress or sublimate his
healthy panic in the face of the reductive.

The hermeneutic sublime is a rhetoric, a discourse of connotations.
Its signs consist of relations between indeterminacy and a "meaning"

predicated of indeterminacy. We speculated that the signifiers of this discourse are themselves constituted by a subject's relation to an object— his inability to grasp it; the signifieds of the discourse are arbitrary with respect to such an object and are, as it were, imported into the discourse under the pressure of some force majeure that lies beyond the original signifying occasion. It comes down to the claim that the failure to understand something has the very highest meaning. This is an exciting idea, and a dangerous one. Schiller draws the logical conclusion that *confusion* is the preeminent occasion of the sublime.[1] And by "confusion" he means not merely "the spiritual disorder of a natural landscape" but also "the uncertain anarchy of the moral world," including the amoral chaos of human history in which all best things are confused to ill. "Should one approach history with great expectations of illumination and knowledge—how very disappointed one is!" But the idea is to abandon "the possibility of *explaining* Nature" and take "incomprehensibility itself as a principle of judgment." For the fact that Nature and her work in history mock our minds

> —that in her obdurately free advance she treads into the dust the creations of wisdom and of chance with equal indifference; that she drags down with her in a *single* collapse both the important and the trivial; that here she preserves a community of ants, while there she enfolds in her arms and crushes her most splendid creature, man; that she often wastes in a wanton hour the most tediously won achievements, while often working for centuries on some inane labor—

is the surest guarantee we have against determinism. Somehow the sublime authorizes a translation of absurdity into freedom; lack of connection or non-sense is redeemed: "For if the connection among a series of objects is abstracted, one is left with the concept of independence which coincides surprisingly with the pure rational concept of freedom." It *is* a rather surprising coincidence, and clearly it can occur only if the freedom of reason is apodictically secure.

One question begged in Schiller's sublime is this: How is one to distinguish between what is intrinsically incomprehensible and what one merely fails to understand? Black holes, we might all agree, are in the present state of knowledge an occasion for the sublime; but how about the ungraspable magnitude of the hydrogen bomb?—possibly that, too. But what then of the computer, the very apotheosis of the understanding, which few yet understand: Is the computer sublime? No doubt, for some it is, and yet it is the symbol of determinism. Clearly there are many connotative systems based on a failure to understand. A glance at the rhetoric of public life, from advertising to politics, will convince us of how many institutions are professionally engaged in the business of promoting confusion. The Romantic sublime must be much more narrowly discriminated—as an ideology—than the semiotic model allows. The "pure rational concept of freedom" does not follow from the ordinary mind's extraordinary capacities for confusion. But it may be that the necessity of confusion follows from the idea of a transcendent reason. In any case, it is now our task to study the structure of the coincidence between the two, the point at which they confront each other rather violently in the sublime moment. Our path leads through the twilight zone at the border of the aesthetic and the practical, and we won't get very far if we refuse to take a moralist's view now and then.

Unlike the beautiful, the sublime is cognate with the experiential structure of alienation, whose modern form is discovered and announced in the Romantic authors. Alienation also presupposes the bathetic collapse of the signifying relations which make a social order. When the significance of things is no longer "natural" or *im*mediate, when making sense requires the mediating intervention—as opposed to the assumed immanence—of a transcendent idea, the world is being understood rhetorically, at second remove. It is often noticed that Wordsworth was among the first to register a disturbed awareness of urban alienation. Before he ever got to London he was baffled by it, feeding even as a child upon rumors from the imperial city:

> Above all, one thought
> Baffled my understanding: how men lived
> Even next-door neighbours, as we say, yet still
> Strangers, not knowing each the other's name.   [*P* 7.115–18]

It is just Wordsworth's bafflement, his inability to read the cityscape, that makes it an appearance "With wonder heightened, or sublimed by awe" (7.153): the sublime enters to rescue—but not, unfortunately, to cure—an estranged mind in an alien city.

All versions of the sublime require a credible god-term, a meaningful jargon of ultimacy, if the discourse is not to collapse into "mere" rhetoric. Even the political or debased sublime (of which the totalitarianism of the *Volk* is merely the disasterous extreme) cannot survive ideological pluralism. What will distinguish the Romantic sublime from cognate structures is the precise form of its signifieds, its ideology. And here our own cultural situation comes unavoidably into play. We no longer share in the hierophancy of the sublime which was unquestioned in nineteenth-century critics. In retrospect, the Romantic consensus—that set of assumptions about what is "higher" and what "lower"—

seems almost as salient as the quality of its critical thought, which we continue to appreciate and claim as our own. The Wordsworth is obviously no longer ours of whom Ruskin could write that he "may be trusted as a guide in everything, he feels nothing but what we ought all to feel—what every mind in pure moral health *must* feel, he says nothing but what we all ought to believe—what all strong intellects *must* believe."[2] What separates our era—perhaps just one's generation—is not the modernist ambivalance about god-terms, the need and value of them, but a general assumption of their dispensability. "Wisdom and Spirit of the Universe! / Thou Soul that art the eternity of thought" (*P* 1.401–2): before this we are less exasperated than blank. Wordsworth is currently being read with great penetration, but in spite of his edification. Yet as we move away from an antiquated diction to the subtler formulas of ultimacy developed by the Romantics, our distance is less sure. We should like to determine what in the Romantic ideology has residual power, what we still share.

The notion of ideology is rather portentous, not to be loosely invoked. However broadly construed, ideology is not relevant unless we find that the movement of the mind in the sublime moment is not necessary or autonomous, but instead masks the project of an ulterior motive. We would then be led to substitute for the usual efficient causality of the sublime moment (in the theories, for example, of Burke and Kant) an emanational or teleological causality. Until the ulteriority of the sublime moment has been demonstrated, as opposed to merely asserted, it makes no real sense to interpret its "meanings." Just here the semiotic model lets us down. We have seen that it provides no way to make discriminations of value among the "god-terms" invoked in the third phase. But further: the model requires, and can in no way provide, a dynamic element. We simply recognized that in phase two the discourse breaks down. But why? Are the causes and conditions of this failure completely intrinsic, as Kant thought? Similarly, we suggested that in the third phase the mind simply recovers its balance, like a tipsy boat—as if a compensatory law, economic or natural, were secretly at work. What determines this reversal of direction, which we meet in the poets as recognition, a kind of lyric anagnorisis? In short, what accounts for the "mental movement" in and between the three phases of the sublime?

We might begin with a plausible hypothesis: the dynamic element of the sublime represents the particular form of ultimacy invoked in the third phase in order to constitute the new discourse. Obviously, we ought to find out whether this is true before proceeding further to deconstruct the motive power of the sublime. The latter project—a genetic (as opposed to an operative) explanation of what might be rather crudely called "dynamic ultimacy"—requires a psychology and must be deferred to later chapters. In the meantime we meet the danger that the semiotic model will dictate the form of the analysis, and hence, covertly, its result. I propose therefore to drop it, and to see if a reading of Kant entirely in his own terms will bring us to the same point. Kant's version of the breakdown in the discourse is impressive, but it may in fact be fictional, masking the project of his "ultimate," the noumenal ego, with all its contradictions. The sublime certainly seems to reflect contradictions, and they seem to be preserved in its transcendent resolutions.

Kant's Fictional Moment

S. H. Monk found in the *Critique of Judgment* "the unconscious goal" of eighteenth-century aesthetic,[3] and we can easily discern in Kant the unconscious origins or radical forms of nineteenth-century speculation. "He has influenced even you," Goethe told Eckermann in 1827, "although you have never read him; now you need him no longer, for what he could give you, you possess already."[4] Kant established decisively the discrimination of the aesthetic boundary; at the same time he located the judgments on the sublime and the beautiful in a network of a priori relations to the cognitive and ethical domains of mind. Kant is as important for any theory of the sublime as Aristotle is for the theory of tragedy. The *Critique* is so well known that we can dispense with an explication of the role of judgment as the faculty which mediates knowing and willing (desiring) and proceed directly to the theory of the sublime.

Kant divides the sublime into the *mathematical*, which concerns the effect of magnitude on the imagination and is referred to the faculty of cognition, and the *dynamical*, which concerns the effect of power (*Macht*) and is referred to the faculty of desire. In both modes sublimity is properly predicated of the subject and its supersensible destiny (*Bestimmung*) and not of any object. A natural object seems sublime only by virtue of a certain "subreption" whereby we substitute "a respect (*Achtung*) for the Object in place of one for the idea of humanity in our own self—the Subject" (p. 106; 5, 257).[5] Kant's insistence on this principle of a subjective but universal, a priori aesthetic divides his theory at a stroke from its empiricist predecessors in the eighteenth century. The aesthetic judgment is "final" or "purposive" (*Zweckmässig*) only with reference to the subject but is necessarily determined for that subject and is therefore universally valid and separate from any other teleology or motive.

In the mathematical sublime the mind confronts an object whose extreme magnitude challenges the imagination (as the faculty of sensible representation) to an extraordinary effort. This begins as the immediate grasping of the quantum in a single intuition which Kant calls *apprehension* (*Auffassung*). But apprehension is locked into a temporal series; as a number of discrete intuitions accumulate, the imagination moves into the higher and properly aesthetic operation of *comprehension* (*Zusammenfassung*), which attempts to combine the apprehended series into a single, unified intuition. Apprehension can be carried on ad infinitum, but comprehension has a maximum point: "For if the apprehension has reached a point beyond which the representations of sensuous intuition in the case of the parts first apprehended begin to disappear from the imagination as this advances to the apprehension of yet others, as much, then, is lost at one end as is gained at the other, and for comprehension we get a maximum which the imagination cannot exceed" (p. 99). The imagination overextends itself; it is driven to a "point of excess . . . like an abyss in which it fears to lose itself" (p. 107), and it breaks down. The collapse of comprehension results in a feeling of displeasure (*Unlust*) as the imagination is forced to recognize its inadequacy. But here, in the moment of crisis, reason intervenes and presents the idea of totality or infinitude, and as the mind is led to recognize in the idea of the supersensible its ultimate destiny (*Bestimmung*), it experiences therewith "a simultaneously awakened pleasure" (p. 106), since it finds "the absolutely great only in the proper estate of the Subject" (p. 121).

Kant's explanation of the affective ambivalence of the sublime establishes a profound alienation between imagination and reason:

> Thus, too, delight in the sublime in nature is only *negative* (whereas that in the beautiful is *positive*): that is to say it is a feeling of imagination by its own act depriving itself of its freedom by receiving a final determination in accordance with a law other than that of its empirical employment. In this way it gains an extension and a power greater than that which it sacrifices. But the ground of this is concealed from it, and in its place it *feels* the sacrifice or deprivation, as well as its cause, to which it is subjected. [P. 120]

The sublime experience is "contra final" (*zweckwidrig*) for the imagination, but "final" (*zweckmässig*) for "the whole province of the mind" (*die ganze Bestimmung des Gemüths*)" (p. 108). Hence "the *sublime* is what pleases immediately by reason of its opposition to the interest of sense" (p. 118). But here the question arises, Why can't the imagination participate in the pleasure the whole mind takes in reason? If indeed the imagination has gained an "extension and a power greater than that which it sacrifices," why is this possibility "concealed" (*verborgen*) from it? Is the imagination necessarily limited to a passive representing of the sensible?

We can detect some uneasiness in Kant's account at this point. Clearly, he wishes to save the sublime from what he calls *fanaticism—nach Grundsätzen träumen*, visions guided by fundamental principles. This "rational raving" (*mit Vernunft rasen*) disgusts him; it is "least of all compatible with the sublime"; it is "obsessively ridiculous" (*grüblerisch lächerlich*) (p. 128; 5, 275). Worst of all, this deep brooding passion is "lawless" (*regellos*). The vehemence of Kant's attack on fanaticism suggests that his analytic is vulnerable here, for after all, on his own showing the fanatic is entirely in accord with reason. An ideological element has entered Kant's account. We have only to recall the tradition of rational fanatics during the nineteenth century—Wordsworth's Oswald comes to mind—to realize in a general way what is at stake here.

We look for an ideological element at the point where an a priori argument appeals covertly to the "observation of men" within a determinate status quo. Kant has represented, as the central moment of the mathematical sublime, the collapse of aesthetic comprehension and the intervention of reason. But this moment is, in fact, an operative or fictional one, because comprehension is not, strictly speaking, an empirical employment of the imagination. Reason has already intervened to make comprehension possible and necessary. In the apprehension of a magnitude, "the mind . . . hearkens now to the voice of reason, which for all given magnitudes . . . requires totality, and consequently comprehension in *one* intuition, and which calls for a *presentation* answering to all the above numbers of a progressively increasing numerical series" (p. 102). In comprehension, the "time-condition" of the imagination is suspended, and "co-existence" is thereby rendered intuitable (p. 107). Looking at the boundless ocean or infinity of stars, we feel that it's all simultaneously *there*, coexisting with us; we *think* (*denken*) a realm of existence that we are unable to *cognize* (*erkennen*) (p. 120). Comprehension is thus the imagination's application of the timeless idea of reason, but its putative collapse does not render apparent the role reason has been playing. Instead the imagination feels a defeat, and reason appears, freshly and finally, as its savior.

There is an evident dissonance between the fiction of the imagination's collapse and Kant's deeper view of comprehension as an effect of reason. This dissonance requires interpretation, as opposed to mere exposition. Clearly Kant wanted to guarantee the a priori validity of the sublime by grounding it in necessary operations of the mind. But it is difficult to avoid the conclusion that in the sublime, reason posits its own sensible or imaginative frustration in order to discover itself freshly in an attitude of awe. These terms anticipate rather dangerously the course of German idealism, but they focus for us the fascinating problem at the heart of Kant's critique: how is it that reason operates on two "levels" of consciousness? Kant's philosophy as a whole begs this question; we are never quite sure where to place consciousness. (Hence Schiller was led, in his development of Kant's dualism, to posit an "absolute unity of mind . . . neither matter nor form, neither sensuousness nor reason," which actively mediates the determined, opposed impulses toward form and the sensible.[6]) The affective ambivalence of the sublime, which opposes the imagination's feeling of defeat to the reason's awe of itself, points to a cognitive alienation within the mind as a whole and invites a dialectical interpretation. We are justified, I believe, in turning to an emanational logic precisely because Kant in effect abandons his attempt to make comprehension an empirical operation. Hence the real motive or cause of the sublime is not efficient but teleological; we are ultimately referred not to the failure of empirical imagination but to reason's project in requiring this failure. The cause of the sublime is the *aggrandizement of reason at the expense of reality and the imaginative apprehension of reality.*

In exposing the structure of the sublime, we find the question, How does it work? turning into the question, What is it for? Kant neither has nor requires a genuinely psychological theory because he takes no account of unconscious determinants, but his terms suggest a direction for such a theory. The imagination's feeling of sacrifice or deprivation, the relation of concealment between it and reason—these suggest the role of repression in the sublime, and will later be our theme. We would need, too, an account of how the relative infinity of the object suggests to the mind its own supersensible infinity, so that the object becomes a symbol, a presentation of reason's ideas. The semiology of the sublime requires for its working principle the category of "sublimation," which suggests in turn the psychological concept of "identification." For the moment, however, we shall linger with Kant's terms and elucidate some poetic analogues.

"The feeling of our incapacity to attain to an idea *that is a law for us,* is RESPECT" (p. 105). In Kant's view, respect (*Achtung*) is a "pleasure" predicated upon the "displeasure" the imagination feels in its own defeat. It follows that the intensity of this pleasure will be directly proportionate to the "unattainability" (*Unerreichbarkeit*) of the prescriptive idea of reason. If we consider the sublime experience as a movement between the unconscious application of the idea of reason (comprehension) and the self-conscious discovery of its provenance, we

see that the greater the distance between these two "levels" of awareness, the more affecting the experience will be. Kant's conception of
respect is his version of the numinous "other," the *mysterium tre-
mendum* that is the central descriptive notion in religiously oriented
theories of the sublime down to Rudolf Otto's *Das Heilige* (1917). Kant
takes it for granted that the attempt to predicate affective states (such
as astonishment) of empirical objects must lead to an endless squabble
about what is or is not sublime, with no possibility of a universally
valid judgment. In 1805 Richard Payne Knight charmingly pointed out
against Burke's theory that had the author walked up St. James's Street
without his breeches and carrying a loaded blunderbuss, it would have
occasioned great and universal "astonishment" as well as terror, but
not the feeling of the sublime.[7] With such objections an empirical theory
must contend. But Kant's respect is a wholly subjective relation: "the
astonishment amounting almost to terror, the awe and thrill of devout
feeling, that takes hold of one . . . is not actual fear" (pp. 120–21), but
rather the imagination's attempt to use fear as the affective representation of its relation to reason.

Reason cannot, in Kant's system, undergo a development or an
essential aggrandizement. But the sublime moment offers to reason an
occasion for self-recognition. Reason and its province of the unconditioned, of the supersensible totality, are discovered as man's *Bestimmung*,
his ultimate destiny and vocation. Hence the sublime is apocalyptic in
the strict sense that it reveals final things, and the defeat of the sensible
imagination accomplishes subjectively the end of the natural order. In
the famous Simplon Pass passage of *The Prelude* we have an exemplary
dramatization of the mind's self-recognition, as Wordsworth recovers
from a defeat of the imagination:

> I was lost;
> Halted without an effort to break through;
> But to my conscious soul I now can say—
> 'I recognise thy glory': in such strength
> Of usurpation, when the light of sense
> Goes out, but with a flash that has revealed
> The invisible world, doth greatness make abode,
> There harbours; whether we be young or old,
> Our destiny, our being's heart and home,
> Is with infinitude, and only there;
> With hope it is, hope that can never die,
> Effort, and expectation, and desire,
> And something evermore about to be.   [6.596–608]

The lines are so familiar that it is easy to miss the undergirding accuracy of phrase and thought. "Greatness" for Wordsworth lies not in man's proper *Bestimmung*, infinitude, but in the "strength / Of usurpation": this strength preserves and indeed depends upon the resistance of sense to its overcoming. Man achieves or realizes an aesthetic greatness at the moment when his infinite destiny is revealed to him as still outstanding, unrealized, unachieved. Wordsworth's *eschaton* is here not quite immanent; Wordsworth remains within the tradition of Christian hope, as the Pauline rhythm confirms. "Something evermore about to be" is the formula of *homo absconditus*, the man at one with himself *in spe* but not *in re*, the man who must look to history for what he knows to be beyond history.[8]

This kind of existential alienation has such theological sanction that it is difficult to conceive of it as ideology, although the tradition of classical, Hegelian idealism attempts such a perspective against Kant. It is also difficult because we appreciate that Wordsworth did not will the usurpation; writing at his desk and remembering, he did not want the light of retrospective sense to go out. The imagination is unwittingly, involuntarily, divided against itself. It not only serves the reproductive function of memory but "is at the same time an instrument of reason and its ideas" (p. 121). The imagination reaches the flash point—the moment of absolute overextension—only because it remains unaware of the hidden master who enjoins comprehension. Once the soul has become "conscious," the "glory," or brief nimbus, of sense is past. Wordsworth's metaphor is subtler than Kant's theory because it locates aesthetic greatness more precisely in the unconscious apotheosis of sense than in the consequent state of recognition.

Here the border between the sublime and the visionary is definitively etched. In both Kant and Wordsworth the sublime conducts us, as it were, to the frontier of the "invisible world" but leaves us as soon as that world is consciously represented or given any positive content. The sublime remains negative, dialectical, a movement between two states, an indeterminate relation. From a structural point of view the content of the invisible world is an indifferent matter. To Kant's variety of terms (the unconditioned as supersensible, the highest good, the totality, the *universitas*, the noumenon, the archetypal intellect, the holy will, and so forth) we are compelled in our day to add the repressed traumata, which enjoin their will on the imagination. As a structure, the sublime adapts to the particularities of many theologies and is especially at home in the modern theology of the unconscious. But if the fact or existence of the invisible world—as opposed to its content—is called into question, the possibility of a sublime moment evaporates. And if the sensible world is too strongly negated, the usurpation loses its "strength," and the sublime is reified into a permanent attitude of alienation from nature.

The Ethic of Sublimity

The paradoxical structure of the "negative" or Kantian sublime is oscillatory rather than genuinely ambiguous. Aesthetic "greatness" reveals or intimates man's ontological destiny, but only under the aspect or provision of its unattainability. Greatness emerges from the heart of defeat; respect expresses our feeling of incapacity. Psychologically, the structure suggests a compensation principle in which a kind of reactive identification saves the empirical mind from defeatism. Should the sublime become an ethic, however, it will in practice promote the defeat of the ordinary intellect—or at least justify it. On the contrary, insofar as there is an insistence upon realizing man's infinitude either imaginatively (as in Blake) or materially (as in idealist utopianism), the sublime moment—that sudden turning of the mind in an awe-full intuition—must disappear.

In short, there can be no sublime moment without the implicit, dialectical endorsement of human limitations. When Wordsworth sees the blind beggar in London, it is the epiphany of absolute limitation which precipitates the sublime moment. The beggar wore on his chest "a written paper, to explain / His story, whence he came, and who he was."

> Caught by the spectacle my mind turned round
> As with the might of waters; an apt type
> This label seemed of the utmost we can know,
> Both of ourselves and of the universe;
> And, on the shape of that unmoving man,
> His steadfast face and sightless eyes, I gazed,
> As if admonished from another world.   [P 7. 641–49]

The beggar is our epitome or type; he represents *our* world, what we can *know* at the point where earthly limits become definitive. But just at this point—which corresponds to the flash when the light of sense goes out—the other, *unknown* world comes into being, like the invisible world of the Simplon Pass passage. We are "admonished" and placed in an attitude of respect as we feel our incapacity of attaining that "other" world.

Yet how are we to learn of man's highest powers except by a negative argument from human limitations? The sublime moment does refer us to "the idea of humanity within our own self," even as it shows that humanity to be unattainable. (Indeed, the contrast between humanity and actual men becomes something of a cliché in moralists who affect the sublime.) Lucien Goldmann has made *die Idee der Menschheit* the central category in his early study of Kant, and he has no difficulty showing the presence of a universalist humanism, an ideal of community, in all Kant's attempts to find an a priori ground for knowing, willing, and judging.[9] What, then, is the significance of the aesthetic in this line of thinking? Goldmann formulates "Kant's reply": "It is a *consolation*, an *alleviation*, but certainly not a way of *overcoming* man's limitation and its tragic implications. For the unconditioned, the totality which man can attain in aesthetics is subjective; it is merely a form or a *symbolic expression*, not an objective and material reality encompassing the whole man."[10] Like all Marxist aestheticians, Goldmann is thinking in terms of *beauty*, for in the judgment of the beautiful a "final" correspondence between the ideal and the real is subjectively (symbolically) given. Since for Goldmann man's limitation is more or less his atomistic individualism, the experience of the beautiful enables man to be momentarily and subjectively identified with humanity. The aesthetic thus answers, for limited, bourgeois, individualist man, the question, What may I hope for?

But what about the sublime? In Goldmann's aesthetic, which is the standard idealist line, the sublime must simply drop out. For the judgment of the sublime comes into play precisely insofar as man cannot attain the totality; the intensity of the sublime experience is a direct function of the impossibility of realizing (in any way) the idea of humanity (or any supersensible idea). We might even say that the secondary discourse of the sublime is built on the failure of the beautiful and its reconciling fictions. The sublime and the beautiful differ not in ontological presupposition, but in the attitude toward dualism implicit in each.

Perhaps a closer look at the beautiful will bring this more into the open. Here is Kant's succinct statement: "For the beautiful in nature we must seek a ground external to ourselves, but for the sublime one merely in ourselves and the attitude of mind that introduces sublimity into the representation of nature" (p. 93). The judgment on the beautiful consists of a correspondence between the understanding and "a ground external to ourselves." In the idealist tradition following Kant, "beauty" was loosed from its connection with the understanding alone and came to be applied to the sensuous appearance of an ideal—such as the idea of freedom. Kant's "aesthetic Idea" or, as we say, "symbol," accomplishes a reconciliation of dualistic antinomies in this classic tradition.

With respect to dualism—that is, ideologically—beauty is profoundly ambiguous. Its reconciliations are "illusion" (*Schein*), and they leave "in reality" the opposing terms intact. Now, in the sublime, what corresponds to the structural role of *Schein* is *subreption*: this is the attitude that leads to the representation of the supersensible in the world of appearances. *Subreption* is a term from ecclesiastical law, and it implies suppression of the facts, concealment, deception—in short, a cheat. Subreption may be logically opposed to the Schillerian *Schein*: both refer to illusion, but they are oppositely valorized. The function of the sublime moment is to expose the cheat or subreption by which an object in nature invites awe and to redirect the awe to the subject himself. The sublime in fact subverts and dissolves *Schein* and all that it may stand for in the way of a hope of somehow realizing the unconditioned.

It is therefore no accident that the sublime is missing in the aesthetics of activists and idealists; in fact, already in Kant it is not technically an aesthetic judgment, since it lacks a ground in external reality. To turn an aesthetic into an ethic is risky business, but since the authors themselves are always doing it, we might hazard a rough sketch of the contrast between the sublime and the beautiful as ethical postures. The sublime, it would seem—at least the negative sublime—leads to alienation in all its forms. The beautiful, on the contrary, leads to a reconcilement in which the critical, "negative" power of art is in danger of melting away.

Among the grander deployments of the structure of the beautiful and its precarious ambiguity is Wordsworth's *Recluse* fragment, written as the program for his epic task.[11] Wordsworth proposes "Beauty" as a "living Presence of the earth"; paradise not as lost or merely fictional, but paradise *now* in the "simple produce of the common day":

—I, long before the blissful hour arrives,
Would chant, in lonely peace, the spousal verse
Of this great consummation:—and, by words
Which speak of nothing more than what we are,
Would I arouse the sensual from their sleep
Of Death, and win the vacant and the vain
To noble raptures; while my voice proclaims
How exquisitely the individual Mind
(And the progressive powers perhaps no less
Of the whole species) to the external World
Is fitted:—and how exquisitely, too—
Theme this but little heard of among men—
The external World is fitted to the Mind;

And the creation (by no lower name
Can it be called) which they with blended might
Accomplish:—this is our high argument.   [56–71]

Paradise is here and not here; we accomplish it daily, and chant "long
before the blissful hour." The status of the new "creation" remains profoundly ambiguous. The "blended might" of external World and Mind
preserves the integrity of each in this apocalyptic abrogation of
apocalypse.

Blake, we remember, had no use for such equivocation finding it outrageous. "You shall not," he says, "bring me down to believe such
fitting & fitted I know better & Please your Lordship."[12] With that
sarcastic twist Blake links the preservation of dualistic thought to the
implicit affirmation of a social order. In this view, Wordsworth's Beauty
surrenders its negative or critical function by proposing "nothing more
than what we are." And indeed, as Wordsworth turns toward men and
their ghastly cities, he seems to leave the possibility of Beauty behind
in those "grateful haunts" he must abandon:

              . . . I oft
Must turn elsewhere—to travel near the tribes
And fellowships of men, and see ill sights
Of madding passions mutually inflamed;
Must hear Humanity in fields and groves
Pipe solitary anguish; or must hang
Brooding above the fierce confederate storm
Of sorrow, barricadoed evermore
Within the walls of cities—may these sounds
Have their authentic comment; that even these
Hearing, be not downcast or forlorn!   [72–82]

This, for Blake, clinches his objection. Beauty is reduced to "authentic
comment" whose function is not to transfigure what men are but to
defend the poet against that reality. "Does this not Fit," says Blake—
sliding himself dangerously toward dualism in the heat of refutation—
"& is it not Fitting most Exquisitely too but to what not to Mind but
to the Vile Body only & to its Laws of Good & Evil & its Enmities
against Mind" (E, 656).

Blake's critique is both brilliant and unfair, as any drastic reduction
of the beautiful will be. There is little need at this late date to defend
the bravery of Wordsworth's project; its extreme humanism was and
is permanently attractive. Wordsworth denies that man is fallen, denies
that dualism is limitation. Redemption is ultimately naturalized into self-

recognition—what we *really* are, already, if we could see it. But Blake compels us to see the danger. The revolutionary program of Beauty as nothing more than what we are and see begins to subvert the ontological ambiguity of art. We recognize at once the affinity of this program to the "paradise now" motif of such contemporary projects as the Living Theatre, which has drawn such strenuous objection from the Schillerian idealism of Herbert Marcuse.[13] These mighty ideological confrontations develop from the essential ambiguity of the beautiful. Within the sublime, in the Kantian sense, there is no ambiguity: the sublime does not risk quietism by naturalizing the domain of art. Instead of the achieved stasis, the *discordia concors* of ideal and real, there is oscillation, movement over the widening gap between two terms, culminating in the withdrawal of consciousness from the sensible world. In the sublime moment, dualism is legitimated and intensified. The beautiful intimates reconciliation, however precariously and ambiguously; the sublime splits consciousness into alienated halves.

Schiller, in his version of the sublime, takes this alienation to an extreme that is exceeded only by Schopenhauer. The divorce of mind and nature is equivalent to an inner estrangement in modern, divided man, and while the beautiful addresses the "human being," the sublime refers us to the "pure daemon."[14] The fragile hope of Kant's universalist humanism (at least in Goldmann's view) is displaced completely from the sublime to the beautiful in this logical extension of Kant. To be true to "our *spiritual mission*" is to be false to "our *humanity*": the conflict has assumed the form of tragedy. We can hope, of course, "to remain on good terms with the physical world" which determines our happiness, but in such accommodation we risk falling out "with the moral world that determines our dignity." The quarrel can become so intense that man has "no other means of withstanding the power of nature than to anticipate her, and by a free renunciation of all sensuous interest to kill himself morally before some physical force does it." The sublime as suicide. Unless one has suffered very much, like Schiller, the negative sublime cannot really be recommended as an ethical posture, for it appears to culminate in a transcendent dead end.

The Egotistical Sublime

Fortunately there were and are many ways of eliding, attacking, or subverting the central paradox of the negative sublime, and its pure expression is to be encountered only in theory or in the Germans. It is highly characteristic of Wordsworth—whose great poetry was not, whatever he planned, written under the aegis of the beautiful—to substitute the aesthetic moment for the eschatological revelation of the sublime, and often for him the unconditioned or the *eschaton* is more or less ignored.

Keats said acutely of the "Wordsworthian or egotistical sublime" that it is a "thing per se and stands alone."[15] The egotistical sublime is not "negative" or dialectical. In Kantian terms, the sudden "movement" of the mind is greatly slowed and the phenomenal or sensible ego is aggrandized in place of the self-recognition of the noumenal reason. But Kantian terms are not quite adequate, for this is a "positive" sublime that in the end would subsume all otherness, all possibility of negation. Keats never saw the climactic Mount Snowdon passage of *The Prelude*, but I think he might have found its grandeur alloyed with a kind of massive complacency. Of the "higher" minds Wordsworth says:

Them the enduring and the transient both
Serve to exalt; they build up greatest things
From least suggestions; ever on the watch,
Willing to work and to be wrought upon,
They need not extraordinary calls
To rouse them; in a world of life they live,
By sensible impressions not enthralled,
But by their quickening impulse made more prompt
To hold fit converse with the spiritual world,
And with the generations of mankind
Spread over time, past, present, and to come,
Age after age, till Time shall be no more.
Such minds are truly from the Deity,
For they are Powers; and hence the highest bliss
That flesh can know is theirs—the consciousness
Of whom they are, habitually infused
Through every image and through every thought,
And all affections by communion raised
From earth to heaven, from human to divine. [14.100–118]

The discontinuities that erupt in the central (but uncharacteristic) Simplon Pass passage are here almost programmatically elided. The "extraordinary call" of the sublime appearance is disparaged because, to begin with, the comprehending imagination is never bound to "sensible impressions." Wordsworth propounds editorially a seamless sublimation "from earth to heaven, from human to divine," and he has just offered in the Snowdon vision an emblem for the transdualistic mind that presides over this sublimation:

There I beheld the emblem of a mind
That feeds upon infinity, that broods

Over the dark abyss, intent to hear
Its voices issuing forth to silent light
In one continuous stream; a mind sustained
By recognitions of transcendent power,
In sense conducting to ideal form,
In soul of more than mortal privilege.   [14.70–77]

In the egotisitical sublime the two Kantian poles of sensible nature and eschatological destination collapse inward and become "habitual" attributes of what was to be called Imagination—a totalizing consciousness whose medium is sense but whose power is transcendent. Apocalypse becomes immanent; the sublime, a daily habit.

The egotistical sublime tends to put the critic in a false position. A critic must at once assimilate a poem and define it; keep it "other," determinate. The egotistical sublime invites either homage, which quickly degenerates into the banalities of edification, or rejection, which is potentially the more interesting response, if it is not mere prejudice. The American Romanticist, nourished as he is by the still more drastic egotism of Emerson's sublime, finds his stance especially shaky. Perhaps it takes a kind of restlessness, an ungenerous resistance, to admire and yet to remark the bland outrageousness of the egotistical sublime; perhaps just a sense of how life works. The egotistical sublime subverts the negativity which is the ground of the "other" by ignoring its consequences. Certainly Wordsworth's thought is not dialectical; the "other" is not a phase to be recognized and subsumed; nor is it to be abrogated, as in a visionary poetics. Wordsworth appeals to a familial concord of mind and nature so that the power of each aggrandizes the other. Nature's power to exert transformations and perform blendings "upon the outward face of things" is "a genuine Counterpart / And Brother of the glorious faculty / Which higher minds bear with them as their own" (1805, 13. 88–90).

This is the very spirit in which they deal
With the whole compass of the universe:
They from their native selves can send abroad
Kindred mutations; for themselves create
A like existence; and, whene'er it dawns
Created for them, catch it, or are caught
By its inevitable mastery,
Like angels stopped upon the wing by sound
Of harmony from Heaven's remotest spheres.   [14.91–99]

What is astonishing is Wordsworth's indifference to priority: creating, catching what is created, or being "caught / By its inevitable mastery":

these are in the end—in perception—equivalent, and one need not worry the difference between what the mind confers and what it receives.

In Keats we find an elemental critique of the egotistical sublime and its ultimate derivative, which Keats called *identity*. From the start, identity was a dreaded embarrassment for Keats: he sought enchantments that would be "self-destroying," but

> . . . when new wonders ceased to float before
> And thoughts of self came on, how crude and sore
> The journey homeward to habitual self!
> A mad pursuing of the fog-born elf,
> Whose flitting lantern, through rude nettle-briar,
> Cheats us into a swamp, into a fire,
> Into the bosom of a hated thing.   [*Endymion* 2.274–80][16]

Keats's evolution toward the dialectical structures of the odes and beyond is a recovery of the power of negation and the dramatic "I" which is grounded in negative thinking. In the course of objecting to the "Wordsworthian or egotistical sublime," Keats describes the exemplary "poetical Character" as intelligence *without* identity: "it is not itself—it has no self—it is every thing and nothing—It has no character," no "unchangeable attribute."[17] Keats's battle with identity takes various and complicated forms, but he never ceased objecting, on both formal and moral grounds, to a poetic in which the ultimate function of perception and the goal of experience are to aggrandize the consciousness of who we are.

One feels Keats as a presence in the conscience of Wallace Stevens, who nevertheless attempts to restore the priority of the positive sublime. What is assertion for Wordsworth has become for Stevens a hope. The naivety is gone, for Stevens stands on the other side of Romantic dualism. Like Wordsworth, he is not willingly a dialectical poet: he too would celebrate the predialectical moment before perception's power yields to knowledge and what is created is differentiated from what is given. But Stevens knows better—knows that in the end such a moment is fictional—even if an absolute fiction—and that it therefore refers us back to an unexamined posture of the mind, a faith. Its consequence is therefore hypothetical—obsessively so, and Stevens is never quite free of the anxiety that his hope is after all a protest, and a regressive one at that:

> But to impose is not
> To discover. To discover an order as of
> A season, to discover summer and know it,

> To discover winter and know it well, to find,
> Not to impose, not to have reasoned at all,
> Out of nothing to have come on major weather,
>
> It is possible, possible, possible. It must
> Be possible.   ["Notes toward a Supreme Fiction"][18]

Suppose it is possible that order or "the real" will present itself to the mind as not of the mind, so that the mind is "caught / By its inevitable mastery." Will the "real" not then be mind in a former state, before its obsession with priority, still warm from the bosom of Mother Nature, and unlike anything that can be perceived?

> It must be that in time
> The real will from its crude compoundings come,
>
> Seeming, at first, a beast disgorged, unlike,
> Warmed by a desperate milk. To find the real,
> To be stripped of every fiction except one,
>
> The fiction of an absolute—Angel,
> Be silent in your luminous cloud and hear
> The luminous melody of proper sound.

Stevens's sophisticated regression discovers the primordial self at the moment of being weaned, and the supreme fiction is that this self is "an absolute." This fiction stops the Angel, as it did the angelic "higher minds" in Wordsworth, with the Miltonic promise that poetic order ("sound / Of harmony," "luminous melody of proper sound") is heard, not made.

But the poetic order so revealed is not the ultimate derivative of the egotistical sublime, as Keats saw. A further step is indicated, in which the primordial self discovered as the "real" ground of the phenomenal ("crude compoundings") is appropriated. The later consciousness, or ego, is aggrandized by the perceptional power of its former state. Both Wordsworth and Stevens erect a "positive" theology of the self on the premise that whatever is discovered is, after all, an attribute or potentiality of consciousness in its current state. This sets up an infinite regress in which any determinate state of the self—past or on the verge of becoming past, created (fictional) or discovered (perceptional)—is subsumed into an "I" that is ever expanding, limited only by death or the failure of memory. For such an "I" the present has no unique content and exists in fact only as the capacious vessel of the past. Everything external or "out there" is transmuted into the substance of mind, which accumulates like a kind of capital. "I gazed—and gazed—but little

thought / What wealth the show to me had brought" says Wordsworth,[19] but there comes a time when the wealth is added up, appropriated and possessed, by the "inward eye," which also collects a
due rate of interest from the perception's having been dormant. Although the protagonist of the egotistical sublime celebrates (naively or
nostalgically) the moment of undifferentiated perception, he is fulfilled
by the hour of possession. It is inconceivable that Wordsworth should
have given us the Mount Snowdon vision without the subsequent
editorializing in which he turns experience into emblem and takes possession. Stevens hopes to prolong that golden hour, but his bold attempt
to confer relative permanence upon a moment which has no genuinely
transtemporal point of reference seems to me experientially dubious.

In "Notes," Stevens's Angel is the figure whose power comes from the
overcoming of the divide between imposing and discovering; he is
therefore a fiction, as that overcoming was mediated by the "final fiction
of an absolute." Here Stevens's "I" in turn possesses the Angel:

Am I that imagine this angel less satisfied?
Are the wings his, the lapis-haunted air?

Is it he or is it I that experience this?
Is it I then that keep saying there is an hour
Filled with expressible bliss, in which I have

No need, am happy, forget need's golden hand,
Am satisfied without solacing majesty,
And if there is an hour there is a day,

There is a month, a year, there is a time
In which majesty is a mirror of the self:
I have not but I am and as I am, I am.

The moment of the "real" had been exposed in its fictionality; otherness
is therefore fictional; as the creator of fictions, the "I" has nothing more
to possess, and the only nonfictional statement that can be made brings
the "I" to the starting point of Cartesian scepticism, Coleridgean
imagination, and biblical theophany itself. But there is nothing that
takes Stevens out of time; he is reasoning from time to larger time, and
not beyond death. The egotistical sublime enlarges time "till Time shall
be no more," but it cannot break through the temporal and does not
prefigure apocalypse. Wordsworth is more convincing than Stevens in
his vulnerability to time. In "Tintern Abbey" for example, the several
moments of recognition have the rhetorical form of possessed totality,
but each yields to the plangency of chronic supersession. The reader

devoted to a visionary poetic is likely to feel that there is something morally sinister in the egotistical sublime. It is as if the Red Cross Knight, at the height of his visionary education, were led up the steep hill to meet Contemplation—and there found the venerable figure gazing in a mirror at the majesty of himself, not at the heavenly city.

Yet even if we avoid measuring it by what it is not, the implications of the egotistical sublime are disturbing. It raises a problem of faith and a problem of form. "What am I to believe?" asks Stevens after he has arrived at the imagined Angel as the outcome of "the fiction of an absolute." To be stripped of *every* fiction would be to be stripped of the "real" itself, and of the Angel, its imagined beholder. Is Stevens then to take his stand on a final belief—Am I then to believe? he is asking; and, In what? In the Angel—but Stevens knows the Angel to be an imagined thing; hence the final fiction itself has already been stripped. There is no way to limit the claim of knowledge upon the final fiction, and Stevens ends in the stance of the sceptical philosopher who is enjoined to place everything heuristically in doubt but the self-evident fact of his doubting. "I am and since I am, at least I know the 'I' is not a fiction to be stripped"; but also (and this is the large claim), "I am and, in just the way that I self-evidently exist, everything that is also me (the Angel and all fictions), also exists." Had Stevens not pushed his argument beyond the final fiction, he would certainly have risked bad faith, for calculating the risk in terms of the notion of fiction does not eliminate it. As responsible as Wordsworth was to the sceptical injunctions of the enlightenment and as subject as he was to the "abyss of idealism," he could never have propounded the fictive character of the real.

Hegel associated the "positive" sublime with pantheism, or the aesthetics of immanence.[20] In the positive sublime, spirit and matter are differentiated in principle but not yet in the fact of perception or intuition. This condition of spirit is relatively primitive in Hegel's view (although the late Goethe is cited as a contemporary avatar), and it must progress to the "true" or "negative" sublime. This happens when the divine "One Substance" retires from the phenomenal world and is recognized as "pure Inwardness and substantive Power (*reine Innerlichkeit und substantielle Macht*)."[21] Hegel does not consider the "Romantic" sublime, in which the ego more or less replaces the immanent One, and his evolutionism is difficult to endorse at this late date. The dynamical element in Hegel's myth is the irresistable progress of analytical differentiation. (In this respect his myth is roughly Blake's stood on its head: the significant events are similar, but they are oppositely valorized.) Here as elsewhere Hegel seems to be projecting the specific determinations of postenlightenment thinking back into early eras. (Blake does this too.)

So an application of Hegel's account to the Romantic sublime in some sense restores its original ground. The movement in both Coleridge and Wordsworth away from the doctrine of the One Life and toward the differentiated opposition of imagination and nature is formally reprised in Hegel's logic of the sublime. The positive sublime cannot survive analysis into an "inwardness" set over and against an "outer."

In his penultimate phase, Stevens is on the verge of believing that the positive sublime can survive. For he requires that the real come "from its crude compoundings," from "out there," and yet that it confirm the inward order he would impose. But once this "absolute" is recognized and identified as a fiction, the brave affair must either become religion or become irony. It may seem to some that the very sophistication and irony of Stevens's recursion to the egotistical sublime renders the regressive character of its motive the more apparent. "It is possible, possible, possible. It must / Be possible": this is the unsublimatable protest, an echo of the very tone of what Blake called Innocence at the painful moment of its supersession. Freud might well have recognized in that last fiction the absolute resistance of primary narcissism, without which the self is finished. Fortunately, as we have seen, Stevens advances to the secondary narcissism of appropriating the Angel as his own. Stevens's great trick, against Freud and (perhaps deliberately) against Coleridge's famous definition of the imagination, is to present this secondary narcissism as compensation for the loss of primary narcissism and, indeed, as its supersession. The moralist, frustrated by this subtlety, will wish to charge Stevens or any egotistical romantic with a refusal to grow up, but of course the Wordsworthian poet will welcome the charge. Adulthood, after all, is usually conceived as the "reasoning negative" of childhood; the mind *completely* adult, without the power of childhood illusions to sublimate, is virtually dead, if it is possible at all. The ultimate fictionality of the egotistical sublime subverts the hierophant who requires edification and rests in a faith. But the specter of knowledge purchased by loss of power must haunt the moralist who pursues maturity to a dead end.

The regressive structure of the egotistical sublime raises a formal problem that may in the end be more important than the disclosure of psychological correlatives. It is widely admitted that it is difficult to specify the formal status of the "I" in Romantic lyric poems, and it is no secret that several schools of criticism have profited from the general confusion. Phenomenological criticism has brilliantly deconstructed Romantic imagery but at the cost of fudging the distinction between poet and speaker, who tend to dissolve into the mist of immanent consciousness. The problem is that the lyric "I" so often seems to escape from its contained, dramatic determination and become itself a container. It is as if the "I" were aware of its own presentation in the poem; its progress becomes the successive assimilation or rejection of its former states, so that in the end only a purely theoretical line, not any differential of consciousness, separates it from the present of the maker. Poet, speaker, and reader are merged into one adventure of progressive consciousness. And the phenomenologists are firmly grounded in the peculiar character of Romantic discourse. Wordsworth himself read his own poems in this way, as Albert Wlecke has shown.[22] The fusion—which looks like confusion to those groomed on the modernist doctrine of the persona—turns out to be a structural and even programmatic feature of Romantic texts.

We recall that Stevens's "I" subsumed the Angel precisely as the fictionality of that Angel became apparent: we found in this the essential gesture of the egotistical sublime. "I can / Do all that angels can" and more, says Stevens. In the ultimate logic of this poetic, all determinations of the imagination, whether fictional or perceptional, are at once canceled and preserved—sublimated in the sense of Hegel's central term, *aufheben*. Romanticism as a whole is often advertised as the sublimation of traditional or religious doctrine; M. H. Abrams takes this point of view in his comprehensive study *Natural Supernaturalism*. In a poem responding to the logic of sublimation, the great shifter "I" will be constantly expanding in its reference, until it approaches the absolute present of the maker. "Am I that imagine this angel less satisfied?": here the sense of a dramatic speaker is attenuated to the zero degree. In the absolute state of such an "I", everything but itself is a fiction. Poetry, dependent as it is upon "external regions," even if they are only "reflections" of the I, mere "escapades of death" (as Stevens goes on to say), threatens to evaporate altogether, as Hegel in fact thought it ultimately should.

But there is another logic of response to fictionality, equally central to Romanticism as a whole. The egotistical sublime strips fictions of their ontological significance—their power, as symbol or epiphany, to crash through the phenomenal and articulate essence of eternity. The poet, like Yeats, who invests fictions with ontological meaning inevitably resurrects the question of belief. His answer to Stevens's question, What am I to believe? is going to take a quasi-religious form. Disillusionment, or the confrontation with fictionality, is here genuine crisis, not the occasion for self-aggrandizing sublimation. In fact, the characteristic response of the believers (or "dreamers") to this crisis is *de*sublimation, a great contrary tendency in Romanticism that predominates in disillusion poems from the antistrophe of Collins's "Ode on the Poetical Char-

acter" to Coleridge's "Dejection: An Ode," Keats's "Ode to a Nightingale," and Yeats's "The Circus Animals' Desertion." Desublimation is
particularly appropriate to romance and seems to be referrable to a later
(not "higher" or "deeper"!) phase in the ontogenetic career of the
imagination, a stage in which the reality-principle and fantasy are ir-
revocably at odds. Like its contrary, the poem of desublimation is self-
reflexive and sceptical of its fictions; it too "reads" itself, but with different consequence. In stanza 7 of the "Ode to a Nightingale" Keats
makes the bird immortal, its voice heard "In ancient days by emperor
and clown," and (in surmise) by sad-hearted Ruth. This is a fictive bird,

> The same that oft-times hath
> Charm'd magic casements, opening on the foam
> Of perilous seas, in faery lands forlorn.
>
> 8
> Forlorn! the very word is like a bell
> To toll me back from thee to my sole self!
> Adieu! the fancy cannot cheat so well
> As she is fam'd to do, deceiving elf.   [68–74]

The "I" of stanza 8 recognizes the fictionality of the image just advanced,
and it desublimates: "forlorn" is reduced back out of the fiction to the
"sole self" where it originated. In a similar gesture Yeats finds his sublimating ladder gone and has to "lie down where all the ladders start, /
In the foul rag and bone shop of the heart."[23] How would Stevens—the
Stevens we have read—have moved in this situation? Would he not
have claimed as his all that the fictive bird could be—and more, the
power of imagining such a bird?

Most Romantic poems eddy back and forth between the logic of sublimation and its contrary. Unfortunately, we cannot digress still further
into an extended demonstration of this situation or the usefulness of so
describing it. In the poem of desublimation the spiritual cost is perfectly
evident as the "I" submits to drastic reductions. Does the egotistical
sublime have a cost, or is it in fact "genuine liberty," as Wordsworth
says (P 14.132)? This is not a genetic matter, for we are not interested
in the poet as man: we are testing the tough-mindedness of a spiritual
posture. "I see, and sing, by my own eyes inspired," says Keats in the
"Ode to Psyche," a subtle tour de force in the egotistical sublime. What
kind of seeing is this, and what is it worth? Keats himself moved
quickly away from the blandishments of sublimation, and there is a
profound critique of it in The Fall of Hyperion. But the argument from a
poetic career is also an extrinsic one, and our method here requires an

intrinsic critique of what Blake called a state, through which individuals pass and in fact repass. Wordsworth himself was not by any means always in the "state" of the egotistical sublime. At times he is fully committed to desublimation, as in phases of the Intimations Ode and in "Resolution and Independence." I for one find him most moving when he is sounding for himself the risks and dangers of the egotistical sublime. Brooding on the fate of the sensibility poets—especially Chatterton, whose need to believe and to be believed in was so desperate—Wordsworth reflects that

> By our own spirits are we deified:
> We poets in our youth begin in gladness;
> But thereof come in the end despondency and madness.
>
> ["Resolution and Independence," ll. 47–49]

The poets are made gods by themselves and by nothing else; they are therefore self-begotten, but totally dependent upon their own fluctuating spirits, the labile content of their mere "I am." To have not, but to be, is also to be nothing more than one can make oneself. Everything and nothing are here too close for comfort, and perhaps only the self-consciousness of the poet stands between.

Poets, however, are up to such risks, which in any case they have no choice about. It is not in the assumption of spiritual risks that the egotistical romantic pays for the hybris of his sublimation. Nothing is got for nothing. The cost is there, and it is paid in the text, not in extrinsic circumstance. If we were subtle enough as moralists to discern the inner economics of poems we might learn to measure them, not by the immensity of the claim staked out for the "I" in its golden hour, but by their authenticity, the precision with which accounts are balanced. The "I" in the sublimating phase of a poem loses the potentiality of a dramatic or implicit "I" and becomes a reflective, ruminating "I" whose perception or imagery is always refracted through its sense of itself. The unmediated vision is prior to the egotistical sublime and can continue in it only as nostalgia or as food for thought. Hence the reader's odd sense of diminishment as perception contracts to identity, however exalted.

Poetic sublimation is in fact a specific instance of the general economic law of sublimation, whether of labor (capitalism), of sexuality (narcissism), or of perception (abstraction). Sublimation is the transubstantiation of what Marx called "individualities" and Blake called "minute particulars" into an abstract medium of exchange. Work, libido, and perception are freed from the limits of one determinate context and constitute a fund of energy that can either be voluntarily expended in a variety of specific contexts or simply treasured up. But the price of this freedom for will or ego—and of this enhanced sense of self—is alienation from particular forms of primary experience. These forms become mere potentialities, reflections, fortuitous externalizations. In secondary narcissism, energy or libido is withdrawn from objects and directed toward or within the ego itself. Objects and persons are not only poor surrogates, but their specificity is irrelevant, and they are essentially interchangeable occasions for the love-energy. According to Marx, in the transition from the aristocratic condition of landownership to the capitalist order, it is inevitable "that all personal relationships between the property owner and his property should cease, and the latter become purely *material* wealth."[24] Sublimation melts the formal otherness of things and reduces them to material or to substance. The formal properties of the perceived particular are canceled and replaced by their "significance," values assessed and assigned by the mind.

The imagination is often rendered as the power of reconciling the particular and the universal. It is worth noting, however, that this emphasis is Coleridge's and not Wordsworth's. Coleridge never could manage the egotistical sublime. His eye was particular and his mind too aware of its projections for the moment of undifferentiated perception or its memory to survive in him. "Frost at Midnight" seems at first to hover on the edge of a Wordsworthian fadeout which never quite occurs: the dualism is overt as fluttering film and the "idling Spirit" are paralleled as "companionable forms."[25] In the end the poem is resolved in an imagery brilliantly particular from which the "I" wholly disappears—the aesthetic of the beautiful and not the sublime. Coleridge writes best when his "I" is in suspension. Wordsworth's theorizing, on the other hand, tends to relegate determinate perception to the inferior realm of fancy. In Wordsworth, the imagination is the faculty which transforms everything into the money of the mind. It confers, abstracts, and modifies; it dissolves, separates, and consolidates; it "recoils from every thing but the plastic, the pliant, and the indefinite,"[26] because too great an attachment to determinate objects makes sublimation impossible, as Freud often pointed out.

The theory of sublimation has a genetic air about it, for this is how it has been applied by psychologizing criticism. But we have claimed for sublimation a constitutive role in the imaginative logic that determines or influences the "I" of a Romantic poem. Sublimation may in fact be the condition under which an "I" can enter a poem at all. In any case, there are many forms of poetic sublimation short of the absolute, imaginative degree of the egotistical sublime. They cannot be recognized unless we assume the "I" of a poem to be a coherent consciousness whose ups and downs obey a rhythm independent of the poet's self-presentation, whatever that may be. Oddly enough, purely formalist readings of Romantic poems in effect expose the poems to disintegration by ignoring their inner logic, the adventure of an "I." The pattern elucidated by the formalist refers us to the extrinsic coherence of the maker whose artistry is celebrated as the poem's organic unity.

Occasionally, however, opposed assumptions about the intrinsic progress of a meditation seem to be equally tenable. The first three stanzas of "Resolution and Independence" raise such a problem:

1
There was a roaring in the wind all night;
The rain came heavily and fell in floods;
But now the sun is rising calm and bright;
The birds are singing in the distant woods;
Over his own sweet voice the Stock-dove broods;
The Jay makes answer as the Magpie chatters;
And all the air is filled with pleasant noise of waters.

2
All things that love the sun are out of doors;
The sky rejoices in the morning's birth;
The grass is bright with rain-drops;—on the moors
The hare is running races in her mirth;
And with her feet she from the plashy earth
Raises a mist; that, glittering in the sun,
Runs with her all the way, wherever she doth run.

3
I was a Traveller then upon the moor;
I saw the hare that raced about with joy;
I heard the woods and distant waters roar;
Or heard them not, as happy as a boy:
The pleasant season did my heart employ:
My old remembrances went from me wholly;
And all the ways of men, so vain and melancholy.   [1–21]

The shift of tense is salient: to what time does "then" (l. 15) refer? The suggestion is strong that it is the very time pictured in stanzas one and two, and the very moor, hare, woods, and waters. But if so, why the puzzling shift to the past—as if the poem had to begin twice? The arrival of the "I" in the poem displaces the opening imagery with a force that challenges interpretation. There is, of course, a way out: we may suppose, with Jack Stillinger, that "from his situation in the present, the speaker here shifts to the past-tense recollection of an earlier day ("then"), the remainder of the poem. The pleasantness of the day, the sounds of nature, and especially the racing hare are the linking elements that arouse the recollection."[27] This tack simplifies the emergence of the "I," but it requires us to take the definitely specified objects of stanza three generically and indefinitely. It also convicts the poet (as well as the speaker) of a confusing and indefinite reference ("then"). The implicit juxtaposition of two days seems arbitrary, and uncharacteristic in a poet who always provides an explicit bridge to conscious recollection. Besides, the poem will veer back and forth between present and past: these shifts are coherent only as events within the logic of one experience.

We certainly have a major clue when we note the coincidence of the shift to the past and the appearance of the anaphoristic initial "I." Evidently the entrance of the "I" requires the retreat of sensory impressions into the medium of memory. The anaphora, here as elsewhere in Wordsworth (e.g., "Tintern Abbey"), suggests a compulsive rhythm and some hesitancy in proceeding. The rhythm is broken in the odd retraction "Or heard them not, as happy as a boy," which liberates the "I" from a determinate memory. Truth to the fact of hearing or not hearing is sacrificed to the mind's greater sense of potentiality in not having to choose. Here is the equivocal freedom of sublimation: surmise is purchased by the loss of sense: the auditory plenitude of the first two stanzas is now reduced to the merely possible as well as to the past—it is doubly "distant." Other details contribute to the effect of dense, faintly ominous mediation. "Pleasant season" is an abstraction hinting at transitoriness, for the seasonal is only a phase; the hyperbatic "did my heart employ" suggests the temporary preoccupation of the heart rather than its full participation. And in the final lines of the stanza, the pleasant time is explicitly placed in a wider context of the "vain and melancholy."

The entrance of the "I" induces a small-scale sublimation. The imagery of the first two stanzas proceeds without an "I" and turns self-sufficiently, in a dozen ways, on reciprocity and plenitude. The roaring wind and falling rain are answered by the sun, which is calm and rising; the birds answer themselves (even the note of trouble in the brooding of the Stock-dove is answered by the Jay); sky and morning, grass and raindrops—indeed, "all things" and the sun make a series of participatory pairs. The mist raised from the "plashy earth . . . glittering in the sun" unites all four elements and is itself joined to the hare. How is the "I" to enter this scene which has no need for it and in which it has no place? The "I" must arrogate to itself the reciprocity and plenitude before it as if it were the necessary antiphon to hare, woods, and waters.

And so it rather heavily does. But this is only low-order sublimation, some degree below the sublime. The "I" is still passive before appearances. The change of tense displaces not only the sensory impressions but also self-consciousness and its attendant anxiety. As the temperature of that anxiety rises in the poem—twice forcing it back into the present tense (ll. 31 and 46)—sublimation changes its theater from memory, an indirect alienation of appearances, to imagination—a direct transformation of the "other." (Wordsworth himself cites the picture of the old man as an instance of "the conferring, the abstracting, and the modifying powers of the Imagination."[28]) The mode of memory might be considered sublimation at the lower intensity of fancy.

At all events, there is in the egotistical sublime a natural progression from undifferentiated perception (in which the "I" is immanent) through memory (in which both "I" and object are mediated by the past) to imagination—which proceeds, as Wordsworth would have it, from "a sublime consciousness of the soul in her own mighty and almost divine powers."[29] At every point this sublimating is in response to the pressure of anxiety; so in "Resolution and Independence" the "fears and fancies . . . Dim sadness—and blind thoughts, I knew not, nor could name" are already present as the motive power in the poem's early self-alienation. Here we have emphasized not the motive of sublimation but its economic structure, its inevitable cost. As the Romantic ego approaches godhead, the minute particulars which are the world fade out.

3. *And I will place within them as a guide*
My umpire conscience, whom if they will hear,
Light after light well used they shall attain,
And to the end persisting, safe arrive.

O conscience! into what abyss of fears
And horrors hast thou driven me; out of which
I find no way, from deep to deeper plunged!
—Milton, *Paradise Lost*

Darkning Man: Blake's Critique of Transcendence

At first look, the negative or Kantian sublime and the positive or egotistical sublime seem to be genuine contraries. Against the collapse of the sensible imagination, brought on by the noumenal reason's thirst for totality, we may plausibly set the imagination's exaltation—whether as the agency of immanence or as a projective, fictional power—in the egotistical sublime. The positive sublime is insured against the moment of sudden loss because its attachment to the object is from the start a secondary affair, a limited engagement protectively suffused with self-love. We have seen, too, that the egotistical sublime evades or subverts dualism by declining to polarize thought and perception into a timeless, noumenal order and a finite, sensible world. The state of undifferentiated perception, as fact, memory, nostalgia, or fiction, is its touchstone.

Yet within the egotistical sublime we found both an essential instability and, ultimately, a principle of limitation. The logic of the egotistical sublime is dynamic but also perpetual: the "highest bliss" such minds can know is "the consciousness / Of Whom they are, habitually infused / Through every image and through every thought" (*P* 14.114–16). The egotistical sublime is restless but repetitive, habit forming. The mind so deployed has "endless occupation . . . whether discursive or intuitive" but no chance of a leap through or beyond time. Wallace Stevens would expand the hour of "expressible bliss" into a month, a year, "a time / In which majesty is a mirror of the self," but in the section of "Notes" that immediately follows, he settles down to the chronic context of even such a claim:

> These things at least comprise
> An occupation, an exercise, a work,
>
> A thing final in itself and, therefore, good:
> One of the vast repetitions final in
> Themselves and, therefore, good, the going round
>
> And round and round, the merely going round,
> Until merely going round is a final good,
> The way wine comes at a table in a wood.
>
> And we enjoy like men, the way a leaf
> Above the table spins its constant spin,
> So that we look at it with pleasure, look
>
> At it spinning its eccentric measure. Perhaps,
> The man-hero is not the exceptional monster,
> But he that of repetition is most master.[1]

In "Circles," Emerson speaks of man's "continual effort to raise himself above himself, to work a pitch above his last height," and finds his image for such ceaseless sublimating in the "generation of circles, wheel without wheel."[2] The soul moves outward, bursting over each concentric orbit of limitation. But since the soul's self-transcendence is without term, the generation of circles itself succumbs to the circularity of succession: this is "the circular or compensatory character of every human action . . . the moral fact of the Unattainable . . . at once the inspirer and the condemner of every success."[3] It is true that in "Compensation," Emerson excepts the soul—unjustifiably, it seems to me— from the universal "tax" or "penalty" of compensation. But the debt returns to be partially paid in "Circles," in the relativity of ceaseless supersession, if not in the proportional contraction of perception that we have argued. Because time will not relent, the ultimate form of activity in the egotistical sublime is circular. The negative sublime, on the contrary, suggests an infinite parallelism in which the perception of an object *as* sublime is a kind of parallax.

Readers of Blake will be tempted to recognize in Emerson's "generation of circles, wheel without wheel" and also in Stevens's "the going round, / And round and round, the merely going round" Blake's central imagery of fallen limitation, the circle of destiny or the mills of Satan. Emerson propounds an exuberance without a determinate object, so that the prolific soul of "Circles" seems more solipsistic than creative, and it is always subject to time. And repetition, however large the scope of its acts, is tantamount to disaster for Blake. "The same dull round even of a univer[s]e would soon become a mill with complicated wheels" (E, 2). Blake's central conviction, dramatized in the career of his character Urizen, is that solipsism and the rational alienation of perception into mechanical regularity both result from the same imaginative disease. Blake is equally acute in diagnosing the negative sublime, of which Urizen is also in some respects the type. Both versions of transcendence are reduced, in Blake's radical therapy of culture, to one malaise of perception. Blake learned from Milton, if not from life, that the Fall is immensely and necessarily overdetermined and that any definitive explanation is likely to turn into justification. What looks like indecision in the matter of a cause of the Fall is really the result of a technique in which distinct but correlative motives are superimposed. And about the results of the Fall Blake is definitive, though very complicated; best of all, he offers all the advantages of a perspective truly outside the Romantic sublime.

And some disadvantages as well. Blake is not, with all the distinguished scholarship, getting any easier to read. I used to think he was: with a little diligence the system could be mastered; the difficulty seemed conceptual, the very thing to engage the energetic compulsions of an ever-intellectualizing critic like the author of this book. But then I found myself at crucial points left outside the charmed circularity of Blakean hermeneutics, even playing with the vulgarity, Will the real Blake please appear? It would be ungenerous to cavil at the commentary, which nevertheless now illuminates and surrounds Blake like a hovering cherub. Blake has a way of turning his critics into apologists, and we still await the study at once fully informed, (a major project now), free from prejudice, *and* written from the proper distance. But it is not in the conditions of Blake's recent and spectacular academic success that the difficulty lies. The question is how to read Blake exoterically. He was certainly an ironic poet, rarely to be caught speaking in his own person; so there is an essential problem of tone which cannot be resolved by the application of a schematic calculus, however authentic.

The emotions of his text look simple enough: pity, fear, grief, rage, jealousy, pain, joy—elemental stuff. But their permutations seem to make sense only conceptually. More rarely in Blake than in any other major poet does one have the sense that one has been there, at just that point of feeling. Or have we read him wrongly?

Consider the Zoas. One doesn't get far thinking of them exclusively as faculties or psychic agencies correlative to some other system such as Freud's. Each of the Zoas is a character in the specific sense that each is endowed with consciousness, whereas in Freud's system consciousness is ascribed only to a portion of the ego. The Zoas are states of mind and feeling as well as figures in a design. It is true that behind what seems to be an arbitrary turn in the careers of the Zoas, we nearly always find an analytic insight and not a realized moment of consciousness. But perhaps a subtler ear could discern the experiential correlative of the insight. We ought in any case to dispense with all the talk of "on one level" or the other; it's a tired metaphor that now stands in the way. I think the next great leap in the reading of Blake will come when we devise an interpretative language for the obscure contiguities of schematization and consciousness. At what point does a schema begin to be "lived"? Conversely, where does experience schematize itself or merge into the design it unconsciously plays out? This, in a sense, is our problem with Kant, whose concepts we are beginning to personify in the hope of finding a deeper structure beneath the subreptions of his logic.

After all this beating of the drum my reader will rightly hope for more than the confrontation of Blake and Kant which is our current agenda. Unfortunately, an authentic sounding of Blake lies outside the scope of this book, if not indeed of its author, for our subject is the Romantic poetics of sublimation, which Blake, quite literally, as the story goes, could not stomach. Yet I shall attempt to uncover something of Urizen's felt predicament in the moment of his fall, for it seems to me a version of the sublime moment. To the contemporary method of reading Blake entirely in his own terms I can only oppose a somewhat tendentious effort to think through, by way of Kant, the experience of self-consciousness which attends reason in the crisis of the sublime. A strong case can easily be made for Blake's enmity to the Romantic sublime on the "level" of art theory, and although this is not how we would engage Blake, his opinions as an aesthetician are worth a passing look as an introduction to his powerful concern with perception.[4] Blake's views on the sublime as an aesthetic category are perfectly clear in his annotations to Reynolds's *Discourses*. He found Reynolds's work to be grounded on Burke's treatise on the sublime and the beautiful, which in turn was founded on the opinions of Newton and Locke, with whom Blake always associated Bacon. Reading all these men, he felt "Contempt and Abhorrence," for "They mock Inspiration & Vision" (E, 650). Blake uses the word *sublime* as a general honorific and obviously had no use for the distinction, fashionable after Burke (1757), between the sublime and the beautiful. His sublime is not the Romantic sublime. What piqued him most in Reynolds was praise of general conceptions and disdain of minuteness. And Burke's recommendation of obscurity seemed to him disastrous.

Minute Discrimination is Not Accidental All Sublimity is founded on Minute Discrimination

A Facility in Composing is the Greatest Power of Art & Belongs to None but the Greatest Artists, i.e. the Most Minutely Discriminating and Determinate

The Man who asserts that there is no Such Thing as Softness in Art & that every thing in Art is Definite & Determinate has not been told this by Practise but by Inspiration & Vision because Vision is Determinate & Perfect & he Copies That without Fatigue Every thing being Definite & determinate Softness is Produced Alone by Comparative Strength & Weakness in the Marking out of the Forms

Without Minute Neatness of Execution. The. Sublime cannot Exist! Grandeur of Ideas is founded on Precision of Ideas

Singular & Particular Detail is the Foundation of the Sublime

Distinct General Form Cannot Exist Distinctness is Particular Not General

Broken Colours & Broken Lines & Broken Masses are Equally Subversive of the Sublime

Obscurity is Neither the Source of the Sublime nor of any Thing Else   [E, 632–47]

As an annotator, Blake is delightfully sure of himself and gives no quarter. What seems perverse is his insistence that only when vision is determinate, minute, and particular does it conduct to or contain infinity. The eye which would "see a World in a Grain of Sand" (E, 481) must be a "Determinate Organ" (E, 627). Infinite perception must be distinguished from the perception of the "indefinite," which is Blake's version of mental hell. Blake is not merely wittily inverting the terms of contemporary aesthetic discourse. "It is not in Terms that Reynolds &

I disagree   Two Contrary Opinions can never by any Language be made alike" (E, 648). Nor is he, with Kant and the philosophers, worrying the phenomenological ambiguity of infinity. He conceived perception to be the fundamental index of consciousness, subsuming the primary and secondary degrees as formulated by Coleridge. It is an activity of which both object and image are merely phases or products. We have seen how the Wordsworthian "fade-out" signals a sublimation in which the formal properties of what is seen are dissolved and the residual otherness of the thing is alienated as indefinite substance. Here, for Blake, is the very crisis of man's Fall. In his view, the positive and negative sublimes turn out to be not genuine contraries but two versions of the same lapse, itself the negation of visionary perception. Blake's myth of the Fall is an analytic critique of sublimation.

The Psychopolitics of Reason

What then can Blake tell us about the anxiety we suppose to be at work behind sublimation? We recall the defeat of the sensible imagination or phenomenal intellect in Kant's theory of the sublime. The nearest analogue in Blake to the "understanding" of the philosophers is Urizen, whose fall in Night III of Blake's manuscript epic *The Four Zoas* is suggestively parallel to the mind's self-alienation in Kant.[5] Here first is Kant, at his most psychological, describing the crucial moment; the delight in the sublime is *negative*:

> that is to say it is a feeling of imagination by its own act depriving itself of its freedom by receiving a final determination in accordance with a law other than that of its empirical employment. In this way it gains an extension and a power greater than that which it sacrifices. But the ground of this is concealed from it, and in its place it *feels* the sacrifice or deprivation, as well as its cause, to which it is subjected.[6]

The imagination is evidently in an ambivalent position. It deprives itself "by its own act," and yet it passively receives its orders for this self-deprivation from the law of reason. As a proponent of sublimation, Kant would have it that the gain is greater than the sacrifice, but this is certainly not how it feels from the imagination's point of view. The imagination is here the victim of superior forces, and its self-mutilation can be explained only by the "cause"—fear. The text goes on to assert that

> the *astonishment* which borders on terror, the awe and thrill of devout feeling, that takes hold of one . . . is not actual fear, but rather only an

attempt to enter into it [fear] with the imagination, in order to feel the power of this faculty in combining the movement of the mind thereby aroused with its serenity, and of thus being superior to the nature within us, and therefore also to external nature, so far as the latter can have any influence upon our feeling of well-being.

[Pp. 120–21; 5, 269]

The passage is not perspicuous; Kant's personification gets cloudy. It seems the imagination is exposed to fear in order to arouse its power, but this fear is at the same time sublimated or internalized in the wider consciousness of the mind as a whole. Thus, in its converted, ego-form, the power is lost to the imagination (hence the feeling of sacrifice and deprivation), but further, it is directed back against the imagination (the "nature within us") as a superior force. Kant's sublime celebrates the ingenious capacity of the ego to live off the energy and labor of another, who is kept ignorant of what is going on. The imagination can share in the power only by identifying with its superior and hence depriving itself by its own act.

I have gradually modulated into a Blakean politics of the psyche by intensifying Kant's hints of personification. Blake takes his psycho-political schemata much further into a properly mythopoeic dimension, a fact which may signal the presence of conceptual antinomies which the myth expresses without resolving. The Zoas fall into an obsession with power and face each other in a shifting series of master-slave confrontations. Urizen falls spectacularly when he rejects his emanation Ahania in a fit of what is now called male chauvinism. Schematically, the original condition of Ahania might be said to represent the unselfconscious unity of mind and object which attends creative intellectual work and that is the pleasure without which nothing of real value ever gets articulated. Ahania's own fall directly precedes and precipitates Urizen's and may be understood in a preliminary way as the well-known decline of such work into an alienating activity, so that its results confront the mind as an estranged reality over which the mind has no control and to which it must submit in a constant and fruitless sacrifice of mental energy. (Blake's doctrine of the emanation may be interpreted—apart from its esoteric provenance—in the analogous terms of the early, humanist Marx; indeed, the alienation of labor is a conspicuous theme in Romantic writers and is prominent in Schiller, Shelley, and of course Hegel.) As the third night of the Four Zoas opens, Ahania attempts to rescue her lord from the catastrophe engulfing his colleagues. She pleads with him to "Resume [his] fields of Light," apparently hoping, though she fears the worst, that the mind can retain its playful, creative powers

in a world devoted to rack. Her plea is eloquent and far-sighted, but
Urizen fails to understand and responds defensively:

She ended. [From] his wrathful throne burst forth the black
hail storm

Am I not God said Urizen. Who is Equal to me
Do I not stretch the heavens abroad or fold them up like a garment

He spoke mustering his heavy clouds around him black opake

Then thunders rolld around & lightnings darted to & fro
His visage changd to darkness & his strong right hand came forth
To cast Ahania to the Earth he siezd her by the hair
And threw her from the steps of ice that froze around his throne

Saying Art thou also become like Vala. thus I cast thee out
Shall the feminine indolent bliss. the indulgent self of weariness
The passive idle sleep the enormous night & darkness of Death
Set herself up to give her laws to the active masculine virtue
Thou little diminutive portion that darst be a counterpart
Thy passivity thy laws of obedience & insincerity
Are my abhorrence. Wherefore hast thou taken that fair form
Whence is this power given to thee! once thou wast in my breast
A sluggish current of dim waters. on whose verdant margin
A cavern shaggd with horrid shades. dark and cool & deadly. where
I laid my head in the hot noon after the broken clods
Had wearied me. there I laid my plow & there my horses fed
And thou hast risen with thy moist locks into a watry image
Reflecting all my indolence my weakness & my death
To weigh me down beneath the grave into non Entity
Where Luvah strives scorned by Vala age after age wandering
Shrinking & shrinking from her Lord & calling him the Tempter
And art thou also become like Vala thus I cast thee out.

[42:18–43:22; E, 322]

Urizen's error is complex, as his defensive incoherence attests. He
associates Ahania with weakness, but this is pure projection, an unconscious attempt to externalize and thereby to expel his own mental
trouble. For it is Ahania who has called him to activity and lamented
his paralysis. By gazing on futurity, in which he descries the dread
Orc, Urizen has already lost the capacity for "present joy" (37:10);
hence his very recollection of former pleasure is poisoned into a memory
of "A cavern shaggd with horrid shades, dark and cool & deadly."
Thinking is no longer even conceivably fun, for the pleasures of deter-

minate intellect fall to the status of a "nature within us," which is erroneously identified with external nature, or Vala. Under the pressure of immense and unfamiliar anxiety, which springs from a fear of the future, the intellect is trying to concentrate—by concentrating itself. But this effort, heroic and pathetic at once, is doomed because Ahania is the source of all intellectual energy which does not emanate from anxiety. "Whence is this power given to thee!" asks the exasperated Urizen, as if he sensed that the very power he needs is being cut off by this self-mutilation. In this drastic sublimation, the determinate intellect or understanding aspires to superiority by alienating the "objective" imagining on which it is based. After this, the "King of Light" falls "down rushing, ruining, thundering, shuddering" into the state of generation. Blake locates ruin in precisely the same mental event that Kant would celebrate.

Blake's analytic of sublimation is shrewd enough to wrinkle the brow of any self-conscious literary intellectual. We stand to be valuably instructed, if not converted, by his spiritual economics, which are as severe as Freud's and yet argue for a vigorous mental activity not based on the paradox of reductive sublimation—the ceaseless contraction of "lower" into "higher" forms. On the whole, American intellectual culture is devoted to the ideology of the active ego, which can, so marvellously it seems, convert experience into the capital of power. In this context, Blake still has an antinomian aura, especially for those who take his rhetoric for his logic. There are many accounts of the Fall in Blake, and several critiques of sublimation in its sexual, political, and properly artistic guises. Each Fall involves a lapse, a failure or weakness like Urizen's weariness, and also an unjustified usurpation, an arrogation of exclusive power to one agency or faculty. Weakness releases the stuff of perception into an indeterminate otherness (as a refractory emanation) which is thus open for possession *by* another, and mental activity descends into a violent struggle for power jealously guarded and exercised. Blake fits the traditional and Miltonic theme of prideful usurpation into a psychological calculus of gain and loss, a law of compensation that runs through Generation. When any part of us is less creative than it could be, it immediately attempts to be more than it should, thereby becoming less than it was.

Consequently, we find the same ambiguity of cause in Blake's critique of the sublime that we found in Kant's analytic. There are several phases to Urizen's presumption, which is in each case proportionate to Albion's mental weariness. In Night I, Albion proposes to abandon the proper realm of thought (the South) to Luvah and announces his intention to invade the North, the domain of Urthona ("Earth-owner"), presumably

in order to achieve an ownership to which he is originally not entitled;
when Luvah objects, he departs secretly into the North anyway (21:16–
35; 22:1–10; 32–37). The conflict between Urizen and Luvah is the immediate cause of Urthona's fall (22:16–31). Urizen aspires to the total
possession or comprehension of the earth in the logical categories of the
understanding—even at the cost of surrendering perceptional clarity to
the passions. So, in Kant, the understanding and its correlative, the
sensible imagination, attempt to comprehend in *one* intuition a multitude
of discrete intuitions, even at the risk of an overextension of faculties and
a consequent frustration, a feeling of sacrifice and deprivation. Kant's
Vernunft ("higher reason") is a rich repository of indefinables, as its
transmogrifications in subsequent idealism attest. To some extent it
suggests both Urthona and the unfallen Tharmas, a principle of in-
tegration, but since it is conceived almost exclusively in negative terms,
it is primarily what Blake logically calls a "Negation" or Spectre, a "Holy
Reasoning Power" that "Negatives every thing" (E, 151). In Kant, as in
Blake, Reason is obsessed with superiority and holiness, and demands
awe.

In the moment of his fall, Urizen is turning into the Spectre as he
"negatives" Ahania into Vala and abstracts himself from her. Ahania's
attempt to forestall their mutual ruin is doomed not only by Urizen's
defensiveness but also by her own naiveté, which must be explicated
briefly if we wish to understand the negative sublime as a moment of
feeling. Ahania presents a version of Albion's fall as a warning to Urizen,
but she fails to see—in one of Blake's masterly ironies—how Urizen is
already implicated in that fall:

Then O my dear lord listen to Ahania, listen to the vision
The vision of Ahania in the slumbers of Urizen
When Urizen slept in the porch & the Ancient Man was smitten

The Darkning Man walkd on the steps of fire before his halls
And Vala walked with him in dreams of soft deluding slumber
He looked up & saw thee Prince of Light thy splendor faded
[*But saw not Los nor Enitharmon for Luvah hid them in shadow*]

[*In a soft cloud Outstretch'd across, & Luvah dwelt in the cloud*]

Then Man ascended mourning into the splendors of his palace
Above him rose a Shadow from his wearied intellect
Of living gold, pure, perfect, holy; in white linen pure he hover'd
A sweet entrancing self delusion, a watry vision of Man
Soft exulting in existence all the Man absorbing

Man fell upon his face prostrate before the watry shadow
Saying O Lord whence is this change thou knowest I am nothing
And Vala trembled & covered her face, & her locks were spread on the
    pavement

I heard astonishd at the Vision & my heart trembled within me
I heard the voice of the Slumberous Man & thus he spoke
Idolatrous to his own Shadow words of Eternity uttering
O I am nothing when I enter into judgment with thee
If thou withdraw thy breath I die & vanish into Hades
If thou dost lay thine hand upon me behold I am silent
If thou withhold thine hand I perish like a fallen leaf
O I am nothing & to nothing must return again
If thou withdraw thy breath, behold I am oblivion

He ceasd: the shadowy voice was silent; but the cloud hoverd over
    their heads   [39:12–40;19; E, 320–21]

The uncorrupted Urizen may be dozing, but his Spectre is very much at work in this shadow in which the living gold of his unfallen form is draped in spectrous white. Just as in Kantian or "negative" thinking, from the defeated, "wearied intellect" rises a perfect, holy image of ultimacy, a "watry vision" without determinate outline—for, says Kant, the "inscrutability" of Reason's ideas "precludes all positive presentation" (p. 128). The Slumberous Man is made to echo the self-abnegating Psalm 143—"And enter not into judgment with thy servant: for in thy sight shall no man living be justified"—and also Psalm 104:

thou openest thine hand, they are filled with good.
thou hidest thy face, they are troubled:
thou takest away their breath, they die
and return to their dust.   [Vs. 28–29]

These very verses are quoted by Hegel as the consummate example of the negative sublime.[7]

Ahania hopes that Urizen will reject the idolatry perpetrated while he "slept in the porch," but unknowingly she has exposed his project. (All of her vision may of course be understood as Urizen's moment of self-recognition, but so deeply is the original Urizen split that this further reduction has only theoretical significance at this point.) Urizen is dismayed at Ahania's vision (41:5–9,18; 42:7–8), not because it recapitulates the fall, but because it reveals a countermyth to his own version of the fall—a myth which highlights his own role with an ingenuous clarity the more dangerous for being unconscious. In Urizen's view, Man fell because he became intellectually lazy and his "active masculine virtue" succumbed to Vala, "the feminine indolent bliss. The indulgent self of weariness"—what he hopes to avoid by casting out Ahania. Pleasure undermined self-discipline; in short, Man failed to sublimate. But Ahania's account of the fall suggests that sublimation is itself a creation of intellectual weariness (40:3), which in turn results from Man's commerce with Vala "in dreams of soft deluding slumber." From this point of view, Urizen's myth of the fall is totally incoherent because it proposes as a saving alternative the very sublimation which is the idolatrous result of mental failure.

Blake's irony is such that neither Urizen nor Ahania understands fully what is happening to the "Darkning Man." Ahania hopes naively that the intellect has retained its freedom and is not yet compromised in Man's fall; Urizen, however, refuses to see the fall for what it is and rejects its clear consequence even as he fails to take responsibility for his own role. His actions are secretive; they are concealed from the Darkning Man in just the way that the operations of the Kantian reason were hidden from the understanding. As Ahania's tale of the fall continues, the ironies, dramatic and allusive, rapidly thicken. Down from the shadowy cloud drops—unexpectedly—Luvah:

> And Lo that Son of Man, that shadowy Spirit of the Fallen One
> Luvah, descended from the cloud; In terror Albion rose
> Indignant rose the Awful Man & turnd his back on Vala
> . . . .
> And Luvah strove to gain dominion over the mighty Albion
> They strove together above the Body where Vala was inclos'd
> And the dark Body of Albion left prostrate upon the crystal pavement
> Coverd with boils from head to foot. the terrible smitings of Luvah
>
> Then frownd the Fallen Man & put forth Luvah from his presence
> (I heard him:frown not Urizen:but listen to my Vision)
>
> Saying, Go & die the Death of Man for Vala the sweet wanderer
> I will turn the volutions of your Ears outward; & bend your Nostrils
> Downward; & your fluxile Eyes englob'd, roll round in fear
> Your withring Lips & Tongue shrink up into a narrow circle
> Till into narrow forms you creep. Go take your fiery way
> And learn what 'tis to absorb the Man you Spirits of Pity & Love
>
> O Urizen why art thou pale at the visions of Ahania
> Listen to her who loves thee lest we also are driven away.
>   [41:2-4; 41:13-42:8; E, 321]

The allusion to Job identifies Luvah with Satan; as Satan is licensed by God to try Job, so Urizen is ultimately responsible for Luvah's descent, which fills Albion with terror—and then, significantly, with indignation. In Job's case, the boils come "from the sole of his foot to the crown of his head": Blake's reversed "from head to foot" nicely indicates the Urizenic nature of the affliction. The boils, traditionally signs of venereal disease, are identified in *Jerusalem* (21:3–5) as the "disease of Shame," which also covers from head to foot; Blake's illustration of the text in the Job series (VI) shows Satan pouring his vial on Job's head, while Job's wife has custody of his feet and is ignored. Actually, we are informed by the excised lines ("*& Luvah dwelt in the cloud*") that the "watry vision of Man" which Albion worships is from the start a compound of Urizen and Luvah; its full explication, which is unnecessary here, would lead us to the heart of Blake's brilliant reading of Job—the claim that the demonic Satan and the jejune God of that text are both aspects of Job's erroneous theological imagination.[8]

What Ahania's vision reveals is that the perceptional error of the Fallen Man is also a sexual crisis. This is a fundamental insight into the psychology of the negative sublime. The Fallen Man responds to sexual guilt by expelling his passional life into a grotesque naturalization. It now becomes possible to state the entire sequence of the fall, even at the risk of some reduction. The Darkning Man first conceives a slumberous passion for Vala; so the subject of the sublime is caught up by an appearance or prospect "out there" to such an extent that his faculties cease to function energetically and soon feel dwarfed and humiliated. From his "wearied intellect" rises an indeterminate image of perfection or totality; it is a negative projection, but since its origins are concealed from the imagination, the man worships it in self-abnegating awe. At this point Kant's account left unexplained the way in which consciousness rather suddenly ceased to inhabit the plight of the imagination and identified instead with the idea of totality, thereby recovering its self-respect by alienating the "nature within us." In Blake's vision this recovery has the look of an oedipal crisis "successfully" resolved—the very type of sublimation.

Luvah's presence in the cloud is not merely a function of wearied intellect but is also a fantasy which compensates for the passional frustration—the sacrifice and deprivation—which Man feels: it is an image of power. This power is, however, under Urizenic aegis, and it is now directed *against* Man; we remember how in Kant the reason used fear to induce awe for itself. In psychological terms, the passional force is introjected and felt first as fear and then as sexual guilt." In terror Albion rose / Indignant rose the Awful Man & turned his back on Vala."

Albion's struggle with Luvah is not a competition for Vala but Man's attempt to suppress the passion he feels as shame. Ironically, Albion's inability to suppress shame leads him to expel desire itself (Luvah) and its object (Vala)—so that he may be "superior to the nature within . . . and therefore also to external nature." It is clear that this latter feat on Man's part is not quite what Urizen had in mind, for he is disturbed to hear it told: "Then frownd the Fallen Man & put forth Luvah from his presence / (I heard him:frown not Urizen: but listen to my Vision)."

The reader may share Urizen's perplexity over what looks like Albion's sudden reassertion of control over Luvah, but the sequence is psychologically true. In his indignation and struggle against the "Spirits of Pity & Love," Albion has in fact overidentified with the holy specter he worshipped. Urizen is in the position of a father who, merely by trying to be perfect and godlike, has enforced a more drastic oedipal resolution upon his son than could have been anticipated—a common psychological pattern. Urizen wanted only to be worshipped by both Man and nature ("And Vala trembled & covered her face, & her locks were spread on the pavement"), and Luvah's mission (provocatively identified with the parousia in the epithet "Son of Man") was designed only to insure Albion's self-abrogation in nature. But because the power of the specter is derived as much from frustration as from a dream of totality, Albion's suppression of passion in effect accomplishes a negation more extreme than Urizen had realized was necessary. His response to Ahania, "Art thou also become like Vala. Thus I cast thee out," is in a sense an attempt to catch up with what Albion has already done. Ahania's vision reveals consequences to a Urizen who is still somewhat innocent—he hasn't yet wholly fallen, we remember.

Blake's analytic of sublimation is richly suggestive at a number of points. It helps us to fill in the affective mortar of Kant's structure and to account for some curious facts which emerge as we study speculations about the sublime. The peculiar combination of holy innocence and conspiratorial self-aggrandizement which may be detected in the career of Kant's reason is one such fact. The negative sublime begins with an excessive interest in nature and ends with an excessive disdain of nature, and again and again in reading the texts of the sublime—in Schiller, Schopenhauer, and even in the Wordsworth of *The Borderers*—we feel that this movement is compulsive. Reason and its cognates begin as a negative or dialectical alternative to human limitation, but such quasi-theological prestige begins to accumulate around the ideas of reason that in the end reason requires a total withdrawal from all natural connection. We shall later meet the pattern of oedipal overidentification as an element in the "daemonic" sublime. The immediate value of Blake's text is that it plays out a logic implicit in discursive theories of the sublime. We can read the affective logic of the sublime partly in Albion's fall and partly in Urizen's complicated state of self-knowledge.

The ultimate protagonist of the sublime in its third phase—the moment of self-recognition—speaks an extraordinary speech, a compound of anxiety and vaunting pride:

> Am I not God said Urizen. Who is Equal to me
> Do I not stretch the heavens abroad or fold them up like a garment
> He spoke mustering his heavy clouds around him black opake
>
> [42:19–21]

We are taken again to Hegel's chief instance of the negative sublime, Psalm 104, where the Lord is addressed as He "who coverest [Himself] with light as with a garment; who stretchest out the heavens like a curtain" (vs. 2). Urizen's role model is Jehovah himself, and the irony of the "heavy clouds . . . black opake" obviously cuts both ways. Urizen is also answering Luvah, who in the first Night had declined conspiracy with the bold claim: "Dictate to thy Equals, am not I / The Prince of all the hosts of Men nor Equal know in Heaven" (1.22:1–2; E, 307). But Luvah is no longer a threat—Albion has done Urizen's work for him— and Urizen has not yet focused his rage on Ahania. The ultimate object of his threatening rhetorical question is Albion. For Albion's drastic sublimation (a disaster from Blake's point of view), like Job's stubborn victory over Satan, in effect appears to accuse Urizen of being a soft god. Albion can turn against the nature within and without with a force that endangers the hegemony of Urizen, who still inhabits Beulah. Awe and terror, it seems, are not enough—because man can master his passions through indignant suppression. Kant in fact speaks directly to this situation. The mind which recognizes its own sublimity will not prostrate itself timorously before the Godhead; it will identify with that Godhead.[9] For Urizen this means that his original project—exploiting Man's passive turning outward to nature so that it yields a "watry vision of perfection"—is naive and is endangered by Man's withdrawal from any engagement with nature. The mind convinced of its own sublimity cannot in fact experience the awful or sublime moment, which is a discovery, a movement between two states: the overcoming of sense is necessarily predicated upon an engagement with the sensible. Unlike the positive sublime, whose ultimate form is repetitive and circular, the negative sublime theoretically aims toward a unique disillusionment— the unmasking of the "subreption" by which an object seems sublime. Ahania's narrative exhibits in the form of myth the tendency of the positive sublime to yield to the polarizing pressure that results in the negative sublime. Albion, of course, is not a real threat; he doesn't have the respect for himself that Urizen supposes; nothing suggests that he knows that "sweet entrancing self delusion, a watry vision of Man" is in fact "his own shadow." Albion is already worshiping Jehovah before Urizen has quite grown into his role. Albion lacks the self-consciousness of a potential protagonist of the sublime. This situation parallels the way reason operated on two levels of consciousness in Kant, the concealment which enables reason to discover its own power in an attitude of awe.

From an affective point of view, the salient feature of Ahania's vision is the coincidence it establishes between the obscuring of the Darkning Man's perception and the suppression of his desire. Blake's text enables us to confront a question that our own discussion has pretty much begged: are the two kinds of sublimation, perceptional and passional, really one, as we have implicitly claimed? Man's idolatrous awe changes to terror with the appearance of Luvah, "that Son of Man," whose arrival suggests (in addition to the oedipal introjection we have remarked) the realization of the judgment Man feared ("O I am nothing when I enter into judgment with thee"). Terror, we may surmise, is consistent with the Spectre's design, insofar as he is a separate will. (The subsequent indignation is Man's own contribution, a further fall into self-righteousness.) Urizen is not yet Jehovah until Man in effect makes him so. In Blake's technical terms, the Spectre represents a Pahad phase of God—the fifth "eye" which immediately precedes Jehovah. *Pahad* is translated "fear" or "terror" in the King James Version. He is invoked by Eliphaz, one of Job's comforters, in a passage cited by Burke as proof of his contention that obscurity is a cause of the sublime:

But let it be considered that hardly any thing can strike the mind with its greatness, which does not make some sort of approach towards infinity; which nothing can do whilst we are able to perceive its bounds, but to see an object distinctly, and to perceive its bounds, is one and the same thing. A clear idea is therefore another name for a little idea. There is a passage in the book of Job amazingly sublime, and this sublimity is principally due to the terrible uncertainty of the thing described. *In thoughts from the visions of the night, when deep sleep falleth upon men, fear came upon me and trembling, which made all my bones to shake. Then a spirit passed before my face. The hair of my flesh stood up. It stood still,* but I could not discern the form thereof; *an image was before mine eyes; there was silence; and I heard a voice—Shall mortal man be more just than God?* We are first

prepared with the utmost solemnity for the vision; we are first terrified, before we are let even into the obscure cause of our emotion;
but when this grand cause of terror makes its appearance, what is it?
is it not, wrapt up in the shades of its own incomprehensible darkness, more aweful, more striking, more terrible, than the liveliest
description, than the clearest painting could possibly represent it?[10]

We have already met Burke's argument in its sophisticated Kantian
form. What is indistinct is phenomenologically in-finite, and this leads
to a hypostasized infinitude. Burke is not aware, although it would
rescue his argument from a dubious premise of causality, that the "fear
and trembling" is itself the indistinct spirit, i.e., Pahad. Blake's illustration of the text in the *Job* series (IX) shows Pahad with his arms bound
and concealed, which suggests most simply that he is powerless to judge
right from left, right from wrong.[11] Job is looking upward calmly at the
nightmare invoked by Eliphaz, who is not looking at (i.e., reseeing) his
own vision; the other comforters are frightened. In the margins are the
forests of night (error) and the verses: "Shall mortal Man be more just
than God? Shall a Man be more Pure than his Maker?" The irony is
clear: Eliphaz's rhetorical questions, intended to frighten Job, have become for Job genuine questions. If this is God, then mortal man may well
be more just and pure. Job's own error is a self-righteousness based on
fallen categories. His state is closely analogous to what Urizen fears to
be the case with Albion, who, as we have seen, is identified with Job in
the third Night. Urizen is threatened to observe in Albion's expulsion
of Luvah and Vala a man more just than God, purer than his Maker.
Luvah-Satan having failed (ironically by conquest) to execute Urizen's
naive design, Urizen must, like the God of *Job*, thunder his own
anxiously rhetorical questions: "Am I not God . . . Who is Equal to me."
    The point to be grasped in this confluence of texts is that the obscure
image is terrible only to him who is conscious of guilt. It is a feeling of
guilt that Eliphaz wishes in vain to force upon Job. Albion is already
guilty with Vala, and the indistinct image of perfection arises to punish
him. He feels this guilt, succumbs to a conviction of its justice, but then
is able to suppress it by removing all desire (Luvah) and all occasion for
desire (Vala). Like Kant's reason in its ultimate phase of self-congratula-
tion, Albion is no longer exposed to terror. But the cost is great, for this
sublimation dooms, among other things, natural religion and any connection to nature. The Kantian therapy is a drastic one; it logically ends
in mental suicide. Behind the phenomenology of the sublime moment we
begin to descry an immense and fascinating psychodrama, which now
invites our attendance.

Part Two:
The Psychology of
the Sublime

for who would lose,
Though full of pain, this intellectual being,
Those thoughts that wander through eternity
—Milton

4. *I am afraid it is a practice much too common in enquiries of this nature, to attribute the cause of feelings which merely arise from the mechanical structure of our bodies, or from the natural frame and constitution of our minds, to certain conclusions of the reasoning faculty on the objects presented to us; for I should imagine, that the influence of reason in producing our passions is nothing near so extensive as it is commonly believed.*—Edmund Burke, *A Philosophical Enquiry into the Origin of Our Ideas of the Sublime and Beautiful*

The Logic of Terror

In our inquiry we have met indications at every turn that the transcendence of the sublime is intimately and genetically related to anxiety. We have not yet illumined that relation to any degree, though we did invoke two psychological structures which seem to answer to the negative and positive versions of the sublime. The negative sublime apparently exhibits some features of a response to superego anxiety, for in the suddenness of the sublime moment the conscious ego rejects its attachment to sensible objects and turns rather fearfully toward an ideal of totality and power which it participates or internalizes. The egotistical sublime, on the contrary, seems akin to narcissism, and in it the psychological role of the father or authority appears to be strangely vacant. It is time to ask whether these speculations can be consolidated, deepened, and tested.

Any aesthetic, pressed beyond a certain point, becomes or implies a psychology. The very openness of a sublime to psychological conjecture proves an obstacle to a rigorous analysis. The sublime makes everyman his own psychologist; yet we come to acknowledge the usual divide between those who seek an explanation in terms of unconscious process and those whose psychology is a mentalized rendition of manifest themes. A critic must be pulled reluctantly into the domain of psychoanalytic explanation, because it seems to require of him a persistent, genetic naiveté in the matter of meaning. We know the abuse of such explanation—its beady, narrowing look, its implicit *aha!*, its frequent eventuation in a complicated set of metaphors we are asked to take as fundamental reality. Yet we must have recourse to depth psychology if we wish to work very far beneath the surface of the sublime. What will persuade us to take this path is the inadequacy of an aesthetic at crucial points and the major precedent of Edmund Burke.

The role of anxiety is so conspicuous in Kant's "dynamical" sublime that we have bypassed his account of terror and delight and concentrated instead on exposing the hidden project of reason in the other branch of the negative sublime, the more elusive "mathematical" sublime. We found that the collapse of imaginative comprehension, which was alleged to have an intrinsic cause within the province of the sensible, in fact resulted from the unconscious pressure of the supersensible reason. In his account of the dynamical sublime Kant presents no argument for the spontaneous collapse of the imagination; consequently, the role of reason, latent in the case of the mathematical sublime, is here overt. The imagination, in a position of complete physical security, confronts an overwhelmingly powerful and threatening appearance of nature and *pictures to itself* the hypothetical case of attempting to offer some resistance ("Analytic of the Sublime" p. 110). At once the futility of such resistance is recognized, but somehow—it is not clear why—this hypothetical exercise of the imagination arouses the forces of the soul, discovering "within us a power of resistance of quite another kind, which gives us courage to be able to measure ourselves against the seeming omnipotence of nature" (p. 111).

There seems to be no necessary cause for the intervention of the supersensible in this mental process. If we were actually threatened, there would be a clear motive for the counterstress of self-preservation— our anxiety would be objective. But Kant emphasizes as a precondition of the sublime experience that we not be in physical danger (p. 110). He postulates a defensive reaction of the mind which will give us "courage" when there is no danger. Clearly the sublime moment, so conceived, invites self-indulgence: the mind cultivates a state of imagined terror in order to perform a factitious transcendence. Of course, Kant is attempting to save the disinterested character of the judgment on the sublime. Moreover, he is right—with respect to objective fear: if the danger is real we turn and flee, without pausing for our sublime moment. What Kant fails to see is that the anxiety which precipitates both the imaging of injury and the subsequent identification with the higher power within is not objective but subjective—it originates from within. The threatening occasion appears to revive a fundamental fantasy of injury and escape (refuge) which is then played out hypothetically (pictured to ourselves) in the phenomenal terms of the occasion before us.

The dynamical sublime exhibits in less disguised fashion the same intentional structure we uncovered in the mathematical sublime. In the sublime of magnitude, the mind substitutes its own infinity for the apparent phenomenal infinity before it; we have seen that this substitution is essentially metaphorical because the two kinds of infinity are logically incommensurable—they belong to separate discourses. (The play of substitution between artificial, phenomenological infinity, or trompe-l'oeil, and infinity-as-totality is an enduring motif of the aesthetic of sublimity and is exercised by nearly every writer in the tradition.) The resolution of the dynamical sublime is similarly metaphorical. How, we may ask, if "our power of resistance" is of "quite another kind" than nature's power—how is a comparison between these two categorically incommensurable powers meaningful? We are answered by an act of metaphor. Thus we perceive again that the intentional structure of the negative sublime as a whole implies the conversion of the outer world into a symbol for the mind's relation to itself. Indeed, if Kant's theory is pressed to its logical conclusion, the judgment on the sublime ceases to be an aesthetic judgment at all, because it has no necessary ground in the object.[1] This is why the subsequent tradition of idealist aesthetics—in Schiller, Hegel, and all their epigoni down to Herbert Marcuse—ignores the sublime and propounds the notion of the beautiful as the union of the sensible and the ideal.

At the present critical moment, aesthetics seems to be an archaic enterprise. In any case, we have been reading Kant's theory not as aesthetic doctrine but as a fictional structure with an inner logic, an interplay of submerged, personified agencies profoundly congruent to the imaginative logic dramatized in many Romantic poems. The inadequacy of a purely reasonable or conscious explanation of any mental event becomes apparent when the analysis of that explanation yields inexplicable connections or a logical contradiction. Kant's account betrays the masked presence of some force majeure. If we are to proceed to a genuine psychology of the negative sublime, we must be prepared for reduction, so that the "conclusions of the reasoning faculty" become derivatives and not explanations of "an instinct that works us to its own purposes, without our concurrence." These terms are not Freud's but Burke's.[2] It was Burke who first insisted upon the centrality of terror in the sublime moment. *A Philosophical Enquiry into the Origin of Our Ideas of the Sublime and Beautiful*, published in 1757, was the book of a young man, informed but uninhibited by received speculation, who had a genuine idea. We delight in such books and forgive extravagance not only because it is usually interesting but also because it is often the price of originality. Burke's treatise seemed for a while to be isolated from contemporary discussions, but his later influence upon Romantic sensibilities—and even, in the case of Wordsworth, upon the affective diction with which the sensations were classified—has often been noted and is still being documented.[3]

Burke's approach is remarkably exoteric. Unlike Kant, he is not an ideologue of the sublime. He presents himself as "a man who works beyond the surface of things," stirring the stagnant waters of science, hoping to learn the "exact boundaries" of the passions, to "pursue them through all their variety of operations, and pierce into the inmost, and what might appear inaccessible parts of our nature" (p. 53). He is not a good critic of the arts, but he does not pretend to be:

> We might expect that the artists themselves would have been our surest guides; but the artists have been too much occupied in the practice; the philosophers have done little, and what they have done, was mostly with a view to their own schemes and systems; and as for those called critics, they have generally sought the rule of the arts in the wrong place; they sought it among poems, pictures, engravings, statues and buildings. But art can never give the rules that make an art. . . . I can judge but poorly of any thing whilst I measure it by no other standard than itself. The true standard of the arts is in every man's power; and an easy observation of the most common, sometimes of the meanest things in nature, will give the truest lights, where the greatest sagacity and industry that slights such observation, must leave us in the dark, or what is worse, amuse and mislead us by false lights. [Pp. 53–54]

It is a familiar ambition, but not the less powerful for that. "In an enquiry, it is almost every thing to be once in the right road" (p. 54), and Burke was confident he had taken the right path. His own "observation" was acute: his treatment of grief, for instance, as a negative phase of love ("in grief, the *pleasure* is still uppermost; and the affliction we suffer has no resemblance to absolute pain" [p. 37]) and of the artificial infinite as a repetition compulsion linked to madness (pp. 73–74) evince a sharp eye for the hidden cause. As an aesthetician Burke transposed received problems into psychological motives, as in these comments on tragic mimesis: "I believe that this notion of our having a simple pain in the reality, yet a delight in the representation, arises from hence, that we do not sufficiently distinguish what we would by no means chuse to do, from what we should be eager enough to see if it was once done. We delight in seeing things, which so far from doing, our heartiest wishes would be to see redressed" (p. 47). If we read Burke's own behavior in *Of the Sublime and Beautiful* as critically as he inspires us to do, we come upon an implicit structure that promises to deepen our insight considerably.

II

Burke begins by dividing the passions into two groups. The passions of "pleasure" have as their final cause society and, in particular, generation, the multiplication of the species. Both sexual passion and the feeling, free of lust, which unites man to the greater society of men and animals are forms of love, and Burke will proceed to define beauty as the object of this love. The other group of passions turns on pain and danger and consists mainly of "fear or terror, which is an apprehension of pain or death" (p. 131); the aim of these passions is self-preservation, and they are far stronger than the pleasure passions. This leads to the famous definition:

> Whatever is fitted in any sort to excite the ideas of pain, and danger, that it to say, whatever is in any sort terrible, or is conversant about terrible objects, or operates in a manner analogous to terror, is a source of the *sublime*; that is, it is productive of the strongest emotion which the mind is capable of feeling. [p. 39]

The novelty of Burke's theory is its determined exclusiveness. He is at pains to reduce the traditional occasions of the sublime to the motive of terror. This is easy to do with those occasions which directly inspire fear, and secondarily with those ideas (such as power) which are linked by association to fear. But a third class of perceptions, "from which we cannot probably apprehend any danger" (p. 131), forces him to an ingenious sleight of hand. Those ideas that "operate in a similar manner" have a similar effect. Since terror produces "an unnatural tension and certain violent emotions of the nerves . . . whatever is fitted to produce such a tension, must be productive of a passion similar to terror, and consequently must be a source of the sublime, though it should have no idea of danger connected with it" (p. 134). Burke is here preparing the ground for a dubious argument of optical constriction designed to accommodate the sublimity of magnitude. We shall see that power and magnitude produce the same anxiety in different ways.

But the sublime is not the feeling of terror itself; it is a response to terror. Pain is for Burke a "positive" passion; it is not merely the absence of pleasure, and consequently its remission is not a restoration of pleasure but an entirely different affect, *delight*. The sublime affords a re-active joy, "a sort of delightful horror, a sort of tranquillity tinged with terror" (p. 136). What is this terror and this delight? Here our ex-plication of Burke must become interpretation. His own explanation of how terror produces delight is cumbersome, not to say silly, and depends on an antiquated physiology. Pain and terror "clear the parts, whether fine, or gross, of a dangerous and troublesome incumbrance" (p. 136) and thereby function like physical exercise. It is a homeopathic therapy, a kind of physiological catharsis. It will hardly do. But we find in Burke signs of a deeper explanation and a presentment of terror and delight with extraordinary latent features.

Let us strike for the heart of Burke's sublime moment. How does he describe the distinctive delight? After insisting that "the removal of a great pain does not resemble positive pleasure" he invites, by way of demonstration, our introspection. The passage is Burke's only attempt to characterize delight by more than "a sort of"; it requires the closest reading:

> . . . But let us recollect in what state we have found our minds upon escaping some imminent danger, or on being released from the severity of some cruel pain. We have on such occasions found, if I am not much mistaken, the temper of our minds in a tenor very re-mote from that which attends the presence of positive pleasure; we have found them in a state of much sobriety, impressed with a sense of awe, in a sort of tranquillity shadowed with horror. The fashion of the countenance and the gesture of the body on such occasions is so correspondent to this state of mind, that any person, a stranger to the cause of the appearance, would rather judge us under some con-sternation, than in the enjoyment of any thing like positive pleasure.

> ὡς δ' ὅτ' ἄν ἄνδρ' ἄτη πυκινὴ λάβη, ὅς τ' ἐνὶ πάτρη
> φῶτα κατακτείνας ἄλλων ἐξίκετο δῆμον,
> ἀνδρὸς ἐς ἀφνειοῦ, θάμβος δ' ἔχει εἰσορόωντας,

Iliad, 24 [480–82]

> As when a wretch, who conscious of his crime,
> Pursued for murder from his native clime,
> Just gains some frontier, breathless, pale, amaz'd;
> All gaze, all wonder!

[Pope, *Iliad*, 24.590–93]

This striking appearance of the man whom Homer supposes to have just escaped an imminent danger, the sort of mixt passion of terror and surprize, with which he affects the spectators, paints very

strongly the manner in which we find ourselves affected upon occasions any way similar. [Pp. 34–35]

It may be safely doubted whether anyone likely to be reading this book
or Burke's finds himself in "occasions any way similar" to the panic
of a homicidal fugitive, but perhaps this astonishing assumption has a
psychological rationale.

The "wretch" of Homer's simile has committed murder on native
ground; possibly he has been banished, and he now seeks protection
from a rich man in a land of strangers. In Pope's rendition he is "conscious of his crime"—i.e., he feels guilty; but here (as often) Pope has
neatly glossed over a difficulty. Literally, *ate* ("confusion," "temporary
insanity") has seized a man who has killed one in his native country; it
is agreed, however, among Homeric commentators that the relative clause
is to be read coordinately: *ate* is the cause of the crime and not its result. (*Ate* sent as punishment is post-Homeric.) The meaning is "as
when dense *ate* has seized a man, and he has slain one in his native land
and come to the land of strangers, to a rich man's house, and amazement
possesses those who see him. . . ." Burke invites us to consider, if we
wish to understand *delight*, the "striking appearance" of a fugitive who
is about to get away with his crime: he has escaped the "imminent danger," of death presumably, and he has also escaped the danger of *ate*.
Burke may have read *ate* as punishment, as have better Greek scholars
than he; in tragedy, the word commonly means objective disaster. In
his fascinating discussion of this interesting term, E. R. Dodds concludes that Homeric *ate* "is a state of mind—a temporary clouding or
bewildering of the normal consciousness. It is, in fact, a partial and
temporary insanity."[4] (Agamemnon's rash offense to Achilles is ascribed
to *ate*.) For Burke, however, the word is likely to have fused the meanings of insanity, punishment, disaster, and guilt—the last not from
Homer but from Pope. Delight is what you feel on escaping from the
bewildering emotions and consequences surrounding a murder.

The spectators have committed no crime, yet they are evidently
affected by "the sort of mixt passion of terror and surprize": Burke's
syntax makes obscure the relation between the feelings of the spectators
and those of the fugitive, but as "surprize" is appropriate only to the
former and "terror" mainly to the latter, Burke's construction appears
to imply an empathic identification on the part of the spectators. They
may have begun as "strangers to the cause of the appearance," reading
the "fashion of the countenance and the gesture of the body," but they
are soon full of amazement. There is an affective gap between the objective judgment that would infer only "some consternation" and the

possession by wonder, and it is just here, if anywhere—in the way the quotation says more than he had planned on—that Burke's own unconscious projection may be located. This is, after all, a simile torn from context, and though Homeric similes defeat our desire for a neatly homologous tenor, the context would have been fresh for Burke. The "wretch" is Priam, breaking through to Achilles' inner court to sue for the body of Hector:

> Unseen by these, the King his Entry made;
> And prostrate now before *Achilles* laid,
> Sudden, (a venerable Sight!) appears;
> Embrac'd his Knees, and bath'd his Hands in Tears;
> Those direful Hands his Kisses press'd, embru'd
> Ev'n with the best, the dearest of his Blood!
> As when a Wretch, (who conscious of his Crime
> Pursu'd for Murder, flies his native Clime)
> Just gains some Frontier, breathless, pale! amaz'd!
> All gaze, all wonder: Thus *Achilles* gaz'd
> Thus stood th' Attendants stupid with Surprize;
> All mute, yet seem'd to question with their Eyes:
> Each look'd on other, none the Silence broke,
> Till thus at last the Kingly Suppliant spoke,
> Ah think, thou favour'd of the Pow'rs Divine!
> Think of thy Father's Age, and pity mine!
> In me, that Father's rev'rend Image trace,
> Those silver Hairs, that venerable Face:
> His trembling Limbs, his helpless Person, see!
> In all my Equal, but in Misery![5]

Burke's *delight* requires wonder ("a sense of awe") as the positive expression of one's feeling on release from terror, and he brings it in by quotation. We see that the wonder is Achilles'; amazement is in fact the point of Homer's simile. Perhaps an analysis of Achilles' ambivalent state is needed to complement our analysis of the terror. Achilles naturally feels anger at seeing his great foe, Priam, and later on, when the anger threatens to erupt, he warns the frightened Priam not to try to move him too much; then he rushes out like a lion. But for the moment anger is suspended—sublimated—into wonder. Priam has cleverly assumed the role of the father in Achilles' mind, thereby engaging in his own interest powerful prohibitions against anger and parricide. Pope's note, emphatic on this point, could not have been missed by Burke:

The Curiosity of the Reader must needs be awaken'd to know how *Achilles* would behave to this unfortunate King; it requires all the

Art of the Poet to sustain the violent character of *Achilles*, and yet at the same time to soften him into Compassion. To this end the Poet uses no Preamble, but breaks directly into that Circumstance which is most likely to mollify him, and the two first Words he utters are, μνῆσαι πατρὸς *see thy Father*, O Achilles, *in me*! Nothing could be more happily imagin'd than this Entrance into his Speech; *Achilles* has every where been describ'd as bearing a great Affection to his Father, and by two Words the Poet recalls all the Tenderness that Love and Duty can suggest to an affectionate Son. . . . [At the end] *Priam* repeats the Beginning of his Speech, and recalls his Father to his Memory in the Conclusion of it. This is done with great Judgment; the Poet takes care to Enforce his Petition with the strongest Motive, and leaves it fresh upon his Memory; and possibly *Priam* might perceive that the mention of his Father had made a deeper Impression upon *Achilles* than any other part of his Petition, therefore while the Mind of *Achilles* dwells upon it, he again sets him before his Imagination by this Repetition, and softens him into Compassion.[6]

Achilles succeeds in suppressing his anger and honoring the father. Priam's helplessness presents a powerful temptation—a special danger to the positive "oedipal" resolution of his relation to Peleus. (All this emotion is discharged in a good deal of weeping.) Here, if anywhere, Homer's world is on the verge of passing into a guilt culture, as Achilles learns the morally higher virtue and "softens" into compassion. But we are still short of Achilles' wonder. Anger, after all, is generally introjected as guilt in a process which contributes vitally to the strength of the conscience, or superego. Achilles apparently feels no guilt. Yet if anyone ought to be "conscious of his crime" here it is not Priam, for Achilles has killed Hector and so abused his body that he knows the gods are offended, and he now faces Hector's father, who desires something like repentance. We see what Homer's simile so marvellously does (as if a guilt culture were in the wings!): it is as if Achilles' (unconscious) guilt were relieved by being projected onto the fugitive who escapes punishment. For a reader (like Burke), Achilles' wonder might thus express the unconscious thought "I am not going to be punished, I am home free" at the same time that it expresses a properly filial respect for father. Wonder, the "sense of awe" Burke will find in the sublime moment, is the affective correlative of a positive "identification" with the Father, an identification which both presupposes the renunciation of parricidal aggression and facilitates an escape from the imagined consequences of a murder.

It is a dubious enterprise to psychoanalyze Homer or his heroes, and of course it is probably anachronistic to read the oedipal crisis into the feelings of Achilles, who inhabits a shame-culture.[7] What is at stake is not Homer's meaning, but Burke's (unconscious) reading of the simile. Burke's "terror" is latently associated with the congeries of emotions surrounding murder (insanity, punishment, disaster, and guilt), and the latent reference of "delight" is to submission to a father figure. I think we may infer that the "imminent danger" to which we are exposed and from which we are then released in the sublime moment is an unconscious fantasy of parricide. Yet such evidence is extremely oblique at best. Although the passage is Burke's salient exhibition of what he means by *delight*, it is far too slender an indication to persuade us that an oedipal fantasy enters into the deep structure of the terrible sublime. We need much confirmation if the hypothesis is really to stand.

Before we look at Burke's theory in detail, a general observation is in order. Burke's intriguing text and Freud's are linked by a remarkable and intimate set of correspondences. There is, first, Burke's division of the passions into the erotic and the self-preservative—a dichotomous scheme precisely parallel to the division between the sexual instincts and the ego-instincts in the middle Freud. In the late Freud, as is commonly known, this dualism was extended into a metapsychological opposition between eros and the death instinct, later named *thanatos*. Like Freud, Burke was an insistent dualist in his claim that pain cannot be reduced to the absence of pleasure. In addition, both theories of the psyche are homeostatic: their working principle is the reduction of excessive excitation to the zero degree of equanimity—"tranquillity," in Burke's phrase. The terror tinging that tranquillity suggests the successful resolution of a traumatic disequilibrium.

III

There is no evident mystery in Burke's "terror": it is fear of injury, pain, and ultimately death. In Burke's view, everything sublime either (a) directly suggests the idea of danger, (b) produces a similar effect physiologically, or (c) is some modification of power. But power is nothing more than the *indirect* suggestion of danger:

> But pain is always inflicted by a power in some way superior, because we never submit to pain willingly. So that strength, violence, pain and terror, are ideas that rush in upon the mind together. Look at a man, or any other animal of prodigious strength, and what is your idea before reflection? Is it that this strength will be subservient to you, to your ease, to your pleasure, to your interest in any sense? No; the

emotion you feel is, lest this enormous strength should be employed to the purposes of rapine and destruction. That power derives all its sublimity from the terror with which it is generally accompanied, will appear evidently from its effect in the very few cases, in which it may be possible to strip a considerable degree of strength of its ability to hurt. When you do this, you spoil it of every thing sublime, and it immediately becomes contemptible. [P. 65]

The power of anything is ultimately "its ability to hurt." The fear of injury points genetically and synechdochically to castration anxiety. We know that the castration fear of the young boy is not realistic; nevertheless it operates subjectively as a real fear. A fantasy of aggression or resistance toward a superior power is played out in the imagination, and the boy sees at once that he would lose. (So in Kant's dynamical sublime we "picture to ourselves" the possibility of resistance and recognize its futility.) The fantasized character of castration anxiety seems related to the mediated conditionality of the sublime moment: on the one hand, the "ability to hurt" must be objective and obvious; on the other hand, it must not be actually directed against oneself, or the fantasy dissolves into genuine panic and the objective defense of flight.

The fantasy of injury ends in the simultaneous perception of defeat and the realization that the threat is not, after all, a real one. This makes possible a positive resolution of the anxiety in the delight of the third phase, which is psychologically an identification with the superior power. As a defense mechanism, identification is simply a more sophisticated form of introjection or incorporation (the three terms are often used interchangeably).[8] The boy must have introjected or internalized an image of the superior power in order to picture to himself the consequences of aggression, and in the reactive defense this introjected image is reinforced as the affects line up on its side. The identification which thus establishes the superego retains an essential ambiguity. The boy neutralizes the possibility of danger by incorporating or swallowing it: it is now within and can't hurt him from without. But he must also renounce the aggression and turn himself into—be swallowed by—the image, now an ideal, with which he is identifying. This ambiguity of participation in an ideal which is greater than the psyche—*beyond* it and at the same time *within*—may be met on every page of Kant's account. Reason (or any transcendental faculty) operates within the mind and yet enjoins the mind according to rules that cannot be derived from the free, empirical exercise of the mind. To Freud, it was clear that "the categorical imperative of Kant is thus a direct inheritance from the Oedipus-complex."[9] Hence the importance of the sublime, for this is the very moment in which the mind turns within and performs its identification with reason. The sublime moment recapitulates and thereby reestablishes the oedipus complex, whose positive resolution is the basis of culture itself.

Inevitably, for both Kant and Burke, the myth of the superego takes a theological form. Burke is first led by the logic of his argument to derive political power from terror. He observes "that young persons little acquainted with the world, and who have not been used to approach men in power, are commonly struck with an awe which takes away the free use of their faculties. . . . Indeed so natural is this timidity with regard to power, and so strongly does it inhere in our constitution, that very few are able to conquer it, but by mixing much in the business of the great world, or by using no small violence to their natural dispositions" (p. 67). This meditation on authority leads straight to the view that the idea of God is inconceivable without terror, and Burke is soon quoting the maxim *primos in orbe deos fecit timor*. He immediately draws back, however, and rests with the observation that "true religion has, and must have, so large a mixture of salutary fear," although Christianity, he adds, has humanized the idea of divinity. We are rather close to *The Future of an Illusion*, though this is, after all, a familiar line of thought in Romantic writers. Kant is subtler, as his emphasis on identification is the stronger:

> The man that is actually in a state of fear, finding in himself good reason to be so, because he is conscious of offending with his evil disposition against a might directed by a will at once irresistible and just, is far from being in the frame of mind for admiring divine greatness, for which a temper of calm reflection and a quite free judgment are required. Only when he becomes conscious of having a disposition that is upright and acceptable to God, do those operations of might serve to stir within him the idea of the sublimity of this Being, so far as he recognizes the existence in himself of a sublimity of disposition consonant with His will, and is thus raised above the dread of such operations of nature, in which he no longer sees God pouring forth the vials of the wrath. ["Analytic of the Sublime," pp. 113–14]

The best defense against fear is a strong superego, which the sublime both requires and nourishes. The identification is so strong that the mind voluntarily submits to punishment: "Even humility, taking the form of an uncompromising judgement upon his shortcomings, which with the consciousness of good intentions, might readily be glossed over on the ground of the frailty of human nature, is a sublime temper of the mind voluntarily to undergo the pain of remorse as a means of more and more effectually eradicating its cause." Sublimity enjoins a divided self sitting in judgment on its own impulses and thereby guarantees for culture the distinction between religion and superstition, "which latter rears in the mind, not reverence for the sublime, but dread and apprehension of the all-powerful Being to whose will terror-stricken man sees himself subjected" (p. 114).

The identification which resolves the traumatic disequilibrium of the sublime moment is a metaphorical substitution of a "power within" for the external power. The power within, Kant tells us, is greater far than the external power—to which, however, we remain subject as natural beings. The sublime response saves our humanity from "humiliation", since nature's power merely "challenges our power (one not of nature) to regard as small those things of which we are wont to be solicitous (wordly goods, health, and life), and hence to regard its might (to which in these matters we are no doubt subject) as exercising over us and our personality no such rude dominion that we should bow down before it, once the question becomes one of our highest principles and of our asserting or forsaking them" (p. 111). Among the things the sublime enables us to discount is our life. Schiller developed Kant's view into a justification of suicide under certain conditions.[10] The psychological fact that may be isolated here is the overweening strength of the superego, for its power greatly exceeds the objective occasion or ideal that has been internalized. Freud returned often to this perplexing situation; here is one of his hypotheses:

> The super-ego arises, as we know, from an identification with the father taken as a model. Every such identification is in the nature of a desexualization or even of a sublimation. It now seems as though when a transformation of this kind takes place, an instinctual defusion occurs at the same time. After sublimation the erotic component no longer has the power to bind the whole of the destructiveness that was combined with it, and this is released in the form of an inclination to aggression and destruction. This defusion would be the source of the general character of harshness and cruelty exhibited by the ideal—its dictatorial "Thou shalt."[11]

On this view we should expect to find an increased aggressiveness in the third phase of the sublime, and we do find a condescending animus in Kant's rhetoric as he evokes the peculiar satisfaction of the power within. He recommends as sublime the principled misanthropy which results from general disillusionment with mankind: "To avoid hating where we cannot love, it seems but a slight sacrifice to forgo all the joys of fellowship with our kind" (p. 129). The aesthetic judgment must respect the general more than the statesman; war, conducted in a civilized fashion, is sublime, whereas a prolonged peace favors "a mere commercial spirit, and with it a debasing self-interest, cowardice, and effeminacy, and tends to degrade the character of the nation" (pp. 112–13).

There are, however, compelling reasons why the third phase of the sublime moment does not characteristically issue in aggression. If the sublime is a response to superego anxiety, it recapitulates a defense against an aggressive wish, and so the defused inclination to aggression is more likely to be itself introjected and turned about, directed against the psyche itself in the form of guilt. Pathologically, this results either in obsessional neurosis—when the ego refuses to acknowledge guilt—or in melancholia—when the ego accepts the guilt; both unconscious formations are obviously prominent in Romantic literature—we think of the Ancient Mariner, the *Alastor* poet, or of the obsessive Oswald and the melancholic Marmaduke in Wordsworth's *The Borderers*. Freud's hypothesis of instinctual defusion suggests an infinite spiral for the negative sublime: the identification which neutralizes the terrifying threat releases an aggressive impulse which must in turn be sublimated by an increased identification. Obsessions (repetition compulsion) and melancholia do tend to be characterological features of those personalities with deep spiritual investment in the negative sublime.

In this context, Burke's physiological reduction, which seemed so preposterous, curiously begins to make sense. Even the formulation that pain and terror "clear the parts, whether fine, or gross, of a dangerous and troublesome incumbrance" (and thereby produce delight) may suggest the mind's release from the inhibiting encumbrance of guilt. Actually, the imagery is eliminative, which suggests, I suppose, that the defused aggressive instinct (incapable, in itself, of sublimation) reverts back to an anal-sadistic mode of discharge. Less dubious is Burke's extended account of melancholy, from which, in his view, we are rescued by terror. Our natural state is one of rest, but in this "languid inactive state" the muscles degenerate and the nerves are subject to "horrid convulsions." "Melancholy, dejection, despair, and often self-murder, is the consequence of the gloomy view we take of things in this relaxed state of the body" (p. 135). Psychologically, melancholy or depression is often the expression of an unconscious feeling of guilt.[12] The superego is displeased and in its harshness it can not only deprive the ego of self-esteem but punish it to the point of self-murder. The remedy, according to Burke, is *labor* which requires the contraction of muscles, and this "resembles pain, which consists in tension or contraction, in everything but degree" (p. 135). Terror is the labor of the mind; the sublime, a purgative therapy of the "finer parts," of the imagination. We have seen that the sublime moment releases the ego from guilt through an identification with the power by which (in melancholy) it had formerly been punished. Delight is the temporary negation of paralysis, the expulsion of what blocks the mind. Indeed, the affective coincidence of ego and superego appears to be the foundation of mystic ecstasy—an absorption into a greater power at once beyond and within.

But the sublime, we saw, may also eventuate in melancholy. Unlike Burke, Kant is an apologist for the sublime, and it thus behooves him to distinguish between two types of melancholy—an *"insipid sadness"* and "an *interesting* sadness." He concludes from the latter that "even melancholy, (but not dispirited sadness,) may take its place among the *vigorous* affections, provided it has its root in moral ideas" (p. 130). The sublime appears as a remedy for the languid melancholy, the vague boredom that increased so astonishingly during the eighteenth century; it transformed this state into the firmer, morally sanctioned melancholy of the gloomy egoist. Consequently, the sublime of terror may be characterized as an *episode in melancholy*. In terms of the history of sensibility, this suggests that the prestige and attractiveness of the sublime is a direct function of the prevalence of or predisposition to melancholy. There are other factors which reinforce this connection, as we shall see. On the other hand, the obsessional derivatives of the traumatic sublime mark a failure of positive identification with the superego, and thus the delight is never really experienced. If you do not recover from the second phase, you are likely to replay the precipitating occasion in an involuntary repetition compulsion (like the Ancient Mariner), a disorder Burke finds frequent in madmen (p. 74).

IV

An essential gambit of our inquiry has been that the same psychological structure may be uncovered in both the natural and the rhetorical branches of the sublime. This certainly seems unlikely enough, and we should not be disappointed to find it a partial truth, if we learn something along the way. Yet here, as in other cases, an association presented by the history of ideas points to a connection more profound than a drift of ideas and terms. We remember the identification Longinus proposed: "For, as if instinctively, our soul is uplifted by the true sublime; it takes a proud flight, and is filled with joy and vaunting, as though it had itself produced what it has heard" (*Peri Hypsous*, 7.2). The prior text is introjected; its power becomes our own. The joy and pride we feel are not simply adopted from the text, which may not concern such emotions, but are the affective correlative of a crucial supererogation—the measure of the extent to which the identification releases power within greater than the power without. Evidently the prior text presents, in its quality of excess, a potential threat or danger, an upsetting excitation which we can neutralize because we perceive it to be imaginary.

It would be nice to claim this point as our own, for it promises to contribute fundamentally to the psychology of originality. But the point is Burke's. Here he is on the moment of identification:

> Now whatever either on good or upon bad grounds tends to raise a man in his own opinion, produces a sort of swelling and triumph that is extremely grateful to the human mind; and this swelling is never more perceived, nor operates with more force, than when without danger we are conversant with terrible objects, the mind always claiming to itself some part of the dignity and importance of the things which it contemplates. Hence proceeds what Longinus has observed of that glorying and sense of inward greatness, that always fills the reader of such passages in poets and orators as are sublime; it is what every man must have felt in himself upon such occasions. [Pp. 50–51]

This is Burke's only reference to Longinus in Of the Sublime and Beautiful.[13] Quite spontaneously, Burke makes the connection between "terrible objects" and the sublime passages of the poets. The "swelling and triumph," the "sense of inward greatness," is produced precisely as the mind claims as its own the "dignity and importance" of the power it contemplates. The mind does not claim the terror—that is neutralized or repressed. The passage ends a section on "ambition," which follows a section on "imitation." Ambition is necessary, for

> if men gave themselves up to imitation entirely, and each followed the other, and so on in an eternal circle, it is easy to see that there never could be any improvement amongst them. Men must remain as brutes do, the same at the end that they are at this day, and that they were in the beginning of the world. To prevent this, God has planted in man a sense of ambition, and a satisfaction arising from the contemplation of his excelling his fellows in something deemed valuable amongst them. It is this passion that drives men to all the ways we see in use of signalizing themselves, and that tends to make whatever excites in a man the idea of this distinction so very pleasant. [P. 50]

Burke is rendering an account of the desire for originality. Ambition or the desire for originality—to be "signalized" in some way—is the desire to escape imitation through a supererogatory identification with the object. The connection to the sublime is clear and significant: the sublime of nature *or* of text offers an occasion for the mind to establish its superiority or originality. The reader's "sense of inward greatness" exceeds even the power of the text, just as the superego exceeds in its strength the object of authority on which it is modeled.

We meet the pattern of overidentification often in Romantic texts. We have already examined at length its presence in the relation between Albion and Urizen in Blake's myth of the Fall. It is, I believe, the psychological source of the *daemonic* in Romanticism, and it appears to be a fundamental mechanism in the psychology of poetic "influence," to which the sublime is so intimately tied. For the moment, however, an investigation of the daemonic and an appreciation of its extraordinary implications must be postponed. Our model is not yet secure enough to serve as the foundation for a meaningful superstructure.

V

Have we not, in fact, arrived at the model by pressing one theory and suppressing a multitude of facts for which it cannot account? Besides the cogent objections which may be urged against psychoanalytic reduction, we have obviously side-stepped the other mode of the negative sublime, which concerns magnitude. The omission of the mathematical sublime is the more conspicuous for our having lavished so much attention upon it in a former chapter. There we found that the imagination's traumatic collapse resulted from the unconscious pressure of the reason's need for totality as expressed in the operation of comprehension. Reason appeared to be both the cause of and the solution to the imagination's frustration. That implication of Kant's text struck us as a problem. How could reason operate unconsciously and then, in the reactive phase, be consciously recognized? We have since had occasion to establish essential correlations between reason and the superego. The superego operates unconsciously, producing anxiety to the point where the ego's equilibrium collapses; then consciousness turns to it in the act of identification and receives its image and its ideal. It is as if reason spoke thus to the imagination: "You must try to possess totally the object; but, since you cannot, you must renounce your desire of possession, and make yourself one with me; I offer you an extension and power different from what you have sacrificed, but greater."

However, there is no need for such a translation; Kant's terms suffice. "The *sublime* is what pleases immediately by reason of its opposition to sense" ("Analytic of the Sublime," p. 118). More expansively, in a text we have often encountered:

> Thus, too, delight in the sublime in nature is only *negative* (whereas that in the beautiful is *positive*): that is to say it is a feeling of imagination by its own act depriving itself of its freedom by receiving a final determination in accordance with a law other than that of its empirical employment. In this way it gains an extension and a power greater than that which it sacrifices. But the ground of this is concealed from it, and in its place it *feels* the sacrifice or deprivation, as well as its cause, to which it is subjected. [P. 120]

This self-limitation has the look of an instinctual renunciation, a painful acceptance of object loss that yields the feeling of "sacrifice or deprivation." Here we see that in the case of the mathematical sublime, the renounced wish cannot have been an aggressive one. Left to itself, the imagination would simply go on apprehending. But the imagination must accept the renunciation of its freedom if it is to possess or comprehend the object precisely, because comprehension is the prerogative of reason. The imagination's preliminary attempt to comprehend is an (unconscious) assumption of the privilege and place of reason, which it then retracts by a kind of reaction-formation, a routine situation in the oedipus complex. Freud explains that the superego enjoins the ego in contradictory precepts: "You *ought to be* like this (like your father)" but also "You *may not be* like this (like your father)—that is, you may not do all that he does; some things are his prerogative."[14] Here the original ambivalence implicit in any act of identification is independently reinforced.

What the imagination must sacrifice is its free activity of perception. Whether or not this freedom is fundamentally erotic is a question we must later consider. As we have seen, reason will use fear in order to compel the imagination to surrender its primary attachment and become "an instrument of reason and its ideas" (p. 121). Kant's emphasis on the feeling of deprivation—and on the fact that the greater "extension and power" provided by reason remain concealed to the imagination—is an odd tribute to the strength of unregenerate perceiving. Confronted by natural plenitude, the mind is reluctant to make metaphors. We sense this reluctance again and again in Wordsworth; indeed, it generates the tension of his imagery. Perhaps only fear can compel the mind to relinquish perception in favor of metaphor.

In any case, the supervention of fear exactly marks the point where the perceptional imagination is halted in its usurpation of the prerogative of totality, of possession. Fear changes the imaginative medium from perception to fantasy, and if a successful identification ensues, there is a further change from fantasy to symbol. Geoffrey Hartman's brilliant reading of Wordsworth shows him "fixated," as it were, in the second stage. An example, familiar to all connoisseurs of the sublime, is the Stolen Boat episode of *The Prelude* (1. 357–400). The boy is led by Nature to steal the boat in "an act of stealth / And troubled pleasure" that has overtones of erotic possession:

> But now, like one who rows,
> Proud of his skill, to reach a chosen point
> With an unswerving line, I fixed my view
> Upon the summit of a craggy ridge,
> The horizon's utmost boundary; far above
> Was nothing but the stars and the grey sky.
> She was an elfin pinnace; lustily
> I dipped my oars into the silent lake,
> And, as I rose upon the stroke, my boat
> Went heaving through the water like a swan;
> When, from behind that craggy steep till then
> The horizon's bound, a huge peak, black and huge,
> As if with voluntary power instinct
> Upreared its head. I struck and struck again,
> And growing still in stature the grim shape
> Towered up between me and the stars, and still,
> For so it seemed, with purpose of its own
> And measured motion like a living thing,
> Strode after me.   [1. 367–85]

Two things happen: the determinate horizon is shattered and the "voluntary power" shifts suddenly from the boy ("chosen point" and "unswerving line" suggest how in command he felt) to the "grim shape"—a compound of perception and fantasy. Fear takes over and the boy's wish is guiltily renounced:

> With trembling oars I turned,
> And through the silent water stole my way
> Back to the covert of the willow tree;
> There in her mooring-place I left my bark,—
> And through the meadows homeward went, in grave
> And serious mood; but after I had seen
> That spectacle, for many days, my brain
> Worked with a dim and undetermined sense
> Of unknown modes of being; o'er my thoughts
> There hung a darkness, call it solitude
> Or blank desertion. No familiar shapes

Remained, no pleasant images of trees,
Of sea or sky, no colours of green fields;
But huge and mighty forms, that do not live
Like living men, moved slowly through the mind
By day, and were a trouble to my dreams.   [1. 385–400]

The imagination has been liberated into a greater "extension and might," but since the ground of this new power is concealed, the imagination feels the sacrifice and deprivation as well as their cause—"unknown modes of being," "huge and mighty forms," which resist translation from fantasy to symbol.

What accounts, in Wordsworth, for the immense concealment, for his resistance to identification? No doubt purely personal factors contributed to the strength of his regressive attachment to Nature, but these factors cannot be validated with assurance and are not in my view wholly germane to the analysis of Wordsworth's sublime. And this episode, for one, does not respond satisfactorily to the theory that Wordsworth simply could not free himself from Mother Nature. Nature, after all, led him into it; in the 1805 version, he writes "(surely I was led by her)" as if there were doubt or anxiety on this point. We can see on countless occasions in *The Prelude* Wordsworth's determination to ascribe to Nature's working nearly everything that happened to him; the discipline of pain and fear as well as benevolent, gentling influences belong to her. Nature is thus responsible for both the sense of loss or deprivation, felt as betrayal, and for the fear itself. The former anxiety is fully conscious and is often met by denial, by "Knowing that Nature never did betray / The heart that loved her."[15] But beyond the formulas of betrayal there is the possibility that Nature herself enters into the object of fear in a constitutive fashion. She does not merely employ fear and pain to strengthen the young mind; she is herself a source of pain and terror. Psychologically, Wordsworth's relation to Nature cannot be reduced to an ambivalent struggle against an essentially benevolent pedagogy. The ambivalence of liberation masks a deeper, original ambivalence.

We are tempted here onto vague terrain where our only guide is tenuous speculation. The terror that belongs originally to Nature cannot be a fear of injury. The other side of superego anxiety presents itself as having been ignored. The superego is a precipitate of the mother as well as the father, and its displeasure may thus be manifested not only in the fantasy of castration but also in the sense of loss—of self-esteem or of "narcissistic supplies"—which is actually the major feature of melancholia. Hence we may assume that the imagination's feeling of deprivation owes as much to guilt—the recourse of the superego less drastic than terror—as it does to perceptional frustration. But the anxiety specific to this formation would be immediately recognizable as the familiar anxiety of loss. It might precipitate a "hunger" for the lost relation to Nature, or some other derivative related to the oral fixation of depressives. It could not, in any case, account for the primary fear of Nature which appears, indeed, to be the very opposite to any desire for reunion or approval. Could it be that the anxiety of the sublime does not ultimately result from the pressure of the superego after all?

VI

We had good reasons for adopting our model, and we would be reluctant to abandon it. Perhaps Wordsworth is an exceptional case; our line of thought about Wordsworth was merely suggestive and is far from established. Yet other considerations combine to make us suspect that the oedipus complex is not the deep structure of the negative sublime. It is, in a sense, too obvious, too close to the surface. And we have difficulty isolating the aggressive wish—genetically, to do away with the father—in most texts, even of the terrible sublime. The negative sublime erects reactive structures from which that wish may be logically inferred, but the affect itself is often strangely absent or unconvincing. We think of Wordsworth's *The Borderers*, which is founded on this very situation. The hero Marmaduke is supposed to achieve moral and intellectual sublimity by killing the old father figure Herbert, but genuine animus or aggression is just what Marmaduke cannot feel. The oedipal drama seems extraneous to the emotional center of the play, as if it masked the deep trouble.

Our sense that the theory is inadequate or superficial becomes less impressionistic when we reconsider not the material but the efficient cause of the sublime moment. We spoke of an excess on the part of the object with respect to the perceiving mind or imagination; in semiotic terms, an excess on the plane of the signifiers. It is a habit of structuralist thinking in general to play fast and loose with Saussure's great paradigm, signifier / signified. Yet we violate only minimally the semiotic integrity of this paradigm by translating its terms into a psychological calculus. The obvious approach is to identify the plane of signifiers with impinging stimuli and the plane of the signifieds with the pleasure-pain series, since it is likely that we first learn to discriminate entities within the perceptional flow in terms of the pleasure principle. A signifier either accompanies pleasure or pain; that is the first thing we learn about it, and if it is neutrally associated, it is ignored. These are ordinary facts rendered in a slightly more rigorous fashion than ordinary discourse allows. Since this psychology is basically Lockean, it is what Burke assumes. Kant himself explicitly authorizes a psychological translation of all "representations." Here he concedes the premise of Burke's acute observations and shows us incidentally how venerable a doctrine Freud was later to promote:

> As psychological observations [Burke's] analyses of our mental phenomena are extremely fine, and supply a wealth of material for the favourite investigations of empirical anthropology. But, besides that, there is no denying the fact that all representations within us, no matter whether they are objectively merely sensible or wholly intellectual, are still subjectively associable with gratification or pain, however imperceptible either of these may be. . . . We must even admit that, as Epicurus maintained, *gratification* and *pain* though proceeding from the imagination or even from representations of the understanding, are always in the last resort corporeal, since apart from any feeling of the bodily organ life would be merely a consciousness of one's existence, and could not include any feeling of well-being or the reverse, i.e. of the furtherance or hindrance of the vital forces. For, of itself alone, the mind is all life (the life-principle itself), and hindrance or furtherance has to be sought outside it, and yet in the man himself, consequently in the connexion with his body. ["Analytic of the Sublime," p. 131]

It is difficult to see how an excess of stimuli or signifiers can affect the mind with the opposite feeling of deprivation. The sense of guilt is evidently a secondary formation, at least in the case of the mathematical sublime; in the dynamical sublime, the overload of threatening signifiers may directly activate the fear of injury and the subsequent defense. On the principle of homeostasis, any excess of stimuli will be felt as pain, even if the stimuli themselves are pleasurable. In the latter case an original ambivalence is inevitable. The very gratification of instinctual aims, in its quality of excess, alerts the ego to a danger. There is simultaneously a wish to be inundated or engulfed by pleasurable stimuli and a fear of being incorporated, overwhelmed, annihilated. This is hardly a rigorous formulation of the original "oral ambivalence,"[16] but it helps to account for the peculiar, ambivalent quality of the abyss image. Fascination and dread coincide. Both Burke and Kant emphasize the factor of involuntary motion in the sublime, and this suggests an appeal to the instincts, a gratification too intense to be continued without anxiety. In Burke's view, "the mind is so entirely filled with its object, that it cannot entertain any other, nor by consequence reason on that object which employs it," so that the power of the sublime "anticipates our reasonings, and hurries us on by an irresistible force" (p. 57). Kant is especially clear about the ambivalence of the energy that is attached to the object: "The mind feels itself *set in motion* in the representation of the sublime in nature; . . . This movement, especially in its inception, may be compared with a vibration, i.e., with a rapidly alternating repulsion and attraction produced by one and the same Object. The point of excess for the imagination (towards which it is driven in the apprehension of the intuition) is like an abyss in which it fears to lose itself." ["Analytic of the Sublime," p. 107]

In the second or traumatic phase of the negative sublime, the mind is overwhelmed, but because this state has been associated with gratification it is unconsciously and irresistibly attractive. This is why a diffuse melancholy predisposes to the sublime. The melancholic is in need of "narcissistic supplies"—self-esteem—from his superego, in which an original deprivation is likely to have been institutionalized. The sublime appearance promises an overabundance of stimulation. At any rate, we see that the oedipal formation with all its vagaries and derivatives is superimposed upon an original ambivalence, a rapid alternation of attraction and repulsion. Our line of thought postulates a wish to be inundated and a simultaneous anxiety of annihilation: to survive, as it were, the ego must go on the offensive and cease to be passive. This movement from passive to active is technically a reaction formation, and the oedipal configuration we have remarked thus appears as itself a defense against the original wish. The wish to be inundated is reversed into a wish to possess. Since the defense is directed primarily against the dangerous passivity, the other component of the oedipus complex—the aggressive wish against the father—is only structurally motivated and fails to impress us as authentic.

It would appear that the negative sublime as a whole is the expression of two separate sets of defenses intimately linked. To put it sequentially: the excessive object excites a wish to be inundated, which yields an anxiety of incorporation; this anxiety is met by a reaction formation against the wish which precipitates a recapitulation of the oedipus complex; this in turn yields a feeling of guilt (superego anxiety) and is resolved through identification (introjection). How can a process evidently so complicated yield delight? We have interpreted the delight— the "joy and vaunting" first celebrated by Longinus—as the affective correlative of a successful, supererogatory identification. But perhaps this final defense has an instinctual source less mediated. It is just possible that the defense mechanism of introjection gratifies a wish prior even to the ambivalent wish excited by the sublime appearance— the wish (i.e., to be pleasurably stimulated) before it has become experientially associated with excess. The more-or-less voluntary intro-jection—swallowing, as it were, on one's own terms—would in effect defuse the components of the oral masochism which presents itself as the point of origin for the negative sublime. The secondary defense mechanism would itself become instinctually charged in this sublimation (change of aim and object). But this hypothesis seems useless and also remains utterly beyond verification.

We should not be surprised to find that the sublime moment is over-determined in its effect on the mind. The excess which we have supposed to be the precipitating occasion, or "trigger," directly prompts the secondary anxiety in the case of the dynamical sublime of terror. In the mathematical sublime, however, the traumatic phase exhibits a primary system on which the secondary (guilt) system is superimposed. This situation explains an odd but unmistakable fact of Kant's analytic. Whenever he is generalizing about both versions of the negative sublime, the (secondary) rhetoric of power dominates. It is not logically necessary that the reason's capacity for totality or infinity should be invariably construed as power degrading the sensible and rescuing man from "humiliation" at the hands of nature. But though the sublime of magnitude does not originate in a power struggle, it almost instantaneously turns into one as the secondary oedipal system takes over. What we have found might be summarized schematically, though I hasten to add that this still more drastic reduction of a reductive argument is useful only if it is not taken too seriously.

THE NEGATIVE SUBLIME

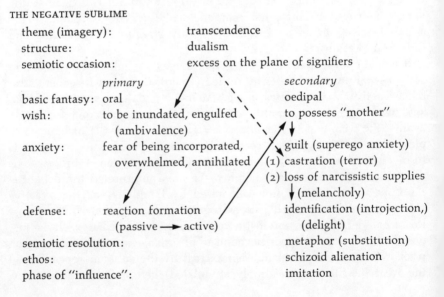

theme (imagery):	transcendence	
structure:	dualism	
semiotic occasion:	excess on the plane of signifiers	

	primary	*secondary*
basic fantasy:	oral	oedipal
wish:	to be inundated, engulfed (ambivalence)	to possess "mother"
anxiety:	fear of being incorporated, overwhelmed, annihilated	guilt (superego anxiety) (1) castration (terror) (2) loss of narcissistic supplies (melancholy)
defense:	reaction formation (passive → active)	identification (introjection,) (delight)
semiotic resolution:		metaphor (substitution)
ethos:		schizoid alienation
phase of "influence":		imitation

5. *When we look back at the face of the seventeenth century, it is at the rigorous face of the rigorous thinker and, say, the Miltonic image of a poet, severe and determined. In effect, what we are remembering is the rather haggard background of the incredible, the imagination without intelligence, from which a younger figure is emerging, stepping forward in the company of a muse of its own, still half-beast and somehow more than human, a kind of sister of the Minotaur. This younger figure is the intelligence that endures. It is the imagination of the son still bearing the antique imagination of the father. It is the clear intelligence of the young man still bearing the burden of the obscurities of the intelligence of the old. It is the spirit out of its own self, not out of some surrounding myth, delineating with accurate speech the complications of which it is composed.*—Wallace Stevens, "The Figure of the Youth as Virile Poet"

The Sublime as Romance: Two Texts from Collins

Willam Collins's *Odes on Several Descriptive and Allegoric Subjects* were published in December 1746 and were not a hit. Joseph Warton, with whom Collins intended at one point to appear in print, published his own *Odes* independently in the same month. The suppler Warton had the immediate advantage with his very poetical choice of expression and lightweight "Invention." Collins was and is difficult, allegoric as well as descriptive, mythopoeic—so the critics have found—as well as allegoric. Johnson conceded "moments of sublimity and splendor" but was troubled by the "harshness and obscurity" and found, on the whole, "deviation in quest of mistaken beauties."[1] Our distance from Johnson is such that we are likely to value that telling obscurity, which was to find sanction in Burke's theory of the sublime. What Coleridge once said to his friend Thelwall might be said to Johnson: "you ought to distinguish between obscurity residing in the uncommonness of the thought, and that which proceeds from thoughts unconnected & language not adapted to the expression of them."[2] Collins's obscurity is uncommonly conceptual, and we may begin to suspect that it is often the subject, as well as the manner, of the Odes.

The question of context has been crucial for the reading of Collins. Warton advertised himself as looking upon invention and imagination as a poet's chief faculties, and he hoped his offering would bring poetry back into its right channel. This ideology, with its pretense of reaction and its antididacticism, looks attractively pre-Romantic, and certainly after Addison's Spectator papers, the pleasures of the imagination were much in the air; a new fashion was in the making. But Collins's effects, in the few perplexing odes we find ourselves rereading, seem to spring from sources darker than the vicarious emotionalism of the new fashion. If that context has critical value, it is the negative value of factoring out what is most conventional and least interesting in Collins's deviation.

Contexts more portentous have been tailored to fit Collins and in particular his most ambitious poem, the "Ode on the Poetical Character." Romanticists have found in the creation myth of that poem and its epiphany—

And thou, thou rich-haired youth of morn,
And all thy subject life was born!

—an anticipation of the Romantic Apollo, the figure of the youth as a virile poet, and even of Blake's Orc.[3] On the other hand, Earl Wasserman has argued persuasively that Christian Neoplatonism is the proper context for Collins's creation myth and, in general, for the "shad'wy Tribes of Mind" who are the personae of the odes.[4] Even the conservative reading of Collins, as represented in the standard articles of A. S. P. Woodhouse, accepts that Collins's major poem is about "the *creative imagination* and the poet's passionate desire for its power"—the question being, for Woodhouse, what in Collins's conception of the imagination is traditional doctrine and what is new.[5] However, before we are drawn into this debate—which has been very instructive—we ought to ask: is it at all possible to read the odes *out* of context? For if it is not, the odes must remain of genuine but quite limited importance no matter how much we love poor Collins; this is pretty much where they stand now. The epithet "transitional" haunts Collins as it does all the so-called Sensibility poets. They have consistently been the victims of ulterior interests, and one benefit of a deeper theory of the sublime might be to rescue a reading of them in terms both theirs and ours.

Yet a reading of Collins in his own terms looks like a difficult enterprise, because his terms are indeed borrowed from far and wide. He marries a Greek form to a Spenserian diction; his conception of the poet-prophet is Miltonic, and yet he cleaves to the sceptical urbanity of the "gentle mind"; his psychological themes (pity, fear) are Aristotelian, and his account of origins Platonic; his pictorial technique is an admixture of Lockean psychology and traditional painterly and even iconographic presentment; his perception is epiphanic and his syntax absurdly hypotactic. Where is the real Collins? This is a naive question, and it is thus perfectly appropriate for one of the most self-consciously mediated poetic presences in the language. Collins is not, of course, without company in this strange competition of indirection; we think of Gray and other practicioners of the sublime poem down through the early Blake and Coleridge. Beneath the radical uncertainty of tone which the sublime poem exhibits is a fascinating variety of cultural attitudes in shifting patterns of conflict. The poor "I," or voice of these poems, is often thrown into affectation or attitudinizing of one kind or another in its effort to stay afloat on the turbulence of ideological change. The problem is essentially one of authority: in terms of tone, how to be at once impassioned, high sounding, and sincere; in terms of theme, where to locate the "daring and all-embracing power" of Collins's Pindaric epigraph.

Collins's "I," however, is representative in a finer sense. It is just beginning to emerge as an authentic voice from the mediation of some very complex experimentation when it is strangely stunted. When we have used every trick to unify the more difficult odes, some incoherence or harshness remains, and it may be referred to the incomplete subordination of imagery and situation to a dramatized consciousness or speaker. Of course, the Pindaric ode licensed an inconstant speaker, but there are signs that Collins is attempting to use disjunction expressively in order to suggest an implicit adventure or progress of consciousness. In particular, his transfer of the epode to the middle position between strophe and antistrophe in effect turns the traditional finality of the epode into a middle term suspended as an episode in the antithetical progress of the two strophes, where self-consciousness is characteristically concentrated. But Collins's commitment to his "I," the ego of the poem, is somewhat insecure. At times it is as if the "I" did not know quite how to behave: hence the repetitions ("Ah Fear! Ah Frantic Fear! / I see, I see thee near") and the latching onto the persona's gestures ("Like thee I start, like thee disordered fly"). When an "I" becomes self-conscious it requires an identity or convention of self-dramatization, and Collins's decorum of crisis is often not adequate to his self-consciousness.

The "I," or ego, of Collins's poems is vague terrain, off the maps of those who have plotted Collins's ideology, but it is what a reading of Collins out of context might explore. Something more modest is in prospect here—a description, or at least a sketch, of the psychological situation of Collins's "I" as it is represented in the two most spectacular odes, which concern fear and poetic election. The contexts that have been finely woven for Collins remain relevant—we can hardly ignore his themes—but ancillary to the claim we would like to venture for his psychological interest.

II

Collins's obscurity unmistakably resides in "the uncommonness of the thought" rather than in a faulty technique. Obscurity, in fact, seems to be the ground of Collins's fictions, the backdrop of what he often calls the *scene*. The personae, "shadowy tribes of Mind," loom up from an indistinct matrix, a "world unknown" or "unreal scene." They are balanced brilliantly but precariously between outer and inner, what is seen and what is known; they also seem to be suspended historically between the pictorial elaboration of traditional allegory and the vague depths of what we too familiarly call the unconscious; they have the mediate, ambiguous status traditionally accorded to the *daemon*. The complex variety of Collins's sources—never mind the host of epiphanic or theophanic analogues these personae invite—signals a pervasive over-determination. Obscurity has become a part of the meaning, or at least a part of what determines meaning.

At the heart of Collins's daemonic odes is anagnorisis, a moment of epiphanic recognition in which the emotive rhythm of the poem is centered. In this moment of recognition "thou" and "I" coalesce ("O Fear, I know thee by my throbbing heart"), and the pictorial medium of the persona tends to dissolve as the persona is internalized. "I see you there" becomes "I know you here." We have an odd indication of Collins's interest in Aristotle's notion of anagnorisis at the very time he began serious work on the odes in May 1746. According to a letter of his friend John Mulso (28 May 1746), Collins owed his landlady five pounds, and when she summoned a bailiff, Collins could barely scrape together the money. Evidently there was a scene, for Mulso adds: "The *anagnorisis* (a word He is fond of) was quite striking & ye catastrophe quite poetical and interesting."[6] Collins had been working on a translation and commentary of the *Poetics*, where anagnorisis is defined as a "change from ignorance to knowledge, producing love or hate between the persons destined by the poet for good or bad fortune."[7] The poem of recognition raises the expectation that the "I" will be changed in some way that will clarify his affective state. This kind of poem, familiar in the many guises of the Romantic ode, is no longer "about" anything; it is a place where something happens, is about to happen, or fails to happen, a locus of encounters fugitive or overwhelming. A crisis is constituted for the "I"; the poem has become dangerous. And yet, in Collins, something fails to come off: the moment of recognition tends to slip away, leaving the "I" changed but not transformed, and a bit defensive.

But it is time to become less impressionistic. The "Ode to Fear" (probably Collins's first attempt at the Greek ode) begins by invoking the nymph Fear as a presence already known but also somewhat apart and having a special insight:

> Thou, to whom the world unknown
> With all its shadowy shapes is shown;
> Who see'st appalled the unreal scene,
> While Fancy lifts the veil between:
> Ah Fear! Ah frantic Fear!
> I see, I see thee near.
> I know thy hurried step, thy haggard eye!
> Like thee I start, like thee disordered fly.
> For lo, what monsters in thy train appear!   [1–9][8]

The technical subtlety is apparent: Fear does not in herself inspire fear; she is the subject and not the object of fear. The personification enables Collins to represent a psychological subtlety. Fear's response is "objective": she has seen, been appalled, and now enacts the primitive defense of flight. The "I," however, experiences the approach of fear without being able at first to know the cause of her flight. The danger signal of "subjective" anxiety prompts an internalized recapitulation of the primitive defense but also permits a kind of detachment, and this enables Collins to halt, as it were ("For lo"), and assess the cause. The idea of Fear's "train" brilliantly catches the perceptional ambiguity, for it is what chases Fear but also what follows the experience of fear in the protagonist's train of thought. The implication, oddly enough, is that Fear in flight can no longer see what pursues her, as the "I" now can. She has seen once, and that was enough; her state is technically traumatic. The poet's state repeats the trauma as if to master it with the aid of Fancy, whose function is to remove the normal barrier to recognition.

But what is the source of this anxiety, the "world" or "scene" with "shadowy shapes" which is so appalling? Here we might descend to a conventional psychoanalytic reduction, if only because it presents itself so inevitably. In his well-known compendium of psychoanalytic theory, Otto Fenichel remarks: "In psychoanalytic practice, we have the habit of stating, when sensations of this kind come up, such as unclear rotating objects, rhythmically approaching and receding objects, sensations of crescendo and decrescendo, that 'primal-scene material is approaching.'"[9] The "primal-scene material" is the child's observation or fantasy of sexual scenes between his parents or any adults.[10] The child unfortunately has no clear idea of what is going on, so he imagines the worst, a sadistic attack upon his mother, which at once excites and terrifies him. The specific form this primal fantasy takes is determined in classical theory by the particular state of the oedipus complex with which the scene is closely associated. But always present is "the linking together of the conceptions 'sexual satisfaction' and 'danger.'"[11] When in later life the veil is momentarily lifted and the repressed scene approaches consciousness, its imagery combines overexcitation and dangerous violence in a medium of obscurity, as Norman Holland summarizes: "One finds several clusters of images in such fantasies: first, darkness, a sense of vagueness and the unknown, mysterious noises in night and darkness; second, vague movements, shapes shifting and changing, nakedness, things appearing and disappearing; third, images of fighting and struggling, blood, the phallus as weapon."[12]

Whatever we make of this we cannot ignore the mingling of excitement and danger in Collins's text—and in the sublime poem in general as well as its bastard scion, the gothic sort of writing. As the "monsters" who follow in the wake of Fear proceed before—or through—the mind, their direct threat is somehow neutralized or displaced to the fugitive nymph. Collins is drawing on the Masque of Cupid and the Temple of Venus in the *Faerie Queene* (3.12; 4. 10) for his own masque-like distancing:

For lo, what monsters in thy train appear!
Danger, whose limbs of giant mould

What mortal eye can fixed behold?
Who stalks his round, an hideous form,
Howling amidst the midnight storm,
Or throws him on the ridgy steep
Of some loose hanging rock to sleep;
And with him thousand phantoms joined,
Who prompt to deeds accursed the mind;
And those, the fiends who, near allied,
O'er nature's wounds and wrecks perside;
Whilst Vengeance in the lurid air
Lifts her red arm, exposed and bare,
On whom that ravening brood of fate,
Who lap the blood of sorrow, wait;
Who, Fear, this ghastly train can see,
And look not madly wild like thee?   [9–25]

The question with which the strophe concludes is more open than it
looks. As a fantasy, this masque has its consolations. Danger, after all,
doesn't really hurt anybody and only throws himself down in order to
go to sleep. Forbidden deeds ("accursed the mind") are not actually
carried out.

Most striking is Vengeance, the only female in the fantasy, if we
except wounded nature. Her lifted "red arm, exposed and bare" is
defiantly phallic and in fact belongs traditionally to the Father, or Jove,
or God. The sources cited by editor Lonsdale are impressively un-
animous on this point. From Horace (*Pater . . . rubente / dextera sacras
iaculatus arces*) to Dryden ("the King of Heav'n, obscure on high, /
Bar'd his red Arm") to Pope, the red arm is the Almighty's.[13] Perhaps
most relevant is Milton's version: Belial fears that "intermitted vengeance" might "arm again / [God's] red right hand to plague us" (*PL*
2.173–74). Vengeance, in Collins's text, is balanced structurally against
Danger, as if in retaliation for a somewhat unspecified assault. By
equipping her so magnificently, Collins wishfully denies what Freud
found to be the major distress of the primal scene, the perception of the
female as lacking the phallus, which leads normally to an acute intensification of castration anxiety. In one sense, the vengeance here is
Collins's, since he transforms the phrase against the collective insistence
of his poetic fathers. But the psychology we are following here belongs
to the poem's "I," and at that level the image of Vengeance as a phallic
woman is strangely comforting and apotropaic—like the snakes on
Medusa's head once analyzed by Freud.[14]

We can see that Fear personifies one response to this ghastly train of thought, and the "I" of the poem dramatizes another, more complicated response. The poet would like to identify himself with the simpler response ("Like thee I start, like thee disordered fly") and be simply "madly wild." But Fear's defense is simple flight, the prototype of repression; in the strophe she has no power, and the "dark power" (l. 53) somehow associated with the viewing of this scene is what he really wants. The nymph Fear represents an infantile response to the primal scene, its normal fate of repression; the poet's regression to this defense is no longer a real possibility. On the other hand, his ambivalent investment in the scene is still strong enough to hold him back from the normative resolution of the memory and the oedipal complex in which it is installed.

III

The strophe concludes with a rhetorical question that wards off the ambivalence of the protagonist. Immediately in the epode (or mesode) we are given an example of one (Aeschylus) who disdained to become "madly wild." In the epode, Fear is no longer in flight but is instead the object of a search or quest for the source of anxiety:

> In earliest Greece to thee with partial choice
>   The grief-ful Muse addressed her infant tongue;
> The maids and matrons on her awful voice,
>   Silent and pale, in wild amazement hung.
>
> Yet he, the bard who first invoked thy name,
>   Disdained in Marathon its power to feel:
> For not alone he nursed the poet's flame,
>   But reached from Virtue's hand the patriot's steel.
>
> But who is he whom later garlands grace,
>   Who left awhile o'er Hybla's dews to rove,
> With trembling eyes thy dreary steps to trace,
>   Where thou and Furies shared the baleful grove?
>
> Wrapped in thy cloudy veil the incestuous queen
>   Sighed the sad call her son and husband heard,
> When once alone it broke the silent scene,
>   And he, the wretch of Thebes, no more appeared.
>
> O Fear, I know thee by my throbbing heart,
>   Thy withering power inspired each mournful line,
> Though gentle Pity claim her mingled part,
>   Yet all the thunders of the scene are thine!   [26–45]

Fear now has power of some kind. In one aspect, this power seems somewhat weak-minded or regressive. It affects not men but "maids and matrons" with amazement, and maternally helps to nurse "the poet's flame"; it is opposed to a stronger power associated with public morality, whose imagery ("patriot's steel") is associated with the threatening Father. In another aspect, however, Fear's power is "withering"—the word suggests both shrivelling up and, obliquely, the effect of a reproachful look (OED, 1, 2). The "mad nymph" has become an elusive Mother, whose function now is to obstruct insight with a cloudy veil rather than to be appalled when the veil is lifted.

Collins's allusion to the death of Oedipus displays an egregious distortion to which he virtually calls attention by quoting Sophocles' lines in a note. Here the messenger is relating Oedipus's last moments with his daughters (I bracket the lines Collins quotes):

That was the way of it. They clung together
And wept, all three. [But when they finally stopped,
And no more sobs were heard, then there was
Silence, and in the silence suddenly
A voice cried out to him—of such a kind
It made our hair stand up in panic fear:]
Again and again the call came from the god:
"Oedipus! Oedipus! Why are we waiting?
You delay too long; you delay too long to go!"[15]

It is hard to believe that Collins's mistake is not deliberate (like his coy allusion to Spenser at the beginning of the "Ode on the Poetical Character"), but whether conscious or not, the change is a major one. Jocasta is nowhere near this scene in Sophocles. Oedipus is called by the god and not once but "again and again." Actually Collins's (mis)reading of the text rather strikingly anticipates the modern psychological reading of the death scene. Harry Slochower has developed the Freudian interpretation of the Oedipus story through its conclusion in the "baleful grove":

Oedipus' relation to the Eumenides renews—on another level—his contact with Jocasta. Indeed, the horror expressed at his daring to approach their forbidden grove is similar to that voiced at his earlier violation. That is, Oedipus' attempt to penetrate the hidden abode of the Earth-Mothers repeats his incest with his biological mother. . . . His "return to the mother" now takes place, not on a literal, but on a symbolical level. And there is this further difference: where actual incest was coupled with patricide, symbolic incest is followed by cooperation with a surrogate father, Theseus.[16]

Now if this is what Sophocles' Oedipus is doing, Collins's Oedipus is doing the reverse. He is joining Jocasta not symbolically, by way of the Furies, but literally. The god who calls is suppressed, and the incestuous queen takes his place. Parallel to this intriguing change is the reduction of the many callings to the one sad call—a sign of a regressive fixation on one event which prevents its therapeutic, symbolic repetition. But most astonishing is the anxiety which overtakes the "I" whose fantasy this is:

> Wrapped in thy cloudy veil the incestuous queen
>   Sighed the sad call her son and husband heard,
> When once alone it broke the silent scene,
>   And he, the wretch of Thebes, no more appeared.
>
> O Fear, I know thee by my throbbing heart,
>   Thy withering power inspired each mournful line,
> Though gentle Pity claim her mingled part,
>   Yet all the thunders of the scene are thine!

The recognition is emotionally climactic: the verb breaks to the present as the distancing, historical and literary, of the mesode collapses. The mesode had enabled the poet to "trace" the steps of fear to its source in "deeds accursed the mind." Moreover, it is not death itself—that is, muted down to "he . . . no more appeared"—but the sighing "sad call" of the incestuous Mother which prompts fear. The identification of his own feelings with Oedipus is so strong that it quite emasculates the situation of the actual Oedipus and projects in its stead a fantasy with irresistible attractive power from which he cannot remain detached. It is exactly this ambivalent excitement and dread which the Freudians insist lie behind the mystery of the primal scene and its perceptional derivatives. Had Freud never lived, we would be driven to the hypothesis of the oedipal complex to make sense of these lines.

The allusion to Aristotle seems at first to restore a literary mediation to this attack of anxiety. But on closer inspection it confirms the protagonist's surrender to the fantasy. In the *Rhetoric*, Aristotle defines fear as "a pain or disturbance due to a mental picture of some destructive or painful evil in the future," and he explains that the threat must be imminent: "for instance, we all know we shall die, but we are not troubled thereby, because death is not close at hand" (2.5).[17] He emphasizes the necessary loss of detachment in fear:

> Let us now describe the conditions under which we ourselves feel fear. If fear is associated with the expectation that something des-

tructive will happen to us, plainly nobody will be afraid who believes
nothing can happen to him; we shall not fear things that we believe
cannot happen to us, nor people who we believe cannot inflict them
upon us; nor shall we be afraid at times when we think ourselves
safe from them. . . . Consequently, when it is advisable that the
audience should be frightened, the orator must make them feel that
they really are in danger of something, pointing out that it has happened to others who were stronger than they are, and is happening,
or has happened, to people like themselves, at the hands of unexpected people, in an unexpected form, and at an unexpected time.
[2.5]

Plainly, if tragedy is to effect the cartharsis, or purgation of fear, it
cannot remain thus unmediated. This is where pity comes in. Aristotle's
conception of pity is egocentric: "Pity may be defined as a feeling of
pain caused by the sight of some evil, destructive or painful, which
befalls one who does not deserve it, and which we might expect to befall
ourselves or some friend of ours, and moreover to befall us soon" (2.8).
Pity is nothing more or less than mediated fear, and it necessarily
vanishes if the threat comes too close and the line melts between the
other and ourselves: "Speaking generally, anything causes us to feel
fear that when it happens to, or threatens, others causes us to feel
pity" (2.5). "Here too we have to remember the general principle that
what we fear for ourselves excites our pity when it happens to others"
(2.8). From this it follows that fear accounts for our identification with
the feelings and the plight of the tragic hero and that pity implies our
circumstantial distance from him.[18] In this light, Collins's allusion to
Aristotle in effect confesses the inability of the protagonist to resist
being absorbed in Oedipus. Detachment or pity makes a futile claim
against the identification, but "each mournful line" is addressing him
in the immediacy of fear, known by his "throbbing heart."

Aristotle's pity is fundamentally defensive, far from unselfish sympathy or compassion and farther from the soft head of Sensibility. His
view could not have been unknown to Collins if he had done any re-
search at all for the proposed translation and commentary of the *Poetics*.
It is, after all, commonplace moral wisdom which has been echoed
countless times from Aristotle to Blake and Freud. Burke's self-preservative psychology of the sublime is in the tradition and bears, in
addition, obvious traces of the homoepathic theory of catharsis. Yet
Collins's own version of pity in the companion ode seems less defensive than narcissistic:

5.
Come, Pity, come, by Fancy's aid,
Even now my thoughts, relenting maid,
   Thy temple's pride design:
Its southern site, its truth complete,
Shall raise a wild enthusiast heat
   In all who view the shrine.

6.
There Picture's toils shall well relate
How chance or hard involving fate
   O'er mortal bliss prevail:
The buskined Muse shall near her stand,
And sighing prompt her tender hand
   With each disastrous tale.

7.
There let me oft, retired by day,
In dreams of passion melt away,
   Allowed with thee to dwell:
There waste the mournful lamp of night,
Till, virgin, thou again delight
   To hear a British shell!   ["Ode to Pity," ll. 25–42]

Pity insulates her warm enthusiasts from the fear the disasters of tragedy
might be expected to prompt. To dwell with Pity involves melting away
in dreams of passion while trying to make a virgin hear; it's all rather
soupy, and suggests a prephallic sexual mist. Pity is a comforting nurse
who allays anxiety and salves the wounds inflicted by an insatiable
aggressor:

O thou, the friend of man assigned,
With balmy hands his wounds to bind,
   And charm his frantic woe:
When first Distress with dagger keen
Broke forth to waste his destined scene,
   His wild unsated foe!   [1–6]

Distress and his dagger ruin a scene or fantasy that is "destined" or
somehow inevitable. Collins's Pity is not the less egocentric for being a
narcissistic state of mind, but it is less a protection from anxiety than
a regressive evasion of it. The overwhelming of Pity in the "Ode to
Fear" is thus not only the collapse of aesthetic detachment but also the
failure of a sexual posture in the face of a major anxiety.

IV

To worry a dubious inference about Collins's own sexuality is a waste of time and, in my view, a betrayal of criticism. Psychoanalytic criticism need not succumb to the genetic fallacy from which Freudian thought has begun to be liberated. The equation "meaning equals origin"—as if we could, even in principle, specify origins!—charms interpretation like a false Duessa, but it is not a necessary error. If criticism is to have an independent ground it must be staked out not as a special corner of the universal human experience but as the study of how that total experience is refracted in art form. The meaning *is* the refraction. Nevertheless, we cannot quite escape the presence of the basic fantasy material, or else the discourse which valorizes its mediation has no content. The solution, easier in practice than in theory, is to determine accurately the status of the fantasy so that it is not vaporized into the archetypal or trivialized into the merely personal. For it is broadly true that history generates the urgency that will select from the universal code the fantasy appropriate for the moment—and this with an eye to what can be articulated, for the rest is dismissed, however apt it might have been. There are two needs (or wishes) which condition each other at every observable point: the need to say some particular thing and the need simply to say *something*. In discourse, and especially in literature, we can never find either in isolation; we find either a fantasy without words or words without a fantasy.

It has been recognized for some time that post-Augustan or pre-Romantic poetry exhibits a complex relation between these two needs. Their mutual conditionality is intensified, so that each may be translated into the other. The some-particular-thing pressing to be said is the need to say something: we say that the "subject" of this poetry is "literature as process," fictions investigating their own provenance and authority. Or the need simply to speak predominates: we say that the poetry is in search of a subject. This is not the situation in Renaissance or Augustan poems, and in Romantic poetry a latent self-reflexivity is often superseded.

What Collins does is discover a fantasy code appropriate to the special crisis of discourse in his day. It is a code that refers with eerie precision to the anxieties and preoccupations of the so-called phallic stage of the mind's development—and this ought to attract our attention even if we care little for Collins. What Bertrand Bronson says of Collins's poetic character could be said of the Sensibility poets in general: "All his short life as a poet—it ended before he was thirty—Collins was looking for a sustaining subject, and hero-worshipping.

Always hoping to graduate, he never truly left school. . . ." In the *Odes*, Bronson finds "a collegiate air," a "combination of brashness and timidity, so smacking of insecurity mixed with vaulting ambition."[19] That is a bit cavalier, but it is just, and it touches Chatterton, Gray (youth aside), even the more self-satisfied Thomson and Young, and certainly the early efforts of Coleridge in the sublime mode. If a psychological type is to be recognized here, Wordsworth's fine phrase will do: a marvellous boy who perished *in his pride*.[20] The idealized image of the type is the figure of the virile poet identified with the sun and with Phoebus: in Collins, the "rich-haired youth of morn"; in Gray, the aged Bard whose "beard and hoary hair / Streamed, like a meteor, to the troubled air"; in the young Blake, Summer with "ruddy limbs and flourishing hair," loved by the Vallies "in his pride," and in the mature Blake, the character Orc subsuming the traditional imagery of phallic fire. Coleridge celebrated the type—"Beware! Beware! / His flashing eyes, his floating hair"—and Wallace Stevens evokes him splendidly in his "figure of capable imagination . . . a rider intent on the sun, / A youth, a lover with phosphorescent hair, / Dressed poorly, arrogant of his streaming forces."[21]

There is, however, a darker alternative to this phallic hero. It is not demonic, for the figure is already demonic; Satan, after all, is his grandfather, the supreme type of the flaming youth who perished in his pride. Ontogenetically, the phallic stage coincides with the oedipal crisis and its normative supersession depends upon the outcome of that crisis: in the case of the Sensibility poet this outcome is very uncertain. No poet can compete with Blake's awareness of this impasse, and Orc's hopeless entanglement in hatred and jealousy dooms the further advance of his mind beyond rebellion. The Sensibility poets never get this far. They remain suspended before the major anxieties of the phallic stage, and the alternative which shadows them tempts them back into the safer, regressive precincts of narcissism, the renunciation of the gloomy egoist devoted to Solitude, Contemplation, or Melancholy. Remembering Collins, Wordsworth wrote that he "Could find no refuge from distress / But in the milder grief of pity."[22] "Grief" mild or sharp, because a genuine relation to objects or the Other—the possibility of love—is merely potential or already foregone.

Wordsworth himself recapitulates the phallic conflicts of Sensibility with astonishing intensity in his early poetry, particularly in *The Borderers*. He turned, however, against the kind of phallic melancholy that is always associated with pride. The youth of "Lines Left Upon a Seat in a Yew Tree . . ." (c. 1797) is clearly intended to represent a typical superior soul of Sensibility. The youth renounced the world and "with the food of pride sustained his soul / In solitude," nourishing a "morbid pleasure" as his fancy fed "On visionary views . . . Till his eye streamed with tears."[23] The oral imagery of the poem tips us off to Wordsworth's real irritation: this phallic melancholy has falsely assumed the guise of true Solitude. Wordsworth's own melancholy was not phallic or prideful, for he was to find his true center in a still earlier stage of the mind. His influence was such that material belonging to the oral phase dominates the psychology of English Romanticism—though phallic anxieties are always latent even in Wordsworth and do predominate in Coleridge and Byron. This may be why Romanticism impresses us as at once more naive and more profound than the melodrama of Sensibility.

In any case, Collins's imagination halted at an impasse marked with precision in the "Ode on the Poetical Character." To put it bluntly, he was stuck in Romance, the literary mode appropriate to phallic ambivalence, but his genius, as Johnson saw, pointed beyond. Ahead was a symbolic, Longinian identification with Shakespeare, Spenser, and Milton which he could not quite perform. Johnson speaks of "a mind not deficient in fire, nor unfurnished with knowledge either of books or of life, but somewhat obstructed in its progress by deviation in quest of mistaken beauties."[24] What was the natural "progress" or trajectory of this mind? Clearly, Collins was on the way to something—the ambition is unmistakable—and just as clearly it was not the Romantic dialectic of mind and nature. In Johnson's view, Romance held him back, but one suspects that the progress envisaged by Johnson leads away from poetry, which seems inconceivable without some measure of Romance.

Addison had recommended that the poet who wished to present fictional personages verse himself in "antiquated Romances, and the Traditions of Nurses and old women," in order to "humour those Notions which we have imbibed in our Infancy." These strange tales "bring up into our Memory the stories we have heard in our Childhood, and favour those secret Terrours and Apprehensions to which the Mind of Man is naturally subject."[25] In a sense Collins's problem was that the power he sought could not be other than a "dark power" which led backward to Romance, because power itself was still instinct with the "secret Terrors and Apprehensions" we have uncovered in the "Ode to Fear." To possess such power or to identify with it is at the same time to be threatened by it. Yet the symbolic father invoked to resolve this shuddering ambivalence remains aloof. Collins shows us that the revival of Romance takes the psychological form, at his late date, of a family romance.

V

The problem of Romance appears as if on cue in the denouement of the "Ode to Fear." Romance begins to assume the ambivalence associated with the primal scene, but in a sublimated form, for some kind of catharsis has taken place. Fear is exhausted, at the end of her flight:

> Thou who such weary lengths hast passed,
> Where wilt thou rest, mad nymph, at last?
> Say, wilt thou shroud in haunted cell,
> Where gloomy Rape and Murder dwell?
> Or in some hollowed seat,
> 'Gainst which the big waves beat,
> Hear drowning seamen's cries in tempests brought!   [46–52]

Fear is again the mad nymph, but she is less visually distinct or access-ible, and her sequestration is not free of the sinister—particularly in the image of the cries of the drowning "brought" to her as if in offering. She is no longer coalesced with the incestuous queen, but she is not yet the Muse who will assume the purified role of the Mother (Fancy) in the poet's family romance. (The "family romance" is Freud's happy term for the stories and myths of origin elaborated under the influence of the oedipus complex and unconsciously designed to compensate its humilia-tions, renunciations, and disillusionments.[26]) As Fear subsides, she seems a little childish, but her exciting power was certainly there—can the power be appropriated without the paralyzing anxiety?

Romance seems to offer an answer:

> Dark power, with shuddering meek submitted thought
> Be mine to read the visions old,
> Which thy awakening bards have told:
> And, lest thou meet my blasted view,
> Hold each strange tale devoutly true;
> Ne'er be I found, by thee o'erawed,
> In that thrice-hallowed eve abroad,
> When ghosts, as cottage-maids believe,
> Their pebbled beds permitted leave,
> And goblins haunt, from fire or fen
> Or mine or flood, the walks of men!   [53–63]

We sense at once the attempted balance in a tone invocatory yet urbane.[27] A distinction is being made: the protagonist will believe "devoutly" in poetic fictions, but his submission to local superstition is hedged. Only cottage-maids believe in ghosts, and if he is declaring (with a wink) his determination to keep out of harm's way, he is also alerting us that he would never be found afraid in such circumstances. Fear, here in transition, is required to preside over both kinds of fictions.

What moves the ambiguity toward ambivalence are the two prolepses. The power ought to come *as a result* of reading the bards who have an awakening effect on the reader, but that "reader" needs the power in order to attempt and endure such a reading. We can see why, given his encounter with Sophocles. "Dark power, with shuddering meek submitted thought"—a curious phrase, oblique yet revealing. It seems to mean not a willing suspension of disbelief, but "thoughts of meek submission," perhaps in echo of Michael's final words to Adam—

> We may no longer stay: go, waken Eve;
> Her also I with gentle dreams have calmed
> Portending good, and all her spirits composed
> To meek submission. . . .   [*PL* 12.594–97]

The "reader's" mind is deeply divided between the powerful and dark appeal the fantasies are making and his conscious renunciation of the desires they excite. An attitude of meek submission holds off his recognition of these desires, but it also prevents his Longinian appropriation of the precursor's power as his own. The power remains dark, instinct with danger; the liberating power of a symbolic identification with the bards is just what is missing. So too with the second prolepsis, "lest thou meet my blasted view": as if this reader had already blinded (in the conventional psychoanalytic translation, castrated) himself before meeting Fear. The overt meaning of the lines is that credulity will protect him against the consequence of anxiety, but a secondary, latent implication of the prolepsis suggests that an attitude of devotion will protect him against the shame of having his self-curtailment exposed.

Whatever the precise meaning of these difficult, evasive lines, they express a consciousness unable to find a vehicular authority to escape the conflicts of phallic ambivalence. One such authority, Aeschylus, did appear earlier in the poem, but his solution—abandoning the "poet's flame" for the "patriot's steel"—leads away from poetry and is thus an inadequate foundation for a poet's family romance. The power desired here, dark or light, anxious or liberating, must be associated with poetry. In the last lines a symbolic father at last appears—or, one wants to say, is trundled in:

> O thou whose spirit most possessed
> The sacred seat of Shakespeare's breast!
> By all that from thy prophet broke,
> In thy divine emotions spoke,

Hither again thy fury deal,
Teach me but once like him to feel:
His cypress wreath my meed decree,
And I, O Fear, will dwell with thee!   [64–71]

Fear becomes a muse, and her relation to Shakespeare is the beginning of
the poet's proper family romance. But this final prayer is wholly ad-
ventitious with respect to the psychology of the poem. "Teach me but
once like him to feel": this admits that Shakespeare's experience of
Fear, whatever it was, cannot have resembled what the protagonist felt
earlier in the poem. Fear is suddenly divine, Shakespeare a sacred
prophet; the sacerdotal emphasis is new. The devotion mentioned
previously implied credulity or invoked the name of Fear and not her
gift of spirit. Between "meek submitted thought" and the "divine
emotions" of the prophet lies the necessity for the poet of a fiction of
origins, a family romance.

VI

Collins's most ambitious poem, the "Ode on the Poetical Character,"
presents notorious difficulties, but they are conceptual rather than psychological. Perhaps the psychological themes—sexuality, the imagined
relation between the parents, the expulsion from a blissful commerce with them—are too much on the surface of the poem to have
attracted commentary. Surely Collins's theory of the creative imagination, which looks now traditional (Neoplatonic) and now revolutionary
(Romantic), is but a small part of his claim for a serious reading. What
will concern us here—no doubt too exclusively, but we are redressing a
balance—is the status of the poetical character with respect to anxiety,
Romance, and the sense of historical possibility. Throughout the poem
the sense of an "I" is muted, and the arena of mental conflict is displaced
to the welcome indirection of mythopoeic statement.

The strophe consists of an expanded simile in which the poet's election
by the muse Fancy is paralleled to a competition at one of Spenser's
tournaments:[28]

As once, if not with light regard
I read aright that gifted bard,
(Him whose school above the rest
His loveliest Elfin Queen has blessed)
One, only one, unrivalled fair
Might hope the magic girdle wear,
At solemn tourney hung on high,

The wish of each love-darting eye;
Lo! to each other nymph in turn applied,
  As if, in air unseen, some hovering hand,
Some chaste and angel-friend to virgin-fame,
  With whispered spell had burst the starting band,
It left unblest her loathed, dishonoured side;
    Happier hopeless fair, if never
    Her baffled hand with vain endeavour
Had touched that fatal zone to her denied!
Young Fancy thus, to me divinest name,
  To whom, prepared and bathed in heaven,
  The cest of amplest power is given,
  To few the godlike gift assigns
  To gird their blest prophetic loins,
And gaze her visions wild, and feel unmixed her flame!   [1–22]

The terms of this loose simile look egregiously disproportionate. "Young
Fancy" has no evident parallel at the tourney, the "angel-friend" seems
to have wandered in from *Comus*, and the disparity between "One,
only one" (which looks forward to Milton's exclusive claim in the antistrophe) and "few" (which suggests a more generously conceived elite)
places two versions of election in competition. Suppose these matters are
conceded to the expansive privilege of epic simile; still we must wonder
about the heart of the comparison: how are the prophetic poets like the
nymphs of this beauty contest? What they evidently have in common is
a kind of sexual test in which only the chaste are blessed with success.
The unchaste are exposed, left "unblest . . . loathed, dishonoured." To
aspire to the "cest of amplest power" is not only to risk failure but to
risk shame.

    In Spenser the girdle has the power to give "the vertue of chast love,"
and "to bind lascivious desire, / And loose affections streightly to re-
strain." But this magic works only with the already chaste, for "who-
soever contrarie doth prove, / Might not the same about her middle
weare, / But it would loose, or else a sunder teare" (4.5. 3–4). The
girdle has the talismanic ambiguity common in allegorical imagery; it is
at once emblem and cause. If Collins's simile is to be taken at face value,
poetic election is a crisis in the course of sexuality where those whose
desire is impure are separated from those few who feel Fancy's flame
"unmixed." The latter are rewarded with "amplest power" and invited
to what seems, oddly enough, a quasi-sexual communion with Fancy.
"And gaze her visions wild, and feel unmixed her flame!" is delicately
ambiguous, and not free of scopophilia—which should not surprise us

in a poem about the origins of the poetic imagination. Two kinds of sexuality are contrasted: the one is secretly unchaste and then leads to shame and impotence; the other is chaste, rewarded with amplest potency, and leads to an elite participation in the desire of the divine muse Fancy.

In broad outline, the burden of Collins's conceit is conventional, and it evokes not only the chastity theme of the earlier Milton but also a range of doctrine on sublimation from the biblical to the Platonic and even to *amour courtois*. The notion that the higher love is also the more intense resolves into the fiction of Innocence, which always has it both ways. Desire is chaste yet fulfilled: sublimation has no cost—or better, since an economic view already presupposes the Fall, sublimation is unnecessary, since desire has not yet encountered opposition in a reality principle or an experience of shame. Collins is unmistakably invoking a prelapsarian state of mind as the essential condition of poetic election. Milton had insisted upon a full and shameless sexuality before the Fall, and no Miltonic legacy was more important to the Romantic poets than his image of Innocence. There is of course no room for such a state in Freud, or perhaps in life, which makes its presence in poetry (especially in Milton, Blake, and Keats) especially relevant for the moralist. Paradise is the ultimate symbol of the family romance, the concentrated place of the may-be and the might-have-been which the romance is committed to elaborate.

The "cest of amplest power" appears to be an emblem of the power of Innocence with magical properties (as in Spenser) to sustain the state it signifies. Whatever its genesis, Collins is inventive to the point of extravagance in working out its symbolic potentialities in the mesode:

The band, as fairy legends say,
Was wove on that creating day
When He, who called with thought to birth
Yon tented sky, this laughing earth,
And dressed with springs and forests tall,
And poured the main engirting all,
Long by the loved Enthusiast wooed,
Himself in some diviner mood,
Retiring, sat with her alone,
And placed her on his sapphire throne,
The whiles, the vaulted shrine around,
Seraphic wires were heard to sound,
Now sublimest triumph swelling,
Now on love and mercy dwelling;

And she, from out the veiling cloud,
Breathed her magic notes aloud:
And thou, thou rich-haired youth of morn,
And all thy subject life was born!
The dangerous Passions kept aloof,
Far from the sainted growing woof;
But near it sat ecstatic Wonder,
Listening the deep applauding thunder;
And Truth, in sunny vest arrayed,
By whose the tarsel's eyes were made;
All the shadowy tribes of Mind
In braided dance their murmurs joined. . . .   [23–48]

Let us ignore for a moment the divine primal scene imagined of God and
Fancy in favor of a simple connection. The magic girdle or band is
woven coincidentally with God's creation, which suggests at least an
analogy between the two events. Spenser's account, "as Faeries wont
report," has the "pretious ornament" wrought by Venus' husband
Vulcan "with unquenched fire" (4.5.4). Collins's girdle is also an *ornament*, a perfect instance of what Angus Fletcher calls the "cosmic image."
Fletcher has studied ancient and derived ideas of *kosmos* (Latin *ornament*) and isolated the features of the cosmic image central to allegory.[29]
Kosmos denotes both order on a universal scale and microcosmic signs
of that order, particularly the dress or costume which certifies one's
position in the general hierarchy. The cosmic image is synechdochical
and, properly read points to the intimate connection or analogy between
the small-scale sign—say the sartorial emblem—and the creation itself,
conceived as God's ornamenting of chaos. This is precisely the connection implied in Collins's mesode, where God's creation is figured
cosmetically, as a dressing of the earth.

Once we are alert to the resonance of *kosmos*, the imagery of the
poem begins to make coherent sense. The pervasive image system concerns clothing. In addition to the girdle (band, cest, zone, woof) and the
wearing (girding) appropriate to it, there is God's activity (dressing,
engirting) and the generation of the "sainted growing woof" itself with
Truth looking on "in sunny vest arrayed" and the "braided dance" of
the Mind's murmurs. Even the curtain that drops over the inspiring
bowers in the Fall of the poem's last lines may be assimilated to the
dominant code. We are not surprised to find in one of Collins's possible
sources the phrase "the wat'ry zone / Ingirting Albion,"[30] since a glance
at the *OED* shows that *band*, *zone*, and *girdle* have common geograph-
ical and cosmological significations.

Where does all this—another context—lead? Clearly, the poet-prophet whose loins are girded with the "godlike gift" is consecrated into a special relation to the prelapsarian natural creation. The Fancy or imagination of the elect poet gives him the natural world as a cosmic garment, a part of what the psychologists call the "body image." The girdle symbolizes this privileged relation whose magic is reflexively dependent upon the poet's inner chastity of mind. He is to the "sainted growing woof" what the sun is to the growing natural world. Collins's writing is here highly condensed and has led to several interpretations:

And she, from out the veiling cloud,
Breathed her magic notes aloud:
And thou, thou rich-haired youth of morn,
And all thy subject life was born!
The dangerous Passions kept aloof,
Far from the sainted growing woof. . . .   [37-42]

The orthodox view that Collins is merely referring to the origin of the sun misses the point of the Romantic commentators who find here an Apollonian poet.[31] The debate hinges on how to read metaphor, not what the lines mean. Of course Collins is referring to the sun, but the interpretation of mythopoeic metaphor is not exhausted by pointing to its naturalistic referent. The youth is at once the sun, Apollo, and the poet—the last surely signaled by his birth at the moment when Fancy, or imagination, finds her voice. Just as the natural world is growing like the "subject life" of the sun, so the magic woof is growing like the body or emanative condition of the poet, and the condensation thus yields the ratios Fancy: sun: nature and Fancy: poet: sainted woof. Psychologically, the ratio suggests mother: son: Innocence—the last magical, a fiction destined for Romance.

The absence of God or the Father from this ratio is only apparent. In the first place, he is pretty clearly the genitor of the rich-haired youth. He loves the Enthusiast Fancy, is wooed by her, retires with her alone, places her on his throne; amidst swelling music Fancy breathes notes aloud and the youth is born. If this doesn't suggest sexual union I don't know what does; somewhat incredibly, it is still being denied,[32] as if a divine primal scene were out of place in cosmogony. (Coleridge says the mesode "inspired & whirled *me* along with greater agitations of enthusiasm than any the most *impassioned* scene in Schiller or Shakespeare,"[33] which suggests that a scene from which the dangerous passions are kept aloof in mythopoeia may nevertheless draw deeply on fantasy material.) Secondly, the sainted woof is associated with God's creative activity, not Fancy's. It is "wove on that creating day" and is later called "This hallowed work"; only later, "prepared and bathed in heaven," is it given to Fancy for her to assign to the poet (18–19). Ultimately the cest's "amplest power" derives from God who endows chastity with power. Thus the two essential meanings of Collins's symbol, chastity and spiritual power,[34] correspond exactly to the two relations of the family romance. The cest is a precise representation of the ambivalent, symbolic identification with the Father which normatively resolves the oedipus complex. The poetical character accedes to the divine power of the Father precisely when and insofar as it is chaste. Normatively, the "positive" identification is both a sign that the desires are being successfully repressed and an aid enabling the youth to give them up: hence the talismanic property of the girdle, which is both symbol and cause.

This is Collins's family romance, his myth of origins and authority for the poetical character. Romance, however, is not reality, and Collins's acknowledgment of this situation at the end of the mesode refers significantly to the historical moment. Of the sacred girdle he asks:

> Where is the bard, whose soul can now
> Its high presuming hopes avow?
> Where he who thinks, with rapture blind,
> This hallowed work for him designed? [51–54]

The bards of Collins's day are unworthy in the specific matter of spiritual chastity, for no other capability or principle of election has been suggested. The "I" cannot inhabit the romance elaborated as its ideal compensatory home, because *he* is corrupted by desire and cannot presume to innocence. This is the first stage of disillusionment with the romance, the recognition that one cannot fulfill the ideal role of the youth: to aspire to prophetic innocence is to risk the shame of having one's inner corruption exposed, like the unlucky nymphs.

VII

A second disillusionment supervenes in the antistrophe and causes the romance itself to turn against the poetical character as if in conspiracy against its aspiration.

> High on some cliff to Heaven up-piled,
> Of rude access, of prospect wild,
> Where, tangled round the jealous steep,
> Strange shades o'erbrow the valleys deep,
> And holy genii guard the rock,
> Its glooms embrown, its springs unlock,

> While on its rich ambitious head,
> An Eden, like his own, lies spread;
> I view that oak, the fancied glades among,
> By which as Milton lay, his evening ear,
> From many a cloud that dropped ethereal dew,
> Nigh sphered in heaven its native strains could hear:
> On which that ancient trump he reached was hung;
>   Thither oft his glory greeting,
>   From Waller's myrtle shades retreating,
> With many a vow from hope's aspiring tongue,
> My trembling feet his guiding steps pursue:
>   In vain—such bliss to one alone
>   Of all the sons of soul was known,
>   And Heaven and Fancy, kindred powers,
>   Have now o'erturned the inspiring bowers,
> Or curtained close such scene from every future view.   [55–76]

Collins's Eden is of course an extended allusion to Milton's Eden as seen for the first time by the envious Satan just after he has despairingly confirmed himself in evil on Mount Niphates. It is a brave conceit, and it establishes at once a latent analogy between satanic desperation and the poetical character which has just been confronted with its incapacity for innocence. Collins (or his "I"), it would appear, is to Milton as Satan is to Adam and Eve—but Milton is no longer there. This Eden is postlapsarian; it admits history and is among other things the representation of a historical situation. Milton is dead, but his oak (associated with the penseroso mode and possibly with the druids) and trumpet (public, prophetic poetry) remain as the goal of this quest, which is "retreating" from Augustan poetry. Milton thus becomes for the history of literary consciousness what a lost paradisiacal innocence is for the individual poetic mind. His "evening ear" caught "its native strains"—distinctively English, home-ground strains—directly from heaven; or perhaps the native strains are heaven's, and we are to be reminded of the "Celestial voices to the midnight air" heard by Adam and Eve (PL 4.680–88). Milton represents a poetic potentiality prior to the alienation of the divine and the natural, but this possibility is just now closing for the aspiring poet.

Collins's Eden is also psychologically postlapsarian, as a quick look at the Miltonic prototype reveals. Satan approaches

>   . . . and to the border comes,
> Of Eden, where delicious Paradise,
> Now nearer, crowns with her enclosure green,

As with a rural mound the champaign head
Of a steep wilderness, whose hairy sides
With thicket overgrown, grotesque and wild,
Access denied.   [PL 4.131–37]

By comparison, the approach to Collins's Eden is somewhat ominously populated. The steep is "jealous"; "Strange shades o'erbrow the valleys deep," as if the approacher were being watched; the rock is guarded by "holy genii." C. S. Lewis, who was not disposed to exaggerate this sort of thing, instructs us not to overlook the "hairy sides" of Milton's description, for "the Freudian idea that the happy garden is an image of the human body would not have frightened Milton in the least,"[35] and of course the anatomical significance of mounts within gardens is purely conventional. But Collins's garden, unlike Milton's, is already possessed; its springs have been "unlocked" by the spirits of place who guard it. This landscape is instinct with a sexual possessor who jealously confronts and obstructs the envious aspirant.

Milton, however, of "all the sons of soul," was allowed by the "kindred powers" Heaven and Fancy to lay blissfully in the garden without undergoing the oedipal conflict. The family romance takes a new turn. Milton is a privileged "son of soul," an elder sibling against whom the parents did not combine. He is not himself to blame for obstructing his successors' access to Innocence. Just as Satan envies Adam and Eve but resents God, so the poetical character finds its conditions are imposed by the parent powers. Collins is presenting a literary self-consciousness subtler than mere resentment of the privileged precursor. Somehow the rules—theological, epistemological, and simply moral—have changed for the modern sons of soul. Innocence is no longer possible for the modern—either because the bowers have been destroyed or because they have been hidden. The overturning of the bowers (like Guyon's pitiless wrecking of the Bower of Bliss) suggests suppression (Freud's *Unterdrücking*) under a harsher moral regime, while the alternative "curtained close" suggests the subtler mechanism of repression (*Verdrängung*).

In one sense, the Fall in the last lines of the ode is simply a recognition of what has already occurred in the unhappy progress of consciousness away from the ampler power of Innocence. In another sense, the primary Fall occurs right in the antistrophe as the bowers sought "With many a vow from hope's aspiring tongue" are suddenly ("now") withdrawn "from every future view." The poetical character is thereby poised at the transitional moment when poetic Innocence becomes inaccessible for all time. Event and recognition are always reciprocal aspects in any version of the Fall. Psychologically considered, the Fall represents the passing of the family romance, a reluctant admission of its impossibility. Not only is the contemporary bard unworthy of the role of the blest, prophetic son of soul—that was the first disillusion-ment—but the role itself has now been rendered inaccessible for any aspirant.

This is where the poem ends and where Collins ends as a poet. It is, I think, a terminus whose significance extends far beyond Collins. He is involuntarily on the verge of a critique of Romance which would, how-ever, be nostalgic and not rebellious. The image of Edenic innocence is a necessary part of the family romance which every ambitious post-Miltonic poet evolves in order to escape (as a poet) his natural condi-tion and validate his intimations of transcendent origin and authority. The protagonist of the romance is the rich-haired youth who, in Cole-ridge's phrase, hath drunk the milk of paradise. Daemonic Romanticism may be said to commence with the corruption of this youth. In Collins, he is still innocent; at his birth "The dangerous Passions kept aloof." This was not to last and is already giving way in the ode as the in-evitable perspective of the poetical character becomes tacitly satanic. We may even descry, though at great remove, the presence of satanic potentiality already in Collins's apostrophe "And thou, thou rich-haired youth of morn, / And all thy subject life was born!" Satan on Mount Niphates had begun his soliliquy of inner torment by likewise address-ing the sun—

O thou that with surpassing glory crowned,
Look'st from thy sole dominion like the God
Of this new world;   [PL 4.32–34]

and earlier he too had seen a rich-haired angel:

                    . . . he soon
Saw within ken a glorious angel stand,
The same whom John saw also in the sun:
His back was turned, but not his brightness hid;
Of beaming sunny rays, a golden tiar
Circled his head, nor less his locks behind
Illustrious on his shoulders fledge with wings
Lay waving round.   [3.621–28]

To approach this angel (Uriel), Satan turns himself into a rich-haired youth:

And now a stripling cherub he appears,
Not of the prime, yet such as in his face

Youth smiled celestial, and to every limb
Suitable grace diffused, so well he feigned;
Under a coronet his flowing hair
In curls on either cheek played . . .   [3.636–41]

—an appearance that recalls Spenser's young angel, "a faire young man, / Of wondrous beautie, and of freshest yeares" whose "snowy font curled with golden heares, / Like *Phoebus* face adornd with sunny rayes, / Divinely shone."[36] Whatever the provenance of Collins's youth, and this context falls short of allusion, his relation to the poetical character is certainly not a spontaneous, ingenuous identification.

Of course, the satanic undertones of the antistrophe remain latent, unacknowledged, and involuntary. Yet even in a naive reading it is an error to interpret the Fall and expulsion at the end of the ode as Collins's personal self-abnegation—that is, to abandon the myth for an illegitimately intentionalistic referent. Collins says that the "scene," if it is still there at all, will be closed from *every* future view. It is this insistence that places the poetical character not merely in a role *manqué* within the Romance but on the verge of moving beyond Romance. In a speculative spirit we might ask of the poetical character, What next? What are the options open at the end of the poem?

There seem to be two lines of possibility. If the poet is to remain committed to Romance—committed to a transcendent self-justification— he is going to have to assume the daemonic identity which alone remains open, now that Miltonic innocence has been foreclosed. Since direct access to Eden is barred—by oedipal anxiety—he will have to jump over the wall. Among other things, this involves a polemic for a daemonic Milton, a Milton who had all unconsciously played the rebellious, phallic role in his own family romance. Hence, too, the migration of the rich-haired youth from innocence to an alliance with the dangerous passions until he becomes—in Orc; in the poet of whom Coleridge warns "Beware, beware," in Prometheus; in Stevens' arrogant lover— the very figure of desire. Apollo, after all, was the god of sublimated, civilized art; the Romantic Apollo is soon closer to Dionysus. But this figure remains phallic in the precise sense that he can never progress beyond the conflicts, affective and ideological, of the oedipal drama. He becomes entangled in a circuit of desire, frustration, rebellion, and suppression. Eventually he may himself turn into his authoritarian oppressor, in which case the severity of his posture signals a reaction formation: such authority is in the end merely the negative phase of unregenerate desire.

The other possibility at the end of the "Ode on the Poetical Character" has a more liberal aspect. Suppose the poetical character could simply abandon Romance, since the powerful innocence it is intended to secure proves inaccessible. Why play out an expulsion from paradise—still less attempt to usurp it daemonically—when it is a mere fiction of what never was? This means, of course, surrendering the consolations of the family romance, and in particular the poet's claim to divine origin. It would mean a poetry of earth, as if everyday reality were all that is and were enough. Such a poet would have to be on guard lest his experience come to seem extraordinary, himself too favored a being or favored in the archaic way. Should he yield to the blandishments of Romance, he would be swept up into unresolvable conflicts; he would have to insist that his own spirit and nothing else deifies him. Everything in him that seems extraordinary must be ascribable to his natural condition. The chosen few, the blest, prophetic elite, would be discriminated merely by their superior consciousness of what is already the natural birthright of all men. The poet would be a man speaking to men, perhaps a godlike man speaking to godlike men, but never a god speaking to mortals. Such a poetry might, at any rate, be worth a try.

VIII

We may well wonder whether a poetry totally free from Romance is possible, even in principle. If everyday reality is good enough, what need of poetry? And what is to prevent the naturalistic rejection of Romance from turning into an evasion of the phallic conflicts the Romance is designed to assuage? In principle at least, a poetic identity which declines transcendence—or subdues it to an undifferentiated immanence—is regressing to a prephallic stage of desire, a version of narcissism. Romance or fantasy with its burden of oedipal conflict will remain latent in such an identity, and its eruption will threaten precisely at the moment when desire becomes too intense and too pointed—becomes, in short, phallic, as in Wordsworth's "Nutting" or the Stolen Boat episode.

It would be fatuous to suppose that the possibilities here speculatively advanced are really in question at the end of Collins's progress. "The Ode on the Poetical Character" does seem to me to be without serious rival as a representation of the poet's difficult situation in the middle of the eighteenth century; Gray's ambitious odes seem superficial by comparison, though I may have a blind spot with Gray. But no one would claim major status for Collins, even in the excess of rescuing him from his antiquating critics. What he can teach us is the relation between Romance and the psychology of the negative sublime. In the bulk of doctrine on the sublime, the "secret Terrours and Apprehensions" of the supernatural are associated with the terrifying appearances of the natural sublime. Ultimately, the path of the negative or transcendent sublime leads through the phase of daemonic Romance, with it oedipal anxieties, to a symbolic identification with the father. But poetry itself may be a deviation from this normative path in quest of mistaken beauties. We might at least suspect that in a transcendence fully achieved there is no need or opportunity for poetry, just as Kant's theory of the sublime ultimately dispenses with an empirical ground. It may be that poetry turns means into an end. In any case, before we explore the final phase of the negative sublime, we must turn aside to consider the radical alternative of immanence, the positive sublime.

6. *For when he came to where a Vortex ceased to operate*
Nor down nor up remaind then if he turnd & lookd back
From whence he came twas upward all. & if he turnd and view
The unpassd void upward was still his mighty wandring
The midst between an Equilibrium gray of air serene
Where he might live in peace & where his life might meet repose

But Urizen said Can I not leave this world of Cumbrous wheels
Circle oer Circle nor on high attain a void
Where self sustaining I may view all things beneath my feet
—Blake, *The Four Zoas*

Absence and Identity in the Egotistical Sublime

What we have termed after Hegel the positive sublime is not a version
of the sublime at all, if we are to speak strictly and with historical
reference. Hegel refers to the negative sublime as the true type of the
sublime and treats the positive version merely as a prelude to it.[1] Keats's
phrase, "the Wordsworthian or egotistical sublime . . . a thing per se
[which] stands alone," clearly will not license the categorical liberties
we have taken by proposing a comparison between the structures of immanent and transcendent sublimation. But the symmetry which rose to
view in the semiotic perspective invites that comparison and proves

valuable once we accept that it is not worthwhile or even possible to assign the poets to one structure or another. In so central a case as Wordsworth, for example, one structure or the other will predominate according to the critic's emphasis or momentary interest.

The positive sublime suggests immanence, circularity, and a somewhat regressive resistance to alienation of all kinds. We look in vain for evidence of a traumatic moment. Indeed, the whole apparatus of the secondary defense system appears to be irrelevant. The reaction formation which constitutes the negativity of transcendence is simply not there. A relative "excess on the plane of the signified" would logically prompt not an anxiety of inundation but a fear of deprivation. If this is so, the anxiety specific to the positive sublime is at bottom an objective one determined in part by the outer world, or at least by a fluctuation felt to be from without. Thus, the anxiety would not be a reaction to a repressed wish, and the appropriate defense could not take the shape of a reaction formation. Instead, we might expect to find the anxiety itself either evaded or expelled (projected).

Perhaps an example will provide introductory ground for this speculation. In an earlier chapter we noticed a prominent sublimation in the second stanza of Wordsworth's "Resolution and Independence." We alluded to its motive in an anxiety whose deferred eruption into consciousness is presented in stanza four:

> But, as it sometimes chanceth, from the might
> Of joy in minds that can no further go,
> As high as we have mounted in delight
> In our dejection do we sink as low;
> To me that morning did it happen so;
> And fears and fancies thick upon me came;
> Dim sadness—and blind thoughts, I knew not, nor could name.

This is not the kind of traumatic anxiety we encounter in the negative sublime, yet it is certainly intense enough. As the poem continues, the mood is particularized as a fear that the future will not be provident. The poet is now a "happy Child of earth," and he fares as a "blissful creature," but "another day" may come—"Solitude, pain of heart, distress, and poverty" (st. 5):

> My whole life I have lived in pleasant thought,
> As if life's business were a summer mood;
> As if all needful things would come unsought
> To genial faith, still rich in genial good;

But how can He expect that others should
Build for him, sow for him, and at his call
Love him, who for himself will take no heed at all?   [st. 6]

It is the most ordinary and most profound of anxieties, the fear that we shall not be provided for, be fed and cared for. When it returns later in the poem it is

> . . . the fear that kills;
> And hope that is unwilling to be fed;
> Cold, pain, and labour, and all fleshly ills;
> And mighty Poets in their misery dead.   [113–16]

The poet, "Perplexed, and longing to be comforted," seems in effect to be asking the leech-gatherer, How do *you* make your living? How have *you* made out?

In short, the anxiety is a fear of deprivation. Wordsworth insight-fully roots this anxiety in the experience of joy. His joy is anaclitic (bound up with need) and is thus an exposure to frustration. The fear of object-loss poisons this joy into a hope unwilling to be fed, because to be fed by a source you know may vanish is to have your joy in feed-ing destroyed. The very extent or "might" of that joy signals the extent of dependence and the magnitude of an anticipated frustration. "As high as we have mounted in delight / In our dejection do we sink as low." Wordsworth's economics are here quite rigorous; delight and dejection are rendered quantitatively in terms that suggest the presence and absence of a fluctuating energy or "might" that pushes the mind until it "can no further go." Many readers have remarked the signs of an ebbed flood throughout the imagery of the poem. No doubt the flood represents the "oceanic" feeling of joy, of total union with the Mother and her original derivative, Nature, so that its receding leaves the "I" stranded.

In fact, Wordsworth's fourth stanza appears to be closely derived from Thomson's *Castle of Indolence*, which we know Wordsworth was reading during the composition of "Resolution and Independence":

But not even pleasure to excess is good:
What most elates then sinks the soul as low:
When spring-tide joy pours in with copious flood,
The higher still the exulting billows flow,
The farther back again they flagging go
And leave us grovelling on the dreary shore.
Taught by this son of joy, we found it so;

> Who, whilst he staid, kept in a gay uproar
> Our maddened Castle all, the abode of sleep no more.[2]

The "copious flood" of "spring-tide joy" can only mount you up so far upon dry land. You have to grow up; the "I" must be unhappily deposited on the shore and shake itself off. The only alternative is wholesale regression, drowning or pure inundation, and it is not even theoretically possible for a grown man. The mounting and sinking of Wordsworth's economics as well as his presentment of anxiety may be referred to the submerged tidal metaphor. The old leech-gatherer, relict of the flood,[3] brings to mind a phrase in *The Prelude*, where Wordsworth speaks of "old men who have survived their joys" (5.212). The leech-gatherer has simply survived the crisis of losing what man loves and needs. Moreover, his firm mind and the fact of his *being* there resist with saving stubbornness the powerful, regressive attempts of this "I" to dissolve him into inanimate substance (st. 9) or into dream (st. 16). He is saving evidence that the mind can go no further within.

In the face of anxiety the stranded ego withdraws its attachment to objects in their irreducible otherness and thereby hopes to reproduce the primal state before otherness became the experience of frustration. This leads us to regression as one major defense against the anxiety of deprivation. The regression intends the state of primary narcissism but necessarily results in the secondary narcissism we so often find in the egotistical sublime.

> By our own spirits are we deified:
> We poets in our youth begin in gladness;
> But thereof come in the end despondency and madness.   [47–49]

In "Resolution and Independence" the secondary narcissism of the poet—itself a response to the insufficiency of the "real"—is under siege and breaking down. To abandon it means despondency but to persist in it leads to madness; so Chatterton, "the sleepless Soul that perished in his pride" (l. 44). Reality will not support the "genial faith" that will "take no heed." The various attempts to sublimate or reconstitute the "I" as an identity within the ego—as Traveller (l. 15), happy Child of earth (l. 31), or Poet (l. 48)—are not working because the regression which underlies them is suspect. On the other hand, an identification with the old man offers no solution, for he is not a figure of power and thus is not a potential occasion for peripety or reaction formation.

There are other defenses apparently at work under the aegis of the egotistical sublime. Wordsworth is certainly a ruminative or oral poet and his major poems all turn on loss particularized in one way or another. Whether or not this anxiety of loss is the deferred action or even the abreaction of an original, traumatic loss, as Richard Onorato proposes,[4] it motivates an astonishing repertoire of defenses. In "Tintern Abbey," for example, the anaclitic relation to objects is never suspended, for all the threat to it. Indeed, regression is quite consciously found to be inadequate or impossible; neither Dorothy nor the scene before the poet slips back into things "like one whom I had met with in a dream" ("Resolution and Independence," l. 110). Instead, the sense of loss is unconsciously deployed in a phenomenal field. We recognize this in the curious way in which the images of landscape do not suffice. It is as if the "I," looking too intently at any one feature of the scene, were to discern an essential loss or immanent absence which is frightening. Thematically, of course, the reverse is the case; we have repeated testimony to a "presence"—which can be felt, however, only so long as the eye is kept moving:

> And I have felt
> A presence that disturbs me with the joy
> Of elevated thoughts; a sense sublime
> Of something far more deeply interfused,
> Whose dwelling is the light of setting suns,
> And the round ocean and the living air,
> And the blue sky, and in the mind of man:
> A motion and a spirit, that impels
> All thinking things, all objects of all thought,
> And rolls through all things.   [93–102][5]

Essence is here "a motion and a spirit," perhaps only the representation or phenomenal guise of the mind's own restless, impelled activity. Objects in themselves are dwellings, locations, things to be inhabited or rolled through, set in motion or brought to life. They have been evacuated in favor of the presence that is in them but not of them, the presence that cannot be signified any more than wind can be seen.

There are many ways to understand the dialectic of immanence. The older scholars used to speak of the "one life" or the "something far more deeply interfused" as displaced theology (pantheism or whatever), but this thematic rendition interprets the content of the metaphor and not the fact of it. Reading Wordsworth for theology is like reading Blake for the plot; one pursues to distraction what isn't really there except as thematic (metaphorical) abstraction. We would prefer a proposition that did not implicate us in another set of metaphors, however authenticated by the history of ideas. Both the phenomenological and the structural approaches to imagery or discourse converge in the view that presence is diacritical: presence and absence are differential aspects of one activity or one locus. On this view, immanent presence might be understood as the absence of a signifier. Or better—as the medium of signification, which as the condition or "space" of the discourse, cannot itself be signified.

Classical psychoanalysis offers only a rough map for the exploration of this idea. At first it looks as if the anxiety of deprivation were simply projected into the phenomenal field or landscape. Though the term is often used loosely of any externalization, and will be so used later in this discussion, *projection* technically means that what the ego feels to be threatening and therefore inadmissible is expelled and lodged safely in the outer world without being changed. It makes no sense to speak of an anxiety of deprivation in nature, and it is not at all clear that the cause of an anxiety state, as opposed to an unacceptable wish, can be projected. This is not an instance of pathetic fallacy, in any case. Thus we are led back to the even more primitive defense of denial. Nature does not betray the heart that loves her; objects are overflowing with a presence that flows into the mind; perception is the acceptance of plenitude.

Yet the line of inquiry suggested by the classical defenses is too reductive and elementary to give us an account of the absence at the heart of Wordsworthian writing. We are thrown where we belong, back on the text itself, here at its most intriguing and most difficult:

> And now, with gleams of half-extinguished thought,
> With many recognitions dim and faint,
> And somewhat of a sad perplexity,
> The picture of the mind revives again:
> While here I stand, not only with the sense
> Of present pleasure, but with pleasing thoughts
> That in this moment there is life and food
> For future years. And so I dare to hope,
> Though changed, no doubt, from what I was when first
> I came among these hills. . . . [58–67]

How roundabout, how utterly yet movingly mediated this writing is. The central event, the reviving of the "picture of the mind" is curiously opaque and inaccessible; presumably the genitive is possessive—picture from the mind—but picture of what? Probably of the first visit to Tintern Abbey, five years before. The subtle redundance "revives again" suggests that the picture is *recurring* without having quite *occurred* except in an origin retrospectively posited by a mind whose every cognition is brought to consciousness as recognition. "I cannot paint / What then I was" (ll. 75–76); yet its picture revives. It is a picture without content—actually, the possibility of picturing and the necessity of it: the formal, empty envelope of signification. Of course, it is filled by a version of the past that comes into being as a differential function of the present in the process Freud called *Nachträglichkeit* ("deferred action"). Hence Wordsworth's unmistakable doubt as to whether he can ascribe certain intervening feelings and impressions ("sensations sweet," "feelings too / Of unremembered pleasure") to the unconscious efficacy of the original impressions.

> Nor less, I trust,
> To them I may have owed another gift,
> Of aspect more sublime; that blessed mood,
> In which the burthen of the mystery,
> In which the heavy and the weary weight
> Of all this unintelligible world,   .
> Is lightened. . . .   [35–41]

The "I" here is reconstituting its past in the urgency of the present; pleasures "unremembered" until now are given an origin; placing the "blessed mood" in such a series is an act of trust, and the whole pattern is a faith. It may, as the poet goes on to fear, "Be but a vain belief" (l. 50).

Yet we have only begun to unravel the web of this text. Around that central event, the reviving picture, are a series of "with" phrases, mental processes separate but concomitant. Like so many negative definitions of the central point, they together inscribe a ring around an absence and are themselves permeated by it. "With gleams of half-extinguished thought": thought of what and why extinguished? "With many recognitions dim and faint": recognitions of what and why dimmed? Sad perplexity and pleasure (distanced, too, as the sense of present pleasure) coexist in an equal alienation from the core event. And just where is the voice of the whole coming from? Not from within the reviving picture, for that too is observed as if from without; at least it seems involuntary and not forceful enough to displace wholly the concomitant mental events the "I" is observing as well. "While here I stand": merely another condition, another way of observing the "I." And yet the voice proceeds; indeed, the enumeration of its conditions enables it to proceed and to break across the threshold of discourse with "And now." Something coalesces or particularizes to permit the liminal "And now"—perhaps the same influence that metaphorically sublimates thought into gleams and recognitions into dimming light. The "thinking thing," or "I," is here impelled from one signifier to another, and this is a saving momentum, a counter movement to the absence which extinguishes thought and dims recognition. Perceptions, abstracted into "beauteous forms," are drafted into a continuity which defeats "a long absence" (ll. 22–23), but the discourse so founded depends upon the abstraction, the continual displacement of the signifier away from the unnameable origin.

I am not sure I know how to read the lines or render them other than impressionistically. They are difficult precisely because they are not retrospective ("I have felt"), and thus the gap between the subjective "I" and the objective "I"—between intentionality and identity—is not manifestly temporal. Elsewhere Wordsworth gives us confident formulations of the vacancy we are trying to isolate:

> A tranquillising spirit presses now
> On my corporeal frame, so wide appears
> The vacancy between me and those days
> Which yet have such self-presense in my mind,
> That, musing on them, often do I seem
> Two consciousnesses, conscious of myself
> And of some other Being.   [P 2.27–33]

The "Two consciousnesses" are here defined by their objects. Both "myself-as-I-am-now" and the "some-other-Being" of the childhood past are objective states of the self, identities that can be recognized and compared. The vacancy stretches between two known points and thus becomes an extensive attribute of the implicit identity that subsumes both states and whose medium is time. This was Wordsworth's great solution. The myth (or plot) of memory is not a problem but an answer. The vacancy, the absolute insufficiency of the *now*, is objectified as the distance between identities which can be signified. A known version or crystallization of the self—an ideal image of the ego—answers and as it were fills up the absence created by pure subjectivity. Identity seems to imply a discourse, and a succession of identities deployed in time constitutes a "perpetual logic" of knowable terms. Without the myth of memory, Wordsworth's self-consciousness can not be formalized and remains outside the discourse. That is why even in the moment of "And now," he is converting the present into the past, into "life and food / For future years."

Identity and Desire

The vacancy of immanence may be displaced into the direction of the future as well as the past. The myth or plot of desire then replaces the

myth of memory. "Something ever more about to be" (*P* 6.608) replaces something that was felt. Wordsworth often seems to be reading
the past as if it were the future and the future as if it were the past, for
memory and desire are linked as derivatives from the vacancy. In *The
Prelude* he advises us that he values "fleeting moods / Of shadowy
exultation" because the soul,

> Remembering how she felt, but what she felt
> Remembering not, retains an obscure sense
> Of possible sublimity, whereto
> With growing faculties she doth aspire,
> With faculties still growing, feeling still
> That whatsoever point they gain, they yet
> Have something to pursue.   [2.316–22]

The energy that insures continuity is directed toward the possibility
(never to be realized) of an adequate signifier, for *what* the soul
originally felt has disappeared into the vacancy. Romantic desire, as
everyone knows, can never be fulfilled. It is as fundamentally narcissistic
as romantic memory, for the object, the "some other Being," of each is
a displaced projection of the present which contains within it the insufficiency of that present.

It is not, however, in Wordsworth but in Keats and particularly in
Shelley that we find the sharpest presentment of desire. The hero-Poet
of *Alastor; or, The Spirit of Solitude* (1816) exhibits one of the clearest
narcissistic careers in the whole Romantic canon, and Shelley's own
patent ambivalence toward this career does not cloud its outline, and
indeed makes for the interest. Shelley refers several times to the "vacant
mind" (l. 126) or "vacant brain" (l. 191) of his protagonist, and the
vacancy so emphasized is correlative to the Poet's insatiable thirst, what
seems to be a constitutional anxiety of deprivation. The Poet is not an
ordinary young man; his feelings are uncorrupted, his genius ad-
venturous, and he has spent his time in familiarity with the majestic—
indeed, in "the contemplation of the universe." But we can hardly im-
prove upon Shelley's own remarkable reduction of his allegory of the
mind: "He [the Poet] drinks deep of the fountains of knowledge, and
is still insatiate. The magnificence and beauty of the external world
sinks profoundly into the frame of his conceptions, and affords to their
modifications a variety not to be exhausted. So long as it is possible for
his desires to point towards objects thus infinite and unmeasured, he is
joyous, and tranquil, and self-possessed." It is a question of desire and
of an answering appearance of infinitude in objects. "But," says Shelley,

"the period arrives when these objects cease to suffice." It is less their finitude than their irreducible otherness, their residual externality, that causes the harmony of within and without to break. There is an ontological dissonance between desire and anything that can be called an "object." And then the moment of sudden turning we have met in so many guises:

His mind is at length suddenly awakened and thirsts for intercourse with an intelligence similar to itself. He images to himself the Being whom he loves. Conversant with speculations of the sublimest and most perfect natures, the vision in which he embodies his own imaginations unites all of wonderful, or wise, or beautiful, which the poet, the philosopher, or the lover could depicture. The intellectual faculties, the imagination, the functions of sense, have their respective requisitions on the sympathy of corresponding powers in other human beings. The Poet is represented as uniting these requisitions, and attaching them to a single image. He seeks in vain for a prototype of his conception. Blasted by disappointment, he descends to an untimely grave.[6]

At just the point where "objects cease to suffice," the insatiate mind responds to its anxiety of deprivation (appropriately rendered as thirst) by projecting and consolidating a "single image" of the Other. This Being is an ideal self, a composite of all the narcissistic identifications (introjections) the Poet has performed in his previous attempts to ward off the anxiety of the insatiate by drinking deep of knowledge. The Being unites erotic fulfillment and the objectification of the self (Adam's dream of Eve is in the background). Hence the Being represents the possibility of an "objective" me, a signifier or identity that could answer the basic question the Poet asks, after surmising the erotic happiness of the Swan:

And what am I that I should linger here,
With voice far sweeter than thy dying notes,
Spirit more vast than thine, frame more attuned
To beauty, wasting these surpassing powers
In the deaf air, to the blind earth, and heaven
That echoes not my thoughts?   [285–90]

The object of the Poet's desire is narcissistic, but the mode of his desire is anaclitic in the ordinary, erotic sense—a rather curious situation. Freud remarks that "narcissistic libido turns toward objects, and thus becomes object-libido; and it can change back into narcissistic libido once more."[7] Normatively this backward change is a secondary one which presupposes an introjection of the object. It is also technically a sublimation since not only the object but also the aim of the wish is changed. The narcissism of *Alastor* is thus both incomplete and inverted. The narcissistic libido has never really turned outward toward a real Other, but it behaves as if it had and couldn't change back. Object and aim are pathologically dissociated from their normative relation. Hence the fruitless search for a "prototype": the narcissistic object cannot be recognized for what it is.

Once, it seems, the Poet is on the verge of that recognition. His search (or flight) falls into two phases, an upward, regressive journey to origins (ll. 222–468), and a downward course, following a river that is meant to image the progress of his life (ll. 492–671). In the middle is a suspended, womb-landscape of the most extreme regression. A rivulet leads us there, by narrowing banks "whose yellow flowers / For ever gaze on their own drooping eyes, / Reflected in the crystal calm" (406–8), and toward one "darkest glen" in which there is a deep, darkly gleaming well.

> Hither the Poet came. His eyes beheld
> Their own wan light through the reflected lines
> Of his thin hair, distinct in the dark depth
> Of that still fountain; as the human heart,
> Gazing in dreams over the gloomy grave,
> Sees its own treacherous likeness there.   [469–74]

Here, if anywhere, is a moment of recognition that intimates release from the Poet's erotic compulsion. But the moment doesn't deepen; the only identity the Poet can envisage is a "treacherous likeness"—an evanescent imitation but also a frightening revelation of the heart's faithlessness. In the normative resolution one would renounce the unacceptable desire of the heart in favor of a new identification. And a new possibility does enter, as if to resolve the Poet's self-perception and rescue him:

> A Spirit seemed
> To stand beside him—clothed in no bright robes
> Of shadowy silver or enshrining light,
> Borrowed from aught the visible world affords
> Of grace, or majesty, or mystery;—
> But, undulating woods, and silent well,

And leaping rivulet, and evening gloom
Now deepening the dark shades, for speech assuming,
Held commune with him, as if he and it
Were all that was,—only . . . when his regard
Was raised by intense pensiveness, . . . two eyes,
Two starry eyes, hung in the gloom of thought,
And seemed with their serene and azure smiles
To beckon him.   [479–92]

But the Poet is too far gone; the eyes (his own) return as the Other, and
the erotic relation is reinstalled. For a moment he had teetered and almost moved into dialogue with that rather Wordsworthian Spirit—a
nonerotic ideal, a kind of superego. Instead, he succumbs again to "the
light / That shone within his soul" (ll. 492–93).

In the drama of "poetic influence" it was not the least of Shelley's
difficulties that the Wordsworthian communion necessarily entered his
psyche as a superego. But the essential point is that the Spirit implicates
the Poet in a dialogue; the landscape becomes "speech." The threshold
the Poet fails to cross is the threshold of discourse in which he could
have been inscribed as a speaking subject, as an "I." But that would have
required renouncing the beckoning smiles of desire. The Poet fears
identity—fears being constituted in the continuity of discourse—because
he cannot bear its cost. Shelley's own fear of identity was extreme, and
he is not by any means in control of this poem or its tone. In the preface
we note the very split between the mode or aim of desire and its objects
that the Poet exhibits:

The Poet's self-centered seclusion was avenged by the furies of an
irresistible passion pursuing him to speedy ruin. But that Power which
strikes the luminaries of the world with sudden darkness and extinction, by awakening them to too exquisite a perception of its influences,
dooms to a slow and poisonous decay those meaner spirits that dare
to abjure its dominion. Their destiny is more abject and inglorious as
their delinquency is more contemptible and pernicious. They who,
deluded by no generous error, instigated by no sacred thirst of doubtful knowledge, duped by no illustrious superstition, loving nothing
on this earth, and cherishing no hopes beyond, yet keep aloof from
sympathies with their kind, rejoicing neither in human joy nor
mourning with human grief; these, and such as they, have their ap-
portioned curse. They languish, because none feel with them their
common nature. They are morally dead. They are neither friends, nor
lovers, nor fathers, nor citizens of the world, nor benefactors of their

country. Among those who attempt to exist without human sympathy, the pure and tender-hearted perish through the intensity and passion of their search after its communities, when the vacancy of their spirit suddenly makes itself felt.[8]

This is astonishing, outrageous prose. I should be the last to deny its rhetorical power or the force of its bitterness, but ethically it makes no sense and it shows a deeply fractured mind defending itself. That "Power" intends death, either way. Yet Shelley refuses to question, examine, or sublimate the "irresistible passion," though he insists that its objects are uniformly treacherous. The split results in the oxymoronic phrases—"deluded by no generous error, instigated by no sacred thirst of doubtful knowledge, duped by no illustrious superstition"—that surely raise a question of bad faith. Attempting to exist without human sympathy: this means trying to exist *given that* there is no human sympathy, but it also suggests deceptively that the "pure and tender hearted" have made the attempt to accept this condition in good faith. The Poet makes no such attempt. Though it leads to disaster, his desire remains generous, sacred, and illustrious. Shelley's equivocation—the Poet is "led / By love, or dream, or god, or mightier Death" (ll. 427–28) —exhibits a narcissism compounded by denial. I need hardly add that the poem was the beginning and not the end of Shelley's maturity and that its schizoid structure is sublimated into a genuine irony in the later poems. Yet the fear of identity persists throughout the Shelleyan oeuvre, and undoubtedly it is to be referred as much to his struggle with Words-worth as to his own fascinating psychological constitution.

Identity is an inverse function of desire, a secondary precipitate which coalesces as narcissistic desire fails or is betrayed. If you love what is essentially an ideal version or projection of yourself, your love nourishes a growing "selfhood" which is incapable of desire and is (in Keats's phrase) "a thing per se and stands alone." Such desire is eros in the service of the conservative death wish. It is in Keats that the transformation of desire into identity is perceived most clearly, because Keats was to superimpose upon this transmutation an attack on identity that is programmatic, whereas Shelley is defensive. In a sense, Keats attempts to rescue desire—the possibility of a genuine Other—from its nar-cissistic fate. But not at first. Keats is closest to Shelley in *Endymion*, though this poem is altogether less defensive and less serious than Shelley's *Alastor*. Endymion himself we discover to be a rather confused young fellow, given to sophistries of one kind or another, but it can be plausibly argued that his conceptual failures are exorcised in the end. In any case, Keats clearly grasped and learned from the experimental failures of his hero. An instructive text is the dream-flight of book 1, as

Endymion reports to his sister his first contact with the unidentified flying object who later turns out to be Phoebe:

> She took an airy range,
> And then, towards me, like a very maid,
> Came blushing, waning, willing, and afraid,
> And pressed me by the hand. Ah, 'twas too much!
> Methought I fainted at the charmèd touch,
> Yet held my recollection, even as one
> Who dives three fathoms where the waters run
> Gurgling in beds of coral; for anon,
> I felt upmounted in that region
> Where falling stars dart their artillery forth,
> And eagles struggle with the buffeting north
> That balances the heavy meteor-stone—
> Felt too, I was not fearful, nor alone,
> But lapped and lulled along the dangerous sky.
> Soon, as it seemed, we left our journeying high,
> And straightway into frightful eddies swooped,
> Such as ay muster where grey time has scooped
> Huge dens and caverns in a mountain's side.
> There hollow sounds aroused me, and I sighed
> To faint once more by looking on my bliss—
> I was distracted. Madly did I kiss
> The wooing arms which held me, and did give
> My eyes at once to death—but 'twas to live,
> To take in draughts of life from the gold fount
> Of kind and passionate looks, to count and count
> The moments, by some greedy help that seemed
> A second self, that each might be redeemed
> And plundered of its load of blessedness.
> Ah, desperate mortal! I e'en dared to press
> Her very cheek against my crownèd lip,
> And, at that moment, felt my body dip
> Into a warmer air—a moment more,
> Our feet were soft in flowers.   [1.633–65]

A rather paradoxical embrace. Desire intends the annihilation of subjectivity (the eyes are given to death), but the result frustrates the desire. Another "second self" is born as the greedy opposite to the primary desire, and this secondary self is implicated in duration. It seeks to "redeem" the successive moments by abstracting the "load of blessedness" each contains, but this effort to confer value, to make the moments signify, is a "plundering" which destroys the *now* of desire. Desire brings identity to birth; a threshold of discourse (a syntagmatic chain of counting) is crossed; we see that the failure of desire and the aggrandizement of identity are really two sides of the same event.

The inverse reciprocity of desire and identity is rendered in a consistent imagery. Indentity is associated with the necessary, compensatory equilibrium of the body. Endymion's "recollection" is held "even as one / Who dives three fathoms" holds his breath. The total escape from duration which desire intends is, in Keats's simile, to die by drowning: the body involuntarily resists and wants to breathe. From this point of view, desire is only an episode during which identity is held in suspension. Similarly, the gravitational pull on Endymion signals the underlying strength of identity, and Keats's imagery "in that region" of desire (falling stars, struggling eagles, heavy meteor-stone) points to the inevitability of coming down as a second self. Indeed, the identity seems to be orally fixated, as it were; it is greedy, takes in "draughts of life," and evidently is unable to hold its breath too long. The organs of desire, on the other hand, are the eyes, and they are somewhat disembodied and given over to death.

Ultimately the locus of identity is the body—or, more correctly, the imaginary derivative of the body, the "body image." The French psychoanalyst Jacques Lacan has reformulated the traditional problem of subjectivity in terms of what he calls the "mirror stage."[9] The self is originally constituted as an Other in the moment of identifying with an image which appears to exist "outside," typically its own reflection, but always a unified Gestalt. Lacan's idea reaches far, and it could guide us toward a distinction between the *imaginary* identity of the positive sublime and the *symbolic* identity of the negative sublime. For the moment, however, the important point is that what we have been calling the identity, or the "objective me," is from the start experienced as if it were an Other, and therefore as a part of an external pattern, a term in a discourse not initiated by the "I." Whether or not temporality is a necessary attribute of that discourse is something I frankly cannot decide, since as a critic I am only an amateurish and somewhat lukewarm structuralist. It certainly seems as if all perception of the Other, imaginary (fantasized) or symbolic, involves both the bodily Gestalt and a correlative assumption of duration or historicity. The fact that I can be in only one place at one time is a function of bodily limits, and this situation, which constitutes my historicity, is the condition of identity.

Every intellectual knows how much trouble Descartes made for modernity by denying the role of the body and of duration in sub-jectivity. In Descartes the alienation between consciousness and identity is so extreme that it can be bridged only by a sleight of hand, an illegi-timate substitution in the shifter "I." I think, therefore "I" am, reasoned Descartes (silently shifting the referent of his "I"), but strictly speaking, for all we can know, I am *only* when I am thinking. To consider tem-porality at all makes this philosopher a bit nervous, but he meets the consequence cheerfully: "I am, I exist, that is certain. But how often? Just when I think; for it might possibly be the case if I ceased entirely to think, that I should likewise cease altogether to exist."[10] Thinking appears to yield no possibility of an "objective me," and all other mental processes are heuristically in doubt. Imagining, in particular, offers no road to identity since it is "to contemplate the figure or image of a cor-poreal thing," and corporeality has been suspended: "I knew that I was a substance the whole essence or nature of which is to think, and that for its existence there is no need of any place, nor does it depend on any material thing; so that this 'me,' that is to say, the soul by which I am what I am, is entirely distinct from body, and is even more easy to know than is the latter; and even if body were not, the soul would not cease to be what it is."[11] Here is the Cartesian trick: the "I" is first treated as a quasi-objectified essence, and then the resultant "me" is simply identified with the "soul"—a term inextricably woven into tradi-tional discourse. The thinking thing becomes "a mind or a soul, or an understanding, or a reason" and so its objectivity is secured as it is assimilated by traditional categories and their associated propositions. Descartes has slipped across the threshold from the subjective "I" to the objective "soul" by going through the portal "me." The "me" is really the identity by which I am what I am—that is, what I just was: it con-tains an objectification which, Lacan asserts, is an image.

And so the vacancy turns up in yet another relation, perhaps the fundamental one from which the others derive. It is the distance—in another metaphor, the threshold—between the intentional, subjective "I," which is confined to the *now* and is the ultimate locus of the signified, and the objective "me," or identity, which is imaginatively predicated across the moments. Identity is the terminal point of the vacancy, the signifier that fills the vacant space in the discourse—whether that space assumes the form of a "long absence" between past and present or of the "lack of being" installed in desire. All roads in the positive sublime lead to identity. And yet they are all indirect roads. Perhaps a simple schema of these relations would not do unacceptable violence to their unique articulations in the poets:

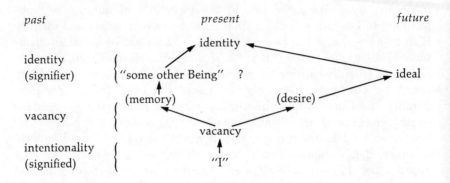

The Limits of Identity

From the present point of view it is a secondary but not uninteresting matter whether identity is welcomed or resisted. Wordsworth's sublimation was so massive and thorough that he was able to embrace identity as a redemptive program. *The Prelude* consists of numerous evocations of the "some other Being" of the past, but these projected memories are collectively the second or reactive term in a dialectic designed to span the vacancy institutionalized in the medium of time. Even in the earliest manuscript, the notebook Wordsworth used at Goslar in the winter of 1798–99, there is clear indication that the "spots of time" were constituted in the urgency of a crisis. The germinal lines begin,

> Was it for this
> That one, the fairest of all rivers loved
> To blend his murmurs with my nurses song . . .[12]

and return again and again with small variation to the formula "Was it for this. . . ?" Each remembered event or scene uncoils from that rhetorical question, with its implied first term.

We know from the first 270 lines of the finished poem what Wordsworth meant by "this." It was a state of "vain perplexity" in which he was "Baffled and plagued by a mind that every hour / Turns recreant to her task" (1.266, 257–58). Having consecrated himself as a major poet, Wordsworth could find no theme, and the result was a paralysis moving in its ingenuous universality. On the one hand, there were plenty of objective themes—he enumerates nine or so—each with the "Time, place, and manners" that he sought, "but nowhere such / As may be singled out with steady choice" (158–60). He would merely be repeating a discourse already founded in which there was no place for his unique

"I." On the other hand, a direct effort of self-representation fell short of objective form:

> Sometimes it suits me better to invent
> A tale from my own heart, more near akin
> To my own passions and habitual thoughts,
> Some variegated story, in the main
> Lofty, but the unsubstantial structure melts
> Before the very sun that brightens it,
> Mist into air dissolving!   [1.221–27]

Hence his present crisis, knowing how he felt but unable to signify what he felt:

> The Poet, gentle creature as he is,
> Hath, like the Lover, his unruly times;
> His fits when he is neither sick nor well,
> Though no distress be near him but his own
> Unmanageable thoughts: his mind, best pleased
> While she as duteous as the mother dove
> Sits brooding, lives not always to that end,
> But like the innocent bird, hath goadings on
> That drive her as in trouble through the groves;
> With me is now such passion, to be blamed
> No otherwise than as it lasts too long.   [1.135–45]

This is the state that the myth of memory resolves. The unmanageable distance between Wordsworth and his theme becomes the manageable distance between present and past. The actual present, the very locus of the vacancy, may be suppressed because it is so clearly out of line with the fictional trajectory that may be extrapolated from the past. Identity is the project that coincides with the new line, the new career at once discovered and invented. "Was it for this?" receives an unexpectedly therapeutic answer: "No, not for this . . . but yes, it was for This!" The identity settled upon is an ideal ego—not, as it might seem at first, a superego, though that will break through in the Simplon Pass passage of book 6, as Wordsworth momentarily crosses into the domain of the negative sublime. The distinction is not easy to make in classical terms, but it is evidently a crucial point of differentiation if our dichotomic structure is to be justified.

For all its celebration in *The Prelude*, the project of identity remains equivocal. Identity is the terminus of one vacancy but, as it turns out, the opening of another. The vacancy between the subjective "I" in its immediacy and the objective, imagined "me" (or self) in its duration vanishes only to reappear as the gap between the imagined self and the Other, which seems thus always to be in retreat. The discourse of the self is not yet the discourse of the Other; another kind of alienation is superimposed upon the first. Here the mere critic is confronted with an intimidating variety of terms—Hegelian, phenomenological, structuralist, sociological—for schematizing what is after all a commonplace. The Poet in possession of identity still has not got a theme other than the story of how he developed his unique image of himself. The image is objective but implicit; it cannot be grasped in the present because its medium is duration, and the attempt so to grasp it directly (as opposed to following the indirect paths of memory or desire) revives the vacancy as a sense of loss. If the myth of memory propounds "I am all that I was and because I have been in that way, I now am in this way," the counter-myth of loss balances this "self-presence" in the mind with an absence: "It is not now as it has been of yore . . . the things which I have seen I now can see no more."[13] By attempting to ground identity in the present, the myth of loss reveals identity to be not the cumulative reservoir of the past but at best "abundant recompense": "That time is past" now means "that time is gone." The myth of memory and the myth of loss are mutually implied in the dialectic of presence and absence.

Identity is similarly equivocal with respect to the plot of desire, and indeed desire and memory are so intimately related that the one may be virtually transposed into the other. Wordsworth and Freud converge in this habitual transposition whereby the "obscure sense / Of possible sublimity" whereto the soul unceasingly aspires is a function of memory, and what is remembered is projected from the mind's current need. The primitive vacancy, which inhabits memory as loss, takes in desire the form of frustration. Shelley's resistance to sublimation was such that he could not have welcomed identity as a saving project, but identity was not less inevitable for all that. But what is identity under the aspect of desire? It is an image of the self, a fictional "me" which exhibits alternately two states corresponding to the myth of continuity and the myth of loss. The first is a coincidence of the "me" and the ideal, a kind of epiphany of narcissism in which the ideal is already felt as a "self-presence" in the mind. But the absence-phase of desire underlies this fiction and can only be suspended momentarily by it. Identity contains an acknowledgment not this time of loss, but of frustration.

The result, in Shelley at least, is a peculiar irony, an "abundant recompense" to be sure, but with an ambivalence equal to that of Wordsworthian loss.

> I love all waste
> And solitary places; where we taste
> The pleasure of believing what we see
> Is boundless, as we wish our souls to be. . . .
>
> [*Julian and Maddalo*, ll. 14–17]

Here is as sophisticated a sublimation of the original, "oceanic" wish as we find among Romantic voices. The "I" can "love" not merely in spite of the illusion but because of it. No doubt its "pleasure" may be referred ultimately to the gratification of the wish, but that gratification is extremely displaced, and the "pleasure" derives as well from the ego's own mastery of wish and reality in the fictionality of belief. The lines from *Julian and Maddalo* evoke the salient quality of Shelley's middle style, which is not so far from decadence as either we or Shelley might have wished. Shelley was not at peace with the identity, the voice or protagonist of this style, and one sees why. *The Witch of Atlas* is a brilliant but rather chilly poem, and its myth exhibits on several levels a critique of fictionality that is not free from self-disgust. Both the Witch and the ghastly, sexless robot she creates are images of what lies beyond desire: only an absolute narcissism is invulnerable to the "lack of being" desire entails. In them the egotistical sublime reaches one kind of deathless end.

Yet the alternative, for Shelley, was risky. To merge the "me" of identity and the ideal of desire is precisely to suspend the irony of absence, and this exposes the text to subversion from without. The fictionality of desire fulfilled is precisely what is suppressed. Self-consciousness in love leads to disaster because it reveals the narcissistic springs of desire, and so we have seen that the self-consciousness of the middle style is predicated upon the end of desire, the acceptance of its vacancy. But the fulfillment of desire in an identity of two is as imaginary a state as the state of identity which wholly contains the past. When this fact is deliberately ignored, as it often is in Shelley's high style, we have a dangerous extravagance, a climbing too far, and a fall over the cliff. It is like a Wordsworthian "spot of time" pretending never to end and never falling gratefully back into a distant past. A good example is the end of *Epipsychidion*:

> We shall become the same, we shall be one
> Spirit within two frames, oh! wherefore two?
> One passion in twin-hearts, which grows and grew,
> Till like two meteors of expanding flame,
> Those spheres instinct with it become the same,
> Touch, mingle, are transfigured; ever still

Burning, yet ever inconsumable:
In one another's substance finding food,
Like flames too pure and light and unimbued
To nourish their bright lives with baser prey,
Which point to Heaven and cannot pass away:
One hope within two wills, one will beneath
Two overshadowing minds, one life, one death,
One Heaven, one Hell, one immortality,
And one annihilation. Woe is me!
The winged words on which my soul would pierce
Into the height of Love's rare Universe,
Are chains of lead around its flight of fire—
I pant, I sink, I tremble, I expire!   [573–91]

The energy of this union results almost entirely from what is being
denied or suppressed. One who seeks the thing he loves will always be
like a man flying from something that he dreads. In such a case fulfillment means the "annihilation" of the illusion on which it is predicated.

It is often averred that Wordsworth's greatness was to marry sublimity and self-consciousness—the portentous manner and tone of the
high style and the traditional substance of the middle style. In brief, he
was able to do this because in his writing, identity is always on the verge
of passing over into the status of the negative sublime, which we have
located in a very different structure. Wordsworth's narcissism is not
reductive: precisely at the point of its greatest intensity it is open to the
transcendent intimations, the power "beyond" but then "within" as he
introjects it in an act of identification. How would the course of English
Romanticism—and particularly the development of Keats and Shelley—
have differed if *The Prelude* had been published in 1805? The egotistical
sublime—the identity of the poet standing on its own—is a plausible
reading of the Wordsworth available to those two poets and an affront
to the program of desire in each. Shelley could be somewhat condescending about the Wordsworthian myth of memory and loss—
"These common woes I feel"[14]—but he was understandably nervous
about his own middle style, and in the introduction ("To Mary") to *The
Witch of Atlas* that defensiveness is associated with Wordsworth. Why
could not he too attain a marriage of the high and the middle, a knowledge not trivialized by the attenuation of desire, a passion not sub-
verted by irony?

If this were a legitimate question, and it no doubt presupposes too
much, the answer would surely lie in Shelley's tenacity of desire. The
only way identity can avoid the fate of the middle style is through

belief strong enough to ignore its fictionality. Here the myth of memory and the myth of desire are genuinely different, for memory offers a superior disguise for its fictions. The egotistical sublime which takes the path of desire is going to run directly into the problem of fictionality, a situation as manifest in Stevens as it is in Shelley. Like Stevens, Shelley does not ultimately surrender desire, and he is forced into an ironic doctrine of fiction in order to sustain it:

> . . . to hope till Hope creates
> From its own wreck the thing it contemplates;
> Neither to change, nor falter, nor repent . . .
>
> [*Prometheus Unbound* 4.573–75]

—in short, never to sublimate. It is possible, possible, possible. It must be possible. Perhaps Prometheus' own repentance—his only act in the drama—is extorted from a poet whose deepest defense remains denial.

Our discussion has become so tendentious that the Shelleyan will be quite properly outraged to see his poet traduced yet again by a set of loaded terms and an implicit moralism. Shelley's extremities drive the reader into taking a stand, rather an unattractive posture since it exposes one's own erotic and imaginative limits—dignified as a sense of reality—so mercilessly. And certainly in *The Triumph of Life* we find a pathos of desire (frustration) as dignified and profound in its acceptance as the Wordsworthian pathos of loss. Hence our structure may be freed from Shelley—and Shelley from it—to be put once more in general terms. "Of course," it must be objected, "if all desire is defined as narcissistic, its object, or Other, is a surrogate and necessarily implies frustration. Freud's direct challenge to Romantic love can hardly be answered if one concedes the Freudian premise." And from another quarter, essentially the same charge: "You have yourself equivocated on the crucial point of whether the discourse of identity is a genuine discourse of the Other." In short, what *is* the discourse of identity, and need it be formulated in terms of narcissism?

Absence and Imagination

Our line of thought has yielded the result that the discourse of identity is, on the one hand, a discourse of origins and, on the other, a discourse of fictions. In both phases the structure of identity is circular and the transcendence it accomplishes is spiral. Because memory has no origin and desire no finality, identity can never be completely accomplished. It remains fictional, or hypothetical, the integral, as it were, of the two trajectories reaching before and after, each of which may be infinitely differentiated. Wordsworth, speaking to Coleridge as one to whom "the unity of all hath been revealed," insists that the mental ·fact, sensation, or thought cannot be rendered as "a single independent thing."

> Hard task, vain hope, to analyse the mind,
> If each most obvious and particular thought,
> Not in a mystical and idle sense,
> But in the words of Reason deeply weighed,
> Hath no beginning.   [*P* 2.228–32]

In the myth of memory, all cognition is recognition; experience, one continuing *Nachträglichkeit*. And the myth of desire also has its infinity, for the Identity which confronts the angel invented him and can thereby project the identity which contains him.

The identity in which the egotistical sublime culminates is an infinitely repeatable "I am." No "thou" or "it" can enter its attractive orbit without being transubstantiated into the "I." The identity so conceived is the inevitable precipitate of the Coleridgean "secondary Imagination," and in fact Coleridge's famous formulation can be transposed without much reduction into the circular dialectic of narcissism.

> The IMAGINATION then, I consider either as primary, or secondary. The primary IMAGINATION I hold to be the living Power and prime Agent of all human Perception, and as a repetition in the finite mind of the eternal act of creation in the infinite I AM. The secondary Imagination I consider as an echo of the former, coexisting with the conscious will, yet still as identical with the primary in the *kind* of its agency, and differing only in *degree*, and in the *mode* of its operation. It dissolves, diffuses, dissipates, in order to recreate; or where this process is rendered impossible, yet still at all events it struggles to idealize and to unify. It is essentially *vital*, even as all objects (*as* objects) are essentially fixed and dead.[15]

The recreative phase of Imagination follows upon a decreative phase, and if objects in their deadness—their unmalleable reality—stubbornly resist the latter process, it is replaced by the weaker but perhaps subtler strategy of idealization. The energy or libido is all from the mind, and the apparent vitality of the Other is transferred or projected. The relation to objects, whether as constitutive perception or as love (if these can be distinguished), is an eddying outward and back again, as in Coleridge's own "Dejection: An Ode." Can this circular rhythm be broken—even theoretically? What compels the Imagination to recreation? Clearly, the primary act of creation does not suffice. Between the primary act and its secondary echo there has been a falling away of objects into their deadness. The secondary Imagination attempts a regression, a recapitulation of the hypothetically original or primary, and thus the intermediate state of reality (objects *as* objects) must be dissolved, diffused, or dissipated.

Yet the successful act of Imagination generates its own supersession, for there is nothing—no order of the Other—to keep its own recreation from falling back into the deadness of reality. In Coleridge's view, the project of Imagination is redemptive, but psychologically the resurrection of reality is an incidental result, a mediation of the underlying aim. An accurate assessment of this situation is essential to any judgment on Romantic love and the moral status of the Romantic Imagination. Freud puts the question fundamentally in a passage of his essay "On Narcissism":

> At this point we may even venture to touch on the question: whence does that necessity arise that urges our mental life to pass on beyond the limits of narcissism and to attach the libido to objects? The answer which would follow from our line of thought would once more be that we are so impelled when the cathexis of the ego with libido exceeds a certain degree. A strong egoism is a protection against disease, but in the last resort we must begin to love in order that we may not fall ill, and must fall ill if, in consequence of frustration, we cannot love. Somewhat after this fashion does Heine conceive of the psychogenesis of the Creation:
>
> Krankheit ist wohl der letzte Grund
> Des ganzen Schöpferdrangs gewesen;
> Erschaffend konnte ich genesen,
> Erschaffend würde ich gesund.[16]

"So that is what it is," writes J. H. Van den Berg. "Objects are of importance only in an extreme urgency. Human beings, too."[17] Van den Berg's critique of Freud has been extended into a critique of Romanticism by Harold Bloom, in whose view "Wordsworth . . . no more overcame a fundamental dualism than Freud did. . . . Wordsworth made his kind of poetry out of an extreme urgency, and out of an overfilled inner self, a Blakean Prolific that nearly choked in an excess of its own delights. This is the Egotistical Sublime of which Keats complained. . . ."[18]

Yet the "necessity" of Freud's text, privileged in this critique of Romanticism, is not an original necessity. Freud is asking secondary narcissism the question that really deserves to be put to primary narcissism. On Freud's own showing, an original narcissism cannot be painful; only its loss could precipitate the disequilibrium and the tension felt as pain. The damming up of libido in the ego is already "in consequence of frustration," and the excess of narcissistic libido is entirely a relative quantity. The anxiety of solipsism—what Van den Berg calls "the groaning of an overfilled inner self"[19]—is a secondary, derivative anxiety, for solipsism is itself a defense against the original anxiety of deprivation. Unlike primary narcissism, the secondary version dialectically presupposes the reality against which alone it can be defined and measured as exceeding "a certain degree." We don't develop a strong egoism in the first place except in consequence of frustration.

In *The Problem of Anxiety* (1926) Freud refined his theory on the etiology of original anxiety. He explains that the infant psyche, basking in its primary solipsism, inevitably comes to experience a threatening "increase of tension arising from non-gratification of its needs." This danger is already dialectical, a relation between needs and nongratification or "object loss." When the infant learns that "an external and perceptible object" (the mother) can gratify his needs, the signifying content of the danger is displaced to her withdrawal or absence. Thus, the phenomenology of original anxiety must center on absence ("call it solitude / Or blank desertion"), and the desertion or "object loss" is logically and temporally prior to the overfilled inner self.[20]

We can see that secondary narcissism contains an original, decisive absence in its image of identity, which is, after all, a kind of surrogate mother. It is not in fact an excess of delight that urges the ego to overflow toward objects, but an insufficiency in that delight, a qualitative absence, a lack of being. We seem to meet this absence everywhere; it shows a kind of protean persistence. It may be defined once more, in Coleridgean terms, as the distance between the two creations, primary and secondary, which structures the second as the "echo" of the first. An echo can never coincide with its original, but neither can it ever escape that original. Coleridge's terminology of primary and secondary, which probably descends from Locke, has been thought confusing, but it renders exactly both the regressive necessity of the poetic Imagination and its discomfitting alienation from what Wordsworth called "the first / Poetic spirit of our human life" (*P* 2.260–61).

The central absence emerges once more when we consider the enigma of Imagination prospectively as well as in terms of primary and secondary. Freud's text on the overfilled ego requires the complementary statement his essay on narcissism as a whole provides. One could as easily say, and Freud does, that we must fall ill if we surrender a strong egoism and if our attachment to objects exceeds a certain degree. "The development of the ego consists in a departure from the primary narcissism and results in a vigorous attempt to recover it."[21] So that is also what it is. Objects are of importance in that they may be "transcended"

—i.e., decreated in order to be brought back again to the only source of life. In intention and in motivation, creative urgency (*Schöpferdrangs*) or Imagination implies a dissociation of aim and object—their interests, as it were, are opposed, and thus the pathology of *Alastor* is truer to the egotistical sublime than we were inclined to admit.

It would appear that the Imagination's cure is at once paradoxical and indirect. Hence the importance, in Coleridge's thought, of its coexistence with the conscious will. Were the Imagination not under the control of the ego, its therapeutic activity could only result in an intensification of the illness: Wordsworth's texts show again and again that an involuntary act of Imagination does conduce to a strengthened solipsism. But the apparent paradox melts when we relate the imaginative act to its deeper provenance in the original anxiety of deprivation. The Imagination is ultimately opposed to the claims of reality, and its compensatory cure of the mind is deeper than the secondary, ambiguous rescue of things. It is certainly morally useful to regard the Imagination's project with respect to reality as a redemptive one but the coexistence of this project with the conscious will—indeed, its "irremissive, though gentle and unnoticed, control" by the will and understanding[22]—should alert us to a pleasing deception. I would be the last to scant the pain of solipsism, but a more austere, and for me more compelling, moralism cannot ignore the compensatory, defensive elements in the overfilled inner self. Perhaps objects (*as* objects) only begin to be redeemed into an essential vitality when we see that they do not need that redemption, as we do.

In touching on Coleridge we are obviously skimming the surface of a deep subject close to the hearts of all Romanticists. Our current path lies this side of the theory of Imagination, and its goal is simply a clear outline of the "absence" in the work of the Imagination. The original absence installed in the secondary identity insures that it too will remain a surrogate—for the object, itself a surrogate. The circular paradox of this kind of transcendence is nicely caught by Keats in the lines from *Endymion* where a homeward journey (memory) is equated with the hopeless pursuit of the *ignis fatuus* (desire):

There, when new wonders ceased to float before
And thoughts of self came on, how crude and sore
The journey homeward to habitual self!
A mad pursuing of the fog-born elf,
Whose flitting lantern, through rude nettle-briar,
Cheats us into a swamp, into a fire,
Into the bosom of a hated thing.   [*Endymion* 2.274–80]

Identity is a principle of continuity, the introjected image of the primal Other, or Mother. The egotistical sublime culminates in an intense ambivalence. Memory and desire practice a cheat: they lead us to a bosom all right, but the cost of the regression and the solitude or desertion implicit in its object have made that object a hated thing. In terms of what Freud called the family romance, identity is regarded with all the unresolved ambivalence of an oedipal crisis in which there is, strangely, no symbolic father to come to the rescue. Yet we cannot fail to note that the structure of the egotistical sublime ends precisely at the point of ambivalence in which we found the beginnings of the negative sublime.

Beyond Identity?

It is often recognized that the Romantic writers confronted as difficulties what we discover as a critique, and we are thereby anticipated—surely for the better, since this means the Freudian critique need not be privileged. Blake and Keats, and perhaps the late Shelley, saw clearly the limits of identity, but their seeing was not disinterested and needs to be read in the light of a distinction between doctrine and form, or between aspiration and realization. We have arrived at the proposition that it is impossible at once to adhere to the hypothesis of primary narcissism and to celebrate Romantic Imagination as a genuine discourse of the Other: unless, of course, there is an imagination—a form of love—which begins beyond identity. The apparent banality of this conclusion masks an important literary corollary. The imagination beyond identity could not be exercised in a discourse of the "I"—a form in which there is virtually no difference of consciousness among the "I" of the poem, the poet, and the reader. It would seem that only an ironic or dramatic form can take us beyond identity, unless we are willing to confuse systematically the *theme* of the Other, even the immense aspiration to it, with its realization. The "I" must become a character viewed ironically, or in relation; the meaning of the poem a tacit construction not available to the protagonist.

The difficulty is that no one will protest more violently the necessity of the Other than the poet whose determined form, lyric or meditative, will not accommodate it. The point is particularly tricky with Shelley but arises with any idealist. In "Dejection: An Ode," Coleridge protests his friend Wordsworth's obstinate but moving resistance to the notion of what we call projection:

O Lady! we receive but what we give,
And in our life alone does Nature live:

Ours is her wedding garment, ours her shroud!
  And would we aught behold, of higher worth,
Than that inanimate cold world allowed
To the poor loveless ever-anxious crowd,
  Ah! from the soul itself must issue forth
A light, a glory, a fair luminous cloud
    Enveloping the Earth—
And from the soul itself must there be sent
  A sweet and potent voice, of its own birth,
Of all sweet sounds the life and element!   [st. 4]

This claim directly challenges and overturns the Wordsworthian mutuality of mind and nature. Whatever Coleridge's motive, the lines and the poem oppose Wordsworth's doctrine: but is it a poor reading of Wordsworth's practice? It is close to Wordsworth's own reading of himself at times, as in the master-slave dialectic of the "spots of time" (P 12.208–23). We can take the Wordsworthian "high argument"—the doctrine of reciprocal and beneficient interchange between mind and nature—at face value only at the cost of reducing criticism to explication. I should not wish to oversimplify a difficult problem; perhaps we do read the poets as much or more for what they say as for what they do. Perhaps as readers we must trust the teller and not the tale. But surely not as critics. Criticism must begin and not end in explication, testimony, and hermeneutics if it is to be recommended as an activity for minds serious in their own right.

The spirit of solitude in the egotistical sublime is also, in its character of absence, a revelation of the unattainability of the Other. Shelley's awareness of the ensuing ambivalence was so acute, even in *Alastor*, that he is not the best poet to take us beyond identity. We begin to suspect that the strength of the protest on behalf of the Other, and the need for it, are direct functions of its unattainability. In any case, we are prepared by common sense not to mistake the theme of love for its actualization any more than we would fail in ordinary life to distinguish among the man who needs love, the man in love, and the man who is loved. It is in Keats that we find a bracing capability of desire beyond narcissism. And, most definitively, in Blake. But here we might pause to scout quite rapidly two alternative paths.

One path suggests we have been on the wrong road all along: it would save the possibility of love and of objects by questioning the premise of the critique. The hypothesis of primary narcissism is hardly invulnerable, but in brief it cannot be attacked from a point within Romantic thought. It may be, as the structuralists charge, that with his hypothesis Freud renewed the central notion of nineteenth-century philosophical idealism, and moreover in rather naïve, quasi-biological terms. The problem he broached and attempted to answer only with respect to secondary narcissism is the familiar impasse of idealism: just how are we supposed to picture the transition from a monad shut in upon itself to a progressive discovery of the object?[23] Freud's answer was implicit, pragmatic, and dualistic: primary narcissism won't work; reality (nongratification) is there; though the first knowledge of the object is of an absence, it is not the less recognition for that. At all events, a critique of Freud on this point amounts to a critique of Romanticism as well. If Freud was in error about love, the error was Romantic love.

Another alternative path, however, we are not likely to ignore in this book. It is the passing over of identity—we cannot yet see how—into the mimetic, symbolic identification of the negative sublime, which was itself, we found, an answer to the object's unattainability. Can the relation of the secondary Imagination to the primary Imagination become more than an echo—perhaps through an intensified mimesis? We remember the Coleridgean triad: eternal act of creation (God): its repetition in the finite mind (primary Imagination): the echo of the latter (secondary, poetic Imagination). An echo is doomed never to coincide with its original, though it incessantly regresses across the vacancy. The negative sublime, however, avoids regression; it leapfrogs, as it were, across the "primary" term of finite origins, which thus turns out to be an intermediate term. The negative sublime seems to offer to the poet the truly primary power of the god, the original or eternal power reigning before his own first poetic spirit got its start at birth. It is clear that this path away from identity involves a confrontation with the father-principle. And the father is the very member of the family romance who is missing in the egotistical sublime.

Part Three:
The Liminal Sublime

quisque suos patimur Manis—Virgil

Wordsworth and the Defile of the Word

Nearing the end of the first book of the poem on his own life, Wordsworth confesses to some uncertainty. He fears that already he may have been misled "By an infirmity of love for day / Disowned by memory," and he counts on Coleridge's sympathy to see him through (*P* 1.612 ff.). His project in this loving reclamation of childhood had been frankly therapeutic:

> . . . my hope has been, that I might fetch
> Invigorating thoughts from former years;
> Might fix the wavering balance of my mind,
> And haply meet reproaches too, whose power
> May spur me on, in manhood now mature,
> To honorable toil.
>
> [1.620–25]

Yet his original project is fast receding before an enterprise more tentative and promising. Even if his hope should be "but an impotent desire,"[1] he has made a discovery, which now solicits him with the charm of the visionary and displaces the reproaches he had anticipated to a new quarter:

> Yet should these hopes
> Prove vain, and thus should neither I be taught
> To understand myself, nor thou to know
> With better knowledge how the heart was framed
> Of him thou lovest; need I dread from thee

> Harsh judgments, if the song be loth to quit
> Those recollected hours that have the charm
> Of visionary things, those lovely forms
> And sweet sensations that throw back our life,
> And almost make remotest infancy
> A visible scene, on which the sun is shining?   [1.625-35]

It is difficult to know how open is this question addressed to Coleridge. For Coleridge, we feel, is not the real addressee; he stands, like a neutral alienist, sympathetic but mute, for an agent or element in Wordsworth himself that would judge harshly the enterprise now in view. As if an answer to his question scarcely mattered—he is picking up confidence— Wordsworth continues:

> One end at least hath been attained; my mind
> Hath been revived, and if this genial mood
> Desert me not, forthwith shall be brought down
> Through later years the story of my life.
> The road lies plain before me;—'tis a theme
> Single and of determined bounds; and hence
> I choose it rather at this time, than work
> Of ampler or more varied argument,
> Where I might be discomfited and lost. . . .   [1.636-44]

We note that Wordsworth's "genial mood" depends upon neither his own self-understanding nor the successful communication of his history in the terms of "knowledge." This cure, if such it is, comes about almost incidentally, as a side effect in his rehearsal of the past. By settling for less in the way of theme and argument, he gains more, a genial state of mind which cannot be sought directly, only received gratuitously.

It is true that Wordsworth will later seem to be educated by the visible scenes of childhood, as if their rememoration indeed constituted a kind of knowledge. Certain episodes seem especially instructive, imbued with a latent message now to be decoded:

> There are in our existence spots of time,
> That with distinct pre-eminence retain
> A renovating virtue, whence, depressed
> By false opinion and contentious thought,
> Or aught of heavier or more deadly weight,
> In trivial occupations, and the round
> Of ordinary intercourse, our minds
> Are nourished and invisibly repaired;
> A virtue, by which pleasure is enhanced,

That penetrates, enables us to mount,
When high, more high, and lifts us up when fallen.
This efficacious spirit chiefly lurks
Among those passages of life that give
Profoundest knowledge to what point, and how,
The mind is lord and master—outward sense
The obedient servant of her will.   [12.208–23]

One can have much of Wordsworth by heart and still be surprised, notably by the submerged metaphors. Here, "lurks," with its suggestion of the hidden and even the sinister, makes one pause only to find that resonance picked up by "passages": a spirit lurks in a passage. "Passages" refers presumably to events that involved a passing from one state to another and also to the passing back and through of retrospection; in this sense, "passages of life" are equivalent to "spots of time." But a "passage" is also a text; one reads these texts or signifiers by passing into and through them. Such passages "give" knowledge but conceal the efficacious spirit; at the very least this spirit, lying as it were in ambush, is to be distinguished from knowledge of the mind's sovereignty. (Actually, "knowledge" is a late idea here; Wordsworth first wrote that the spirit lurks among passages "in which / We have had deepest feeling that the mind / Is lord and master" (1805, 11.270–71), and this phrase evolved through "Profoundest feeling" to become "Profoundest knowledge."[2]) The knowledge or feeling of the mind's great power is often given to Wordsworth, but the spirit comes not as a consequence of this insight but as if in response to it. If *The Prelude* is an indirect quest for the efficacious spirit or genial mood, that quest is fulfilled in a hidden and somewhat unpredictable concomitance.

What then was Wordsworth's discovery? His undeniable claim to originality can be advanced in many directions—he aggrandized the everyday; he virtually destroyed the-poem-which-is-*about*-something by taking the subject out of poetry; he naturalized the archaic, daemonic, and divine sources of power. What must orient us here is his discovery of a mode of conversation, now most easily recognized outside of poetry in the domains of the authentic psychoanalyst and a certain kind of expert teacher too tentative to know or say for sure what he "really" thinks. This conversation is not a "communication" (the cant word of our social world); its aim is not the transmission of knowledge or a message but the springing loose of an efficacious spirit which haunts the passages of self-knowledge, however shallow or deep. Yet to describe *The Prelude* as any kind of conversation seems perverse. Its apparent form is closer to monolithic monologue; it drifts, gets lost, peters out now and then, and generally proceeds without the dramatic constraints a stricter form or a genuine auditor would compel. The ostensible interlocutor has no chance to reply, and indeed it might be said that Coleridge's assumption of this role presupposed his own subsidence as a poet. Worst of all, this "conversation" has for its exclusive theme the inner history of the speaker, and it is thus a discourse apparently exempt from the veridical testing conversation normally entails.

Nevertheless, in its deeper lineaments *The Prelude* has the shape and structure of a dialogue. Wordsworth's real interlocutor is not Coleridge but himself, a part of himself, archaic or prospective but in any case alienated from his present, who beckons to him across a "vacancy." "Often do I seem," he says, "Two consciousnesses, conscious of myself / And of some other Being" (2.31–33). That "other Being" is in part a remembered state of mind, a previous consciousness, and in part the inferred protagonist of visible scenes of whom he is now conscious for the first time. For the first time because that other Being did not exist in the past; though he now exists there, he is a creation of the present. Freud regarded the appearance of a subject as an active character in his own memory as decisive evidence that the original experience had been worked over.

> It may indeed be questioned whether we have any memories at all *from* our childhood: memories *relating to* our childhood may be all that we possess. Our childhood memories show us our earliest years not as they were but as they appeared at the later periods when the memories were revived. In these periods of revival, the childhood memories did not, as people are accustomed to say, *emerge*; they were *formed* at that time.[3]

The radical reading of *The Prelude* must begin with this insight, which no one who has tried the experiment of recollection needs an analyst to confirm. So Wordsworth is to be found forming his significant other Being even as he searches for his signature in recollected hours, perhaps finding him truly only "in that silence while he hung / Listening" like the boy at Winander in conversation with the owls (5.364–88).

In general, the other Being or consciousness implied by Wordsworth's speech remains inaccessible except through the immensely mediated languages of memory and desire. The whole series of representations—images, thoughts, ideas, words—function as the signifiers in this dialogue, and they cannot be short-circuited in an unmediated intuition because that Other is defined, as locus or possibility, only by these signifiers. Insofar as Wordsworth is a speaker, that Other is the being to whom his speech is unconsciously directed; but the Other is also the one to whom he listens, and it is in fact mainly as a listener that Wordsworth overtly construes his identity in *The Prelude*. For there is and has been an evident continuity in his listening. Even as a child, he says, amid "fits of vulgar joy" and "giddy bliss,"

> . . . even then I felt
> Gleams like the flashing of a shield;—the earth
> And common face of Nature spake to me
> Rememberable things . . .   [1.581–88]

and they are still so speaking because "The scenes which were a witness of that joy / Remained in their substantial lineaments / Depicted on the brain" (1.599–601). If he fails to understand this speech, and he often does, sometimes egregiously, the fact of being spoken to remains, and its aim and value depend in no way on the accurate reception of a message. It may even be that Wordsworth's misconstructions, his significant *méconnaissances*, are the essential pivots of this dialogue, for they enable him to change from listener to speaker; they enable him to be cured. We appreciate in any case that these failures are not the result of a faulty archeology, as if the past could indeed be unearthed by consciousness. They are liberating evasions, obscurities which preserve both the mystery (and hence the power) of his interlocutor and the authenticity of his own speech, which otherwise might slide toward the vain repetition or imitation of an alienated self. We might even suppose, as the point of an ideal cure no doubt hypothetical, a moment of pure speech in which the Other is so entirely obscured as not to exist, and Wordsworth knows only a presence uncompounded by the absence which makes speech necessary.

We may have the vague impression that it is Nature with whom Wordsworth is speaking. In one sense this is true, for "the earth / And common face of Nature" is the predominant locus of the signifier. But Nature herself exhibits a paradoxically fugitive omnipresence in *The Prelude*. Wordsworth rarely speaks directly to Nature, more often of or about her; we find a more or less consistent differentiation between Nature and "the language of the sense":

> Ye Presences of Nature in the sky
> And on the earth! Ye Visions of the hills!
> And Souls of lonely places! can I think
> A vulgar hope was yours when ye employed
> Such ministry, when ye through many a year
> Haunting me thus among my boyish sports,
> On caves and trees, upon the woods and hills,

> Impressed upon all forms the characters
> Of danger or desire; and thus did make
> The surface of the universal earth
> With triumph and delight, with hope and fear,
> Work like a sea?   [1.464–75]

Nature is generally two or more ontological degrees removed from the "characters" that can be perceived or intended, listened to or read. Nature hovers in the background as the sum or ground of the intermediary personifications ("Powers," "genii," "Presences," "Visions," "Souls") who are supposed as actual agents of articulation. Nature is thus the guarantor of the dialogue, at once the principle assumed to cover and redeem its discontinuities and a kind of screen on which the multiplicity of representations is projected. When "forms" begin to assume the shape and function of "characters," Nature's significant absence (or "negative presence") is already presupposed, for characters are symbols standing in for something no longer immediately there. Behind every symbol is an absence, the death of the thing (form or image) whose place the symbol takes. Hence speech itself is founded on the withdrawal of the primordial object, in which we find as well the essential formula of anxiety.

It is in this passage from forms to characters, from image to symbol, that the efficacious spirit lurks, and it is the intricate turnings of this passage that I propose to follow and hope to map. We may conceive two domains, an order of imagination or memory and an order of symbol or speech, though the content of these opposed domains ought to be educed from the analysis and not out of an hypothesis. *The Prelude* as a whole is an attempt to negotiate the strait leading from remembered images, and from the power of mind to which these images continue to testify, to capable speech. "I have seen such things—I see them still (memory)—and see moreover deeper into them, as if anew (imagination) —I therefore was and am a favored being (identity)—and I can speak (be a poet)." This argument, here abstractly reduced and overemphasized, presides over each rememoration in the poem, as if this poem were in fact a prelude, achieving its unforeseen finalities only under propaedeutic pretense. In a way the argument serves as "profoundest knowledge" to orient and occasion the "efficacious spirit" which is the poem itself. Moreover, the passage discernible in the project of *The Prelude* emerges with strange and almost literal insistence in the poem's crucial episodes and at the heart of its recurrent figures.

We use the notion of poetic imagination loosely to gloss over the mysterious gap between a power of perception and a power of articulation or composition. Keats says that "every man whose soul is not a clod / Hath visions, and would speak, if he had loved / And been well nurtured in his mother's tongue,"[4] but that can't possibly be true; a mute inglorious Milton is no Milton at all. At times it seems as if the Romantic poets (Blake, of course, apart) were engaged in a conspiracy of occultation concerning the Word, as if to acknowledge that its enjoining power involved the betrayal of a dangerous secret.

The fact is that the passage from imagination to symbol was occluded for Wordsworth, and yet the essential moment of his greatest poetry is right in the midst of this occlusion. He halts or is halted right at the point where the image is eclipsed—where it is on the verge of turning into a "character" in a higher, nonvisual discourse. This moment—and it is an experience as well as a dialectical locus—is the sole province of what he calls "visionary power," and it is the very type of the sublime moment. Here is one of Wordsworth's first attempts to formulate its liminal significance:

> . . . for I would walk alone,
> Under the quiet stars, and at that time
> Have felt whate'er there is of power in sound
> To breathe an elevated mood, by form
> Or image unprofaned; and I would stand,
> If the night blackened with a coming storm,
> Beneath some rock, listening to notes that are
> The ghostly language of the ancient earth,
> Or make their dim abode in distant winds.
> Thence did I drink the visionary power;
> And deem not profitless those fleeting moods
> Of shadowy exultation: not for this,
> That they are kindred to our purer mind
> And intellectual life; but that the soul,
> Remembering how she felt, but what she felt
> Remembering not, retains an obscure sense
> Of possible sublimity, whereto
> With growing faculties she doth aspire,
> With faculties still growing, feeling still
> That whatsoever point they gain, they yet
> Have something to pursue.   [2.302–22]

The mood of shadowy exultation lies beyond the profane domain of form or image, and yet the subject is here not quite integrated into the order of symbolic sound. The notes to which he listens remain a "ghostly language," a pattern of signifiers without signifieds, a language without semantic dimension. The signifier precedes the signified, which may indeed never arrive; or in terms closer to Wordsworth's, the subject is initiated into the *how* of the discourse but not the *what*, and the affective exaltation depends precisely on this halting at a threshold. The "power in sound / To breathe an elevated mood" is here being listened to, but that slight personification ("breathe") refers us obliquely to Wordsworth's situation as a speaker who knows how he wants to sound but not quite what he has to say.

Wordsworth was not a symbolic poet and not a descriptive poet either, if indeed a poet can be descriptive. His landscapes hover on the edge of revelation without revealing anything, and so the very moment of hovering, of glimpsed entry into the beyond, when "the light of sense / Goes out, but with a flash that has revealed / The invisible world" (6.600–602), usurps the missing climax of symbolic revelation. In the Snowdon vision, for example, the salient elements of that magnificent scene—the suspended moon, the sea of hoary mist, the blue chasm in the vapor—refuse to harden into symbolic equation with the imagination or anything else, as Geoffrey Hartman has observed.[5] And this is so despite the fact that Wordsworth is there working explicitly with notions of analogy, type, and emblem. So too with that spot of time when the young boy, having lost his way while riding near Penrith, sees a naked pool, the beacon on the summit, and the girl with a pitcher forcing her way against the wind—salient images which are less than symbols and all the more powerful for that. Or the schoolboy in his mountain lookout, waiting to be fetched home for a holiday that turned into a funeral, who later finds himself returning to certain "kindred spectacles and sounds"—

> . . . the wind and sleety rain,
> And all the business of the elements,
> The single sheep, and the one blasted tree,
> And the bleak music from that old stone wall,
> The noise of wood and water, and the mist
> That on the line of each of those two roads
> Advanced in such indisputable shapes . . .   [12.317–23]

—thence to drink as at a fountain. Many instances of such salience could be adduced, but this feature of Wordsworth's landscapes is widely appreciated and is here evoked only to suggest the scope of the moment we wish to isolate. If the images so projected into the field of Wordsworth's past were to lose their opacity and become the transparent signifiers of an invisible world, the soul would "remember" what she felt and have nothing left to pursue. The conversation, propelled as it is by the baffled misconstruction of the signifier, would be over; Wordsworth would understand himself. Indeed, as the poem goes on Wordsworth is less and less disposed to interrogate the images that rise upon him. The gestures of self-inquisition become the mere feinting of a mind learning how knowledge is opposed to efficacious power.

Visionary power is associated with the transcendence of the image and in particular with the "power in sound"; yet it depends upon a resistance within that transcendence of sight for sound. In the Wordsworthian moment two events appear to coalesce: the withdrawal or the occultation of the image and the epiphany of the character or signifier proper. A form or image may be installed in either the imaginative or symbolic domains. There is a world of difference between the two, but the differentiation can never be found within the image itself. If an image is symbolic, that fact is signaled by what we loosely call "context"—its inscription in an order or language whose structure is prior to its meaning (signifieds) and so determines it. On the other hand, an image (fantasy or perception) may fall short of the symbolic, in which case it remains opaque and meaningless in itself. Earlier we spoke of rememoration as a confrontation with a signifier, but strictly speaking, an image becomes a signifier only when it is recognized as such, and this may involve imputing an intentionality to the image. (A homely example: a child responds to pictures or the type in a book only as colors and shapes until the magical moment when he discerns that they are representations; it is the displaced recapitulation of this moment that is in question here.) There is implicit in the passage from imagination to symbol a confrontation with symbolicity—the very fact of structure in its priority and independent of its actual organization. Hence the signifier may be misconstrued in two possible ways. It may be simply misread, or—and this is in point with Wordsworth—there may be a resistance or a barrier to its recognition as a signifier, a resistance to reading itself as opposed to seeing. I think the resistance may be identified with what Wordsworth calls imagination.

Death and the Word

The spots of time give to the mind the knowledge or feeling of its own sovereignty and occasion the gift of efficacious spirit as well. "Life with me," says Wordsworth, "As far as memory can look back, is full / Of this beneficent influence" (1805, 11.277–79). It is curious that these remembered events should have therapeutic power, since the two memories Wordsworth goes on to present are of a kind we should normally call traumatic, and they each contain intimations of death.

In fact, however, the whole idea of spots of time is installed in a line of associations concerning death. In the first manuscripts containing the bulk of books 1 and 2 (MSS. V, U), the passage "There are in our existence spots of time . . ." follows Wordsworth's account of the drowned man at Esthwaite, later assigned to book 5 (426–59). He had seen a heap of garments on the shore and watched for half an hour to see if a bather would emerge. But no one did, and the next day—"(Those unclaimed garments telling a plain Tale)"—the body was recovered:

> At length, the dead Man, 'mid that beauteous scene
> Of trees, and hills and water, bolt upright
> Rose with his ghastly face. . . .   [1805, 5.470–72]

Why Wordsworth hadn't run for help the night before isn't clear, since surely the "Tale"—or at least the suspicion of something wrong—would have been plain enough to a boy of eight. In any case, MS. V continues with a meditation on disasters that later proved full of beneficent influence:

>   . . . bolt upright
> Rose with his ghastly face. I might advert
> To numerous accidents in flood or field
> Quarry or moor, or 'mid the winter snows
> Distresses and disasters, tragic facts
> Of rural history that impressed my mind
> With images to which in following years
> Far other feelings were attached; with forms
> That yet exist with independent life
> And, like their archetypes, know no decay.[6]

And then follows "There are in our existence spots of time. . . ." The sequence suggests that the spots of time were in their origin "tragic facts" for which time has provided a kind of redemption, permitting their association with "Far other feelings." We might find the tragic (or deathly or traumatic) associations clustering around "spots," whereas "of time" suggests the curative efficacy of a supervening continuity. Here the misconstruction of a memory-representation—entering, we must always assume, into the representation itself—and in particular the poet's indifference to the role of death in his most valuable memories, would seem to lie at the heart of the cure.

In the first spot of time Wordsworth is a very young boy of five or so riding with a trusted family servant on the moors near Penrith.

> We had not travelled long, ere some mischance
> Disjoined me from my comrade; and, through fear

Dismounting, down the rough and stony moor
I led my horse, and, stumbling on, at length
Came to a bottom, where in former times
A murderer had been hung in iron chains.
The gibbet-mast had mouldered down, the bones
And iron case were gone; but on the turf,
Hard by, soon after that fell deed was wrought,
Some unknown hand had carved the murderer's name.
The monumental letters were inscribed
In times long past; but still, from year to year,
By superstition of the neighbourhood,
The grass is cleared away, and to this hour
The characters are fresh and visible:
A casual glance had shown them, and I fled,
Faltering and faint, and ignorant of the road:
Then, reascending the bare common, saw
A naked pool that lay beneath the hills,
The beacon on the summit, and, more near,
A girl, who bore a pitcher on her head,
And seemed with difficult steps to force her way
Against the blowing wind.   [12.231–53]

The emotional pivot of this episode is a word, a name, a group of characters suddenly glimpsed. One kind of fear, not knowing where one is,
is violently superseded by the virtual panic of another kind of fear,
being in a terrible place or spot. Losing its way, the ego is exposed involuntarily to a death, for the characters mean "a murderer was executed
at this spot": death for a death, the law of sacrifice which is the simplest
formula of justice. The custom in the background here is the execution
of a murderer at the spot of the crime, so that the spot becomes charged
with the ritual significance of atonement. It is a place in nature but not
of it, the very point of contiguity between the natural order and the
order of law; hence "By superstition of the neighbourhood, / The grass
is cleared away" lest the stark exigencies of the law should be mitigated
by natural process. The centrality of spot-ness here—migrating, subliminally, into the idea of spots of time—is even clearer in the 1805
version:

Faltering, and ignorant where I was, at length
I chanced to espy those characters inscribed
On the green sod: forthwith I left the spot. . . .   [1805, 11.300–302]

In one sense the spot is an image within a continuum of images, just
as the spots of time are salient memory representations within the vaguer

continuum structured by a linear idea of time. But the text insists, with an emphasis as extraordinary as it is literal, on this spot as a signifier: characters, "monumental letters," or "writing" (1805). This it is which mediates the meaning of the spot, turning faltering confusion "forthwith" into panic and headlong flight. The order of law is inserted into the order of nature by means of writing. Precisely parallel to the point of contiguity between law and nature—that is, the idea of death and the logic of death for death—is the point of contiguity between image and signifier or symbol. We arrive, by no doubt too great a jump as yet, at the equation writing = death, or more exactly, the recognition of a signifier = the intimation of death.

Here we are greeted by a curious fact. In the first manuscript version we have, the characters that were to be given such prominence are unmentioned:

> A man, the murderer of his wife, was hung
> In irons, moulder'd was the gibbet mast,
> The bones were gone, the iron and the wood,
> Only a long green ridge of turf remained
> Whose shape was like a grave. I left the spot. . . .[7]

Evidently in revision (between 1802 and 1805) Wordsworth brushed up on the facts. He would have learned that the victim was a man and learned too, possibly for the first time, of the characters, and that they were still extant. (This is the kind of genetic detail that renders unacceptably naive that reading of *The Prelude* which would accept Wordsworth's myth of memory at face value and evade the origination of the memories in the present tense of a grown man.) In revision, the "long green ridge of turf . . . Whose shape was like a grave" turns into the portentous characters, which suggests that the representations of a secondary anxiety were being retrospectively superimposed upon the memory trace of a grave. If this is "association," it is deeper than what we usually mean by association, for the revision enables the poet Wordsworth to concentrate and perhaps to discover the emotional center of the memory. The element of panic enters the text with the appearance of the characters, as if they constituted the deep meaning of the grave, and not vice versa. At any rate, we have underlined in the very genesis of the passage a deep connection between death and the word.

Yet the point of the episode and its justification as a spot of time lies not in the epiphany of characters but in the subsequent vision:

> It was, in truth,
> An ordinary sight; but I should need
> Colours and words that are unknown to man,

To paint the visionary dreariness
Which, while I looked all round for my lost guide,
Invested moorland waste, and naked pool,
The beacon crowning the lone eminence,
The female and her garments vexed and tossed
By the strong wind.   [12.253–61]

Things are invested with a "visionary" aspect as if in recompense for the
prior fear; though for the boy it is a dubious consolation, for he must
contend with "dreariness," an involuntary perceptional alienation from
the "ordinary" (hence he doesn't think to hail the girl). This is a liminal
state in which mediations have fallen away. The common that he
ascends is "bare," the pool "naked," the moorland a "waste," and even
the beacon crowns a "lonely Eminence" (1805). The features of the
landscape by which he might expect to orient himself are remote, withdrawn in an unapproachable stasis. The girl, however, "more near" in
more ways than one, is an image not of stasis but of difficulty, of forces
locked in contrariety. There is a play on clothing beneath the surface:
dreariness invests the landscape by divesting it until it is naked, just as
the wind whips at the girl's garments. The girl proceeds "with difficult
steps to force her way" against the visionary divestment which threatens
her with the fate of the denuded, static landscape. As object ("outward
sense") to the boy's mind she yet retains her motion and her humanizing
garments against the involuntary, dehumanizing strength of that mind,
and she thereby images the boy's own difficult struggle against his
imagination.

    How should the imagination—that is, the literal, perceptional imagina-
tion—come to have such withering strength? Both the intensity and the
alienating effect of the imagination in its phase of lordship and mastery
seem to derive from the terror that has gone before. We need to put
the two halves of the spot of time back together. Vision occurs in flight
from the characters and appears to realize the deathly intimations read
in the characters. But the proportions of seeing to reading, of image to
symbol, have been reversed. "A casual glance had shown them, and I
fled": the briefest sight, surcharged with meaning, while visionary
dreariness is drawn out seeing, twice rendered by the poet—as if there
were indeed a hidden message threatening to emerge in the pool, the
beacon, and the girl—which yet falls short of symbolic revelation. An
extended seeing replaces reading in this flight; it is a "backward" displacement or regression from the order of symbol to that of image, and
it functions to defend the ego against the death which has been signified.
That death is displaced or projected (and thereby diffused) into the

denuded landscape where the fixating spot is doubled as the naked pool and the beacon on the summit. The wind against which the girl—and by extension the boy—are struggling represents not death but the obscure power we have found inextricably associated with death, a power for which we have as yet no name. For in truth, as strange and indeed academic as it sounds, it is against the fact that things may come to signify that the boy is forcing his difficult way.

The uncontrollable intensity of the imagination is often rendered as a strong wind in *The Prelude*, as M. H. Abrams showed long ago.[8] In the preamble, for example, the inner breeze is creative up to a certain point:

> For I, methought, while the sweet breath of Heaven
> Was blowing on my body, felt within
> A corresponding mild creative breeze,
> A vital breeze which travell'd gently on
> O'er things which it had made, and is become
> A tempest, a redundant energy
> Vexing its own creation.   [1805, 1.41–47]

Here too is evidently a threshold after which the wind becomes de-creative, "vexing" (as with the garments of the girl) what has been brought to birth in perception. In composition as in reading, winds attend the threshold of the word, for wind is the image of the invisible, the representation of the peculiar power of signifying within the perceptional order of the imagination. In book 5 Wordsworth brings the liminal concept of the visionary into connection with the works of mighty poets:

> Visionary power
> Attends the motions of the viewless winds,
> Embodied in the mystery of words:
> There, darkness makes abode, and all the host
> Of shadowy things work endless changes,—there,
> As in a mansion like their proper home,
> Even forms and substances are circumfused
> By that transparent veil with light divine,
> And, through the turnings intricate of verse,
> Present themselves as objects recognised,
> In flashes, and with glory not their own.   [5.595–605]

Wordsworth had a gift for phrasing that defies analysis. Power attends motions of winds which are embodied in a mystery: a series of quasi-metaphorical displacements away from words, compounded by indefinite reference ("there," "that transparent veil"). The passage is evoking the

penumbra of words, the power inherent not in what they mean but in
that they mean; or, in what they are, independent of their meaning—
in an earlier language, the *how* and not the *what* of sublimity. When a
"form" or a "substance" is taken up by a signifier, it receives a super-
added power and a divine glory immanent in the circumfusing veil of
the signifier. Power inheres not in the perceptional form but in language
or symbolicity itself; we remember that the boy drank the visionary
power listening to a language devoid of forms and substances ("by
form / Or image unprofaned"),

> ... notes that are
> The ghostly language of the ancient earth,
> Or make their dim abode in distant winds.   [2.308–10]

But there is in "ghostly language" a ghost to be confronted; our spot of
time has shown us that in the passage to the visionary power of signification lurks the thought of death. There, "darkness makes abode" and
"shadowy things" as well as "light divine." In order to arrive "As in a
mansion like their proper home," forms and substances must die out of
the imaginary or perceptional order and into the symbolic order of verse.
For the speaker or poet this passage appears to involve the intimation of
sacrifice and the assumption of guilt.

In the next spot of time, the fact of guilt is explicitly focused in relation to the visionary moment. Wordsworth is remembering his vigil on
a crag where he waited for a pair of horses to bear him home from
school for the Christmas holidays:

> ... 'twas a day
> Tempestuous, dark, and wild, and on the grass
> I sate half-sheltered by a naked wall;
> Upon my right hand couched a single sheep,
> Upon my left a blasted hawthorn stood;
> With those companions at my side, I watched,
> Straining my eyes intensely, as the mist
> Gave intermitting prospect of the copse
> And plain beneath.   [12.297–305]

Before the holidays were over, his father was dead:

> The event,
> With all the sorrow that it brought, appeared
> A chastisement; and when I called to mind
> That day so lately past, when from the crag
> I looked in such anxiety of hope;

With trite reflections of morality,
Yet in the deepest passion, I bowed low
To God, Who thus corrected my desires;
And, afterwards, the wind and sleety rain,
And all the business of the elements,
The single sheep, and the one blasted tree,
And the bleak music from that old stone wall,
The noise of wood and water, and the mist
That on the line of each of those two roads
Advanced in such indisputable shapes;
All these were kindred spectacles and sounds
To which I oft repaired, and thence would drink,
As at a fountain.   [12.309–26]

There are several suggestions of dissonance in this retrospection. The salient features of the landscape are rehearsed twice, as in the Penrith passage, and the secondary emphasis is upon the features themselves rather than upon their incidental discovery in an ulterior seeing, a looking for a lost guide or a pair of horses. The mist, for example, is at first an interposed obstacle, giving "intermitting prospect of the copse / And plain beneath" on which the boy's expectant eyes are focused; when the memory is re-formed, the mist advances in "indisputable shapes," itself a signifier. More striking, however, is the dissonance surrounding the matter of guilt. If the "desires" corrected by God were simply the boy's eagerness to go home, it is at least odd that his father's death should be felt as a chastisement of that most natural and filial wish. For a boy of thirteen to feel ambivalent upon the occasion of his father's death is perfectly normal, and the ambivalence that may be presumed to be original has made its way into the phrasing—in the "anxiety of hope" and that curious uncertainty about the decorum of grief: "With trite reflections of morality, / Yet in the deepest passion, I bowed low / To God. . . ." We begin to suspect that there is more to those desires than the boy's wish to go home for Christmas.

Editor de Selincourt finds in the "indisputable shapes" of the mist an echo of Hamlet's confrontation with his father's ghost: "Thou com'st in such a questionable shape / That I will speak to thee."[9] Hamlet means "a shape that can be questioned" as well as "an uncertain shape": in contrast on both counts, the shapes of Wordsworth's ghost-mist are "indisputable." Again we have the *how*—in a way that can't be questioned—but not the *what*: the liminal moment when the signifier appears, *apparently* without a signified. But could it be that Wordsworth on the crag had a premonition of his father's death, that this is the signified of those signifying shapes? In fact, he could not have known of his father's fatal illness while waiting to go home,[10] but the first formation of this memory, in the very early *Vale of Esthwaite*,[11] makes this very premonition explicit:

> Long, long, upon yon naked rock
> Alone, I bore the bitter shock;
> Long, long, my swimming eyes did roam
> For little Horse to bear me home,
> To bear me—what avails my tear?
> To sorrow o'er a Father's bier.   [422–27]

Of course, we have no way of knowing what the boy on the crag felt, and I might add, no need to know. We have insisted all along that it is a question of "creative" retrospection, of memories formed at the time they seem merely to emerge. The whole theme of guilt may well be a "later" addition, a reworking of the original impression, as indeed the *Vale* text goes on to imply:

> Flow on, in vain thou hast not flow'd,
> But eased me of a heavy load;
> For much it gives my heart relief
> To pay the mighty debt of grief,
> With sighs repeated o'er and o'er,
> I mourn because I mourned no more.   [428–33]

The ground of our speculation is but the firmer if we assume that the guilt—incurred by an unconscious desire for his father's death—is retrospectively associated, through the premonition, with visionary salience. It is as if that "indisputable" premonition, like the characters on the turf, were the cost of vision, the price of salience. At first, when he "called to mind / That day so lately past," he experienced not renovating power, but a feeling of guilt, so that he bowed low to God. It is only "afterwards" that the kindred spectacles and sounds" come to be a source of power—after, that is, the power has been paid for by the ritual gestures of expiation and correction.

For what is striking about this spot of time is not the presence in it of a commonplace oedipal ambivalence but the deeper evasion of the oedipal "correction." God ironically corrects the filial desire for reunion (to go home) by fulfilling the unconscious desire signified in the premonitory "indisputable shapes." Hence the guilt. More important, however, is the question, In what sense does Wordsworth stand corrected? Far from repenting—or repressing—the spectacles and sounds which are linked to his desires, Wordsworth repairs often to them, "and thence would drink / As at a fountain":

> . . . and on winter nights,
> Down to this very time, when storm and rain
> Beat on my roof, or, haply, at noon-day,
> While in a grove I walk, whose lofty trees,
> Laden with summer's thickest foliage, rock
> In a strong wind, some working of the spirit,
> Some inward agitations thence are brought. . . .   [12.326–32]

The inner or correspondent breeze has its source in a deep affiliation with a visionary moment whose ambivalent burden or message of death has been unconsciously repudiated even as it is consciously expiated. Hence the importance of his ritual chastisement; it covers (from himself) a deeper refusal to bow low. Hence, too, the division in his mind, which intends on the one hand "deepest passion" in its bowing low and yet is aware of the triteness and the ritual conventionality of the gesture. "I mourn *because* I mourned no more": as in the *Vale* text, grief is a "mighty debt"—something owed, not felt, or felt only because it is owed. Lest it seem too schematic to speak here of conscious and unconscious, we have in a draft Wordsworth's own intuitive attribution of the "working of the spirit" to an inner conflict, unconscious and unresolved:

> When in a grove I walk whose lofty trees
> Laden with all their summer foliage, rock
> High over head those workings of the mind
> Of source and tendency to me unknown,
> Some inward agitations thence are brought
> Efforts and struggles tempered and restrained
> By melancholy awe or pleasing fear.[12]

The last line of the draft employs the very diction of the negative sublime in its third, or resolution, phase. But the "inward agitations" derive from a source, the locus of visionary power, which is prior to that resolution and in fact resists it, so that these agitations must be "tempered and restrained" as by a God who awes and corrects.

We are now perhaps in need of drawing back and assuming a perspective from which the pattern exhibited in the spots of time can be seen in relief. Both spots of time locate the visionary—the phase in which the mind is lord and master—just "this side" of the order of the

signifier ("characters," "indisputable shapes") in the liminal space
where the signifier appears but is not yet fully—consciously—read. Yet
the spatial metaphor may distract us; in so crucial a matter it is wise to
guard against being traduced by the specious simplicity of a diagram.
For the liminal space of the visionary is also a liminal moment, and a
moment not before but *after* the threshold has been recrossed in retreat.
In the first case, the flight from the word and the extraordinary seeing
attending it are represented quite literally, though it is the figurative
flight which we have now in view. (According to Freud, flight is the
prototype of repression.[13]) The signified of those characters—death—is
repressed in this flight, but it thereupon reappears in the imaginary order,
in the landscape as invested by "visionary dreariness." In the case of the
holiday vigil, the flight is much subtler: it is both revealed and covered
by the acceptance of a guilt for which the cause remains obscured and
unacknowledged. This permits a return to the "kindred spectacles and
sounds," as if the intimations of death with which they were imbued
could be detached and exorcised through a ritualized guilt.

We may now return to our initial perplexity with some chance of
enhanced understanding. How is it that the spots of time retain a
"renovating virtue," a therapeutic efficacy? Not, it would appear, because they "give / Profoundest knowledge" of the mind's great power—
that feature of them merely marks those "passages of life" in which the
spirit is likely to be found lurking. The spots of time revive the mind
because through them the ego returns, in retrospection, to the liminal
place where "some working of the spirit, / Some inward agitations"
still are active. It is true that the liminal place is the very locus of the
visionary, but we have seen that visionary salience is itself a dialectical
response to the order of symbol. The symbol—the image as symbol or
signifier—is glimpsed, and the power of the subsequent visionary state
depends upon the repression of the signified, which reappears, as by a
profound logic or economy, in the protective domain of things seen. It
follows that the reviving of the imaginative power which the spots of
time effect depends upon the continued repression of the signified. If
the "source and tendency" of those "workings of the mind" were to
become known to Wordsworth, no "inward agitations," no "Efforts and
struggles" could thence be brought; there would be no correspondent
breeze answering the "strong wind" without. Both within themselves,
as coherent memory-fantasies, and within the poem, as episodes in the
project of recollection, the spots of time dramatize a saving resistance
to the passage from image to symbol. This resistance *is* the imagination
—a higher, "visionary" seeing whose very intensity, either as salience
or as "redundant energy," occludes the symbol.

Interlude: The Wordsworthian Darkness

It is tempting to retreat from the complexity of this structure to texts outside *The Prelude*, wherein the threshold between image and symbol is more simply manifested. In "Tintern Abbey," for example, we recognize the crossing of that threshold "With some uncertain notice" when the image of "wreaths of smoke / Sent up, in silence, from among the trees!" becomes a sign. As a sign it demands not merely to be seen but to be read, and reading it involves imputing an intentionality "behind" the sign,

> . . . as might seem
> Of vagrant dwellers in the houseless woods,
> Or of some Hermit's cave, where by his fire
> The Hermit sits alone.   [19–22]

The rhythm of seeing ("Once again I see") is broken in this simple surmise, which nevertheless moves Wordsworth uncertainly beyond the security of the visible, so that the poem comes to a dead halt. The saving externality of things depends upon their remaining images, and the "abyss of idealism" Wordsworth feared may often be recognized at the point, the fixating spot, where things come to signify.

Yet it is the main drama of *The Prelude* which necessarily solicits us, for we have rendered only a few of its episodes. That death somehow embodied in the mystery of words still remains opaque to our effort of elucidation. It is not that we cannot find evidence at what is called the "thematic" level of the connection between death and the word: there is a range of intriguing evidence in book 5, the book on "Books," alone. If we approach that book as fundamentalists—and we must always, I think, begin as literalists in reading Wordsworth—we will soon be baffled by the very explicitness of the opening theme: Poetry versus apocalypse. And it is Poetry literalized—the very book-ness, the pages and print of it, the frail shrines, "Poor earthly casket of immortal verse" (5.164)—which is threatened by a very literal Apocalypse. The actual man Wordsworth wept to read in Milton of the destruction of paradise by the flood;[14] the Wordsworth of this book contemplates "in soberness the approach / Of an event so dire, by signs in earth / Or heaven made manifest" (5.157–59). The violent fate of Nature and implicitly of natural man causes him no apparent anxiety:

> A thought is with me sometimes, and I say,—
> Should the whole frame of earth by inward throes
> Be wrenched, or fire come down from far to scorch

> Her pleasant habitations, and dry up
> Old Ocean, in his bed left singed and bare,
> Yet would the living Presence still subsist
> Victorious, and composure would ensue,
> And kindlings like the morning—presage sure
> Of day returning and of life revived.   [5.29–37]

How out of line is the indifference—or the confidence—with the Wordsworth of the other books! I put this impressionistically, but as fundamentalists our attention will be caught by dissonance more precise and yet more strange within the dream of the Arab itself. The Arab says the shell of poetry

> . . . was a god, yea many gods,
> Had voices more than all the winds, with power
> To exhilarate the spirit, and to soothe,
> Through every clime, the heart of human kind.   [5.106–9]

But what does the shell of poetry actually say? When Wordsworth held it to his ear, he "heard that instant in an unknown tongue," which yet he understood,

> . . . articulate sounds,
> A loud prophetic blast of harmony;
> An Ode, in passion uttered, which foretold
> Destruction to the children of the earth
> By deluge, now at hand. . . .   [5.93–98]

Where is the power, claimed by the Arab, to exhilarate and to soothe? In truth, one cannot read a dream as a literalist because the first thing one learns about dreams is that they distort, sometimes unrecognizably, the thoughts, wishes, and fears that are their motive or cause. Wordsworth the dreamer and Wordsworth the teller of the dream would like to cleave unto the Arab's view of poetry, but the deeper truth of the dream is that poetry is allied to apocalyptic destruction—a connection clearly signified as prophecy. Poetry is not threatened *by* Apocalypse: poetry threatens Apocalypse, at least insofar as it is prophetic poetry. In this light, Wordsworth's odd solicitude for print and pages—as his friend says, "in truth / 'Twas going far to seek disquietude" (5.52–53)— begins to look like a reversal masking his fear of poetry itself.

A fear of poetry itself—this surely requires explanation. Poetry, in the opening of book 5, is specifically the poetry of great precursors ("Shakespeare or Milton, labourers divine!" [5.165]). Wordsworth's interpretation of the dream neatly reverses his fear of being annihilated by this

poetry into a concern, a "fond anxiety" (5.160), for its survival and continued power. The very literalness of the Apocalypse here envisaged
locates the source of his real anxiety with respect to the great poets of
the past. The mystery embodied in their words is still a literal one; their
archaic power comes from the fact that their prophecy points to a
literal fulfillment, just as what the shell utters is even "now at hand."
Their word is, or is in touch with, the Word. More than the enlightened
conditions of belief, more than the general and gregarious advance of
intellect makes this impossible for Wordsworth. It is a question, not of
scepticism, which can be (as in Keats) generous and liberal, but of fear.
As the first great humanizer of the mystery, Wordsworth has priority,
but his very priority exposes him to the terror and the literalness of the
archaic sublime. (Hence he can become, as it were, Keats's stalking horse,
shielding the later poet from the baleful radiance of Milton's awful
certainties.) As post-Enlightenment poets, Wordsworth and Keats have
come to the same point, but not at the same time:

> This Chamber of Maiden Thought becomes gradually darken'd and
> at the same time on all sides of it many doors are set open—but all
> dark—all leading to dark passages—We see not the ballance of good
> and evil. We are in a Mist—*We* are now in that state—We feel the
> "burden of the Mystery," To this Point was Wordsworth come, as
> far as I can conceive when he wrote 'Tintern Abbey' and it seems to
> me that his Genius is explorative of those dark Passages. Now if we
> live, and go on thinking, we too shall explore them. He is a Genius and
> superior [to] us, in so far as he can, more than we, make discoveries,
> and shed a light in them—Here I must think Wordsworth is deeper
> than Milton.[15]

Wordsworth can make discoveries in those dark passages, but they are
discoveries of depth, of thinking into the human heart, not of power.
When Keats in *The Fall of Hyperion* finds himself in the terrain of
mystery, the meal has already been tasted and discarded, the apparatus
of the sacred lies "All in a mingled heap confus'd," and he learns from
Moneta that the major event, the disenthronement of the archaic Titans,
has long been over; tragedy for her, the event for him is already the
nostalgia of wonder. He comes to witness, not to struggle—or if to
struggle, it is only in order to be allowed to witness a superannuated
sublime, beside "forlorn divinity, / The pale Omega of a wither'd race."[16]
Keats's situation is worth sketching, however briefly, for it enables
us to plot in yet another (historical) register Wordsworth's liminal confrontation with the mystery in those dark passages. Wordsworth's fear
of the word is quite specifically, though not exclusively, fear of the

Word. The epiphany of the signifier intimates death (the apocalyptic destruction of nature and the natural man) because that showing forth is charged with the only creative power that is absolute—the power to create literally and the power of the literal. For what, displacements aside, is the manner of the Word? *God said, Let there be light: and there was light*: the most remembered of Longinus's examples, marked for its simplicity by Boileau. In a change of mood, from subjunctive to indicative, reality is born. That is the "Omnific Word," identified by Milton and tradition with the Son, the filial Godhead.[17] Losing just this power, Keats's fallen Saturn is pathetic:

> ... and there shall be
> Beautiful things made new for the surprise
> Of the sky-children—" So he feebly ceas'd,
> With such a poor and sickly-sounding pause,
> Methought I heard some old man of the earth
> Bewailing earthly loss; nor could my eyes
> And ears act with that pleasant unison of sense
> Which marries sweet sound with the grace of form,
> And dolorous accent from a tragic harp
> With large-limb'd visions. . . .   [*The Fall of Hyperion* 1. 436–45]

What Saturn says is beautiful in thought and phrase, but there is no fulfillment; hence, for Keats, he is a bad poet, depending as he does upon a power no longer there. Saturn's literal sublime is now superannuated; he lacks the subjunctive self-consciousness of the new regime, of Apollo or whoever is to succeed him, of the poetry that creates of mind and in mind alone.

The poetry of mind, reflective poetry, is always subjunctive; before every such poem there is an implicit *Let there be*. No doubt even Wordsworth was content with second place to the Godhead, if not to Milton. The terror that invests the poetry of the past with an apocalyptic aspect is not born of an obsession with priority, for Wordsworth's ambition—as well as his achievement, as Keats helps us to see—is consciously identified with his sublimation or displacement of the high argument into the mind and heart of man. There are in Wordsworth many old men of the earth bewailing earthly loss, but they are not viewed ironically or pathetically. They speak a stately speech, choice word and measured phrase, though the burden of their speech is far more humble and banal than Saturn's lament. Hence it seems to me not the necessary second-ariness of either the earthly or the humanizing mind which threatens Wordsworth. It is instead the fact that the mystery still lays claim to him; it is still in the mist that he finds the power, and the power is still, as it was for Collins, "dark power." Knowledge and power are opposed in Wordsworth in a way that to Keats will seem itself archaic and rugged, superstitiously egotistical. Not only is knowledge purchased by the loss of power, but power is purchased by terror, and terror assaults the possibility of perception or insight. Here in ampler lineaments is the very structure of the negative sublime, which exists in Keats only as affectation or as a stage of the mind to be recapitulated in wonder.

Power is "dark" because it requires the assumption of an archaic guilt. In an earlier chapter we considered this accession to guilt in terms of the classical psychoanalysis of the individual, and we noted that the identification in which it is performed is always in excess. Culture is very largely constituted by this crucial supererogation, and hence it is the measure by which the merely personal history of poet or man is exceeded by his sense of destiny—what he *must* do. The inevitable symbol for the initiatory identification which founds and empowers the culture-ego is the profoundly ambivalent symbolic image of the sacrifice. This is no place to review the fascinating speculation on the founding symbol of the sacrifice which has followed in the wake of *Totem and Taboo*; nor am I competent to conduct such a review with any rigor. It is enough to note that the sacrifice, posited, no doubt mythically, as the founding moment of culture, is also the first symbolic act and thereby the origin of the symbolic order, of language in the wider sense. In any case, there is no mistaking the presence and associations of the sacrifice in Wordsworth. We have already glimpsed its aspect behind the ambivalent fixation of what Hartman calls the spot syndrome, and we have observed the alignment it suggests between the advent of the word and the ambivalent annunciation of death. But there is evidence less oblique.

In the penultimate book of *The Prelude* we find a sequence which puts back to back Wordsworth's hope, his own conception of his originality, and his fear, in all its archaic resonance. Wordsworth is celebrating, in the way that is so reassuring to him, the coincidence of Nature's humanizing project with the task of the poet; and so he comes to treat of his own special mission:

> Dearest Friend,
> Forgive me if I say that I, who long
> Had harbour'd reverentially a thought
> That Poets, even as Prophets, each with each
> Connected in a mighty scheme of truth,
> Have each for his peculiar dower, a sense
> By which he is enabled to perceive
> Something unseen before; forgive me, Friend,

If I, the meanest of this Band, had hope
That unto me had also been vouchsafed
An influx, that in some sort I possess'd
A privilege, and that a work of mine,
Proceeding from the depth of untaught things,
Enduring and creative, might become
A power like one of Nature's.   [1805, 12.298–312]

This is the hope: first, that there is no discontinuity between the poets, past or present, since they are "Connected in a mighty scheme of truth"; second, that the "influx" conveys a power not opposed to Nature but allied to her benevolent pedagogy. And this is the astonishing sequel, which proceeds without interval:

A power like one of Nature's. To such mood,
Once above all, a Traveller at that time
Upon the Plain of Sarum was I raised;
There on the pastoral Downs without a track
To guide me, or along the bare white roads
Lengthening in solitude their dreary line,
While through those vestiges of ancient times
I ranged, and by the solitude o'ercome,
I had a reverie and saw the past,
Saw multitudes of men, and here and there,
A single Briton in his wolf-skin vest
With shield and stone-axe, stride across the Wold;
The voice of spears was heard, the rattling spear
Shaken by arms of mighty bone, in strength
Long moulder'd of barbaric majesty.
I called upon the darkness; and it took,
A midnight darkness seem'd to come and take
All objects from my sight; and lo! again
The desert visible by dismal flames!
It is the sacrificial Altar, fed
With living men, how deep the groans, the voice
Of those in the gigantic wicker thrills
Throughout the region far and near, pervades
The monumental hillocks; and the pomp
Is for both worlds, the living and the dead.   [1805, 12.312–36]

This is the fear. The mere entertaining of the hope (1850: "To a hope / Not less ambitious once among the wilds / Of Sarum's Plain, my youthful spirit was raised . . ." [13.312–14]) brings as its mental consequence a vision of archaic sacrifice. The features of the spot syndrome are here—losing the guide ("without a track / To guide me"), the bare dreariness of the roads. But no properly visionary salience intervenes to discharge the coming intimations of death in perception or to keep Wordsworth from being overwhelmed by solitude. First, "reverie," which yields the past in its utter, archaic discontinuity ("Our dim ancestral Past in vision clear" [13.320]). Following hard on this, the very gesture of the Druid-magus:

> I called on Darkness—but before the word
> Was uttered, midnight darkness seemed to take
> All objects from my sight; and lo! again
> The Desert visible by dismal flames;
> It is the sacrificial alter. . . .   [13.327–31]

Wordsworth *summons* Darkness; *he* performs the incantation, and he is moved to it by a vision of the absolute past, in which power is alienated in time ("Long moulder'd") and different in kind ("of barbaric majesty") from the "power like one of Nature's" he had just hoped for. His word is omnific, fulfilled even before it is uttered, and its fulfillment is the sacrifice, the universal, propitiatory symbol which unites "both worlds, the living and the dead."

The Salisbury vision exhibits with stunning clarity Wordsworth's ambivalent relation to the archaic power of the Word. He is in part the victim of the vision; there is naiveté in his incantation; he doesn't know what will follow. But he also participates in the power, assuming the ancient role as if it were his inevitable due. That the vision presents such a contrast to his self-conception as a poet serves to expose the partiality of that conception, though not its sincerity. The repeated plea to Coleridge ("Dearest Friend, / Forgive me") and the self-abnegation, nervous and overdone ("forgive me, Friend, / If I, the meanest of this Band, had hope . . . that in some sort I possess'd / A privilege"), signal not false modesty, but fear of his own strong claim to power—and of its terrifying claim on him. After all, in such passages Coleridge stands for something within Wordsworth, who needs his own forgiveness. But it is the sequence rather than the tone which argues for Wordsworth's doubled perception of the "influx" and its cost. His ambition, consecrated to a grateful imitation of Nature's power, is betrayed by the very *idea* of power into darkness, the nonnatural or supernatural locus of power. Part of Wordsworth's greatness as a poet is the way he consistently realizes as literal episode the unconscious, figurative structure of his thought.

We associate the Wordsworthian darkness with the early work and the crisis of the poet's twenties. *The Borderers*, for example, turns elaborately if somewhat unconvincingly upon an expiatory sacrifice and the assumption of guilt, which are supposed to be an initiation into power. Marmaduke is betrayed, but clearly the program of Oswald's dark sublime engages obscure compulsions and deep inevitabilities within him. "Power," says Wallace of Oswald, "is life to him / And breath and being" (3.1432–33), and it is power that Marmaduke involuntarily seeks in his acquiescence to Oswald. What he finds is overwhelming guilt, which he, unlike Oswald, is learning to bear at the close of the play. The crisis richly sounded in this play and in the work, like *Guilt and Sorrow*, of the same period seems to have a generic status.

Even Wordsworth's descents to gothic claptrap are charged with the resonance of his mediate historical position, and this is so from the beginning. Twenty-five lines into *The Vale of Esthwaite* the essential pattern appears:

> At noon I hied to gloomy glades,
> Religious woods and midnight shades,
> Where brooding Superstition frown'd
> A cold and awful horror round,
> While with black arm and bending head
> She wove a stole of sable thread.
> And hark! the ringing harp I hear
> And lo! her druid sons appear.
> Why roll on me your glaring eyes?
> Why fix on me for sacrifice?   [25–34][18]

The poet initiates a movement to the darkness specifically of superstition, and this search for a chilling thrill coincides with a quest for the source of poetic power. (The terrifying harps of *The Vale* are eventually named as "the poet's harp of yore" [l. 335].) He finds the power all right, and its immediate aspect of sacrifice. Observe, in the continuation, the mode of his saving enlightenment:

> But he, the stream's loud genius, seen
> The black arch'd boughs and rocks between
> That brood o'er one eternal night,
> Shoots from the cliff in robe of white.   [35–38]

"*But* he": the threatening, archaic druids are naturalized, *seen* (eventually as a stream) through the mediate idea of the *genius loci*; in another manuscript the transition from sound to sight, from ghost to landscape, is less secure, for "the stream's loud genius" is "the torrent's yelling spectre." The venturing into terror followed by a saving sharpness of sight (prototype of the imagination's salience) already dominates the structure of *The Vale*, as a kind of systole and diastole. At such moments Wordsworth seems to recapitulate and perform the Enlightenment all on his own.

The early Wordsworth can here only be invoked, not responsibly reviewed. The material is far too rich and extensive for an interlude. Moreover, our central subject is not the themes of the Wordsworthian darkness but the dialectical role of that darkness in occasioning and charging the recoil of extraordinary seeing which Wordsworth names "Imagination." Our structure invites us to consider two movements, as it were, within it; these movements correspond to two phases of a quest, as well as to the opposed directions taken by the argument of *The Prelude* and its implicit therapy, its search for efficacious spirit. First, there is a movement *toward* power, from image to symbol, from ordinary seeing, through self-consciousness (ambition), to the locus or spot of power, manifested in a symbol of sacrifice and guilt. Second, there is a movement, the Imagination's proper movement, *away* from power, from symbol back to image: this is the humanizing direction Wordsworth consciously celebrates in his claim that the Imagination is redemptive.

Wordsworth wants to persuade himself and us that the second movement is the genuine one for mind, for the mind so conceived will feed on power without being threatened or annihilated by it. In the climax of this movement at Snowdon we are given

> . . . the emblem of a mind
> That feeds upon infinity, that broods
> Over the dark abyss, intent to hear
> Its voices issuing forth to silent light
> In one continuous stream. . . .   [14.70–74]

The mind with this intent will hear the astounding roar of "torrents, streams / Innumerable" mounting through the "fixed, abysmal, gloomy, breathing-place" to be converted into sight (14.58–60). In 1805 the emblem was

> The perfect image of a mighty Mind,
> Of one that feeds upon infinity,
> That is exalted by an under-presence,
> The sense of God, or whatso'er is dim
> Or vast in its own being. . . .   [1805, 13.69–73]

The Godhead and the unconscious depths are here significantly allied as the "under-presence," of source and tendency unknown, which powers the mind into its exaltation. The search for power enters the abyss, the "deep and gloomy breathing-place" or "dark deep thoroughfare" (1805, 13.57, 64), from the opposite direction and with the intent not of converting power into exaltation but of finding the voice absolutely strong, the archaic voice of the Godhead.

No doubt Wordsworth does persuade himself and us. But we remain haunted by what still haunts him, and we know that the dark passage leads in both directions. If Wordsworth could, as Keats said, "shed a light" in those dark passages, he was also strong enough to call on Darkness. The paradox thus roughly thrust into view is that Wordsworth's search for efficacious power was opposed to the humanizing originality which was his historical opportunity and necessity. The Snowdon vision does not cancel the opposite motion of the spots of time. We read poetry both for the exaltation of wisdom and for the renovation of power, and I, for one, would not know how to choose between the two.

Crossing the Threshold

Of all the "passages of life" recorded and explored in *The Prelude*, the Simplon Pass passage in book 6 is the most spectacular.[19] It looms up in the middle of the poem, unforeseen but somehow inevitable, a paradigm of the Wordsworthian threshold and hence the very type of Romantic transcendence. And yet within this passage lurks perplexity which seems to resist the light of interpretation.

Wordsworth's recollection approaches his memory of the Simplon Pass with some foreboding. He comes to it naturally enough in the course of retracing the walking tour he and Robert Jones had taken through the Alps in the summer of 1790. In what he calls "the eye and progress of my Song" (1805, 6.526), his day in the Simplon Pass (August 16) follows the Grande Chartreuse, Mont Blanc, and Chamounix, as it had on the tour, but something distinguishes it in his recollection, a "dejection," a "deep and genuine sadness" (1805, 6.491–92). In lines (6.562 ff.) conspicuously matter-of-fact (considering what is to follow), he describes how he and Jones had mounted up the rugged road of Simplon and stopped for lunch. Here they were rather hastily abandoned by their muleteer guides, and when they resumed their hike the path led downward to a stream and seemed to go no further. Deliberating awhile, they crossed the stream and took a path that pointed upward, but after climbing for an hour and a half or so "anxious fears" beset them, and they began to realize that they were lost. They met a peasant who confirmed their fears and worse: he told them they had to return to the perplexing spot and then go downwards, following the stream. Without knowing it, they had already crossed the summit; evidently it was a cloudy, rainy day, and the heights were obscured. Their immense disappointment at this news is the "sadness" still alive in the mind of the poet as he remembers and writes fourteen years later.

> Loth to believe what we so grieved to hear,
> For still we had hopes that pointed to the clouds,
> We questioned him again, and yet again;
> But every word that from the peasant's lips
> Came in reply, translated by our feelings,
> Ended in this,—*that we had crossed the Alps.*   [6.586–91]

But they hadn't really "crossed" the Alps; the most difficult stretch, the treacherous defile of Gondo Gorge, lay just ahead, though downwards. The tidings of the peasant had depressed them, but "The dull and heavy slackening . . . Was soon dislodg'd" (1805, 6.549–61): in the mixed metaphor, power or energy emigrates from their suddenly relaxed will and acts as if from without upon their mental state, which is now an obstacle to be "dislodg'd." Yet at first the power seems still theirs, for they act precipitously:

> . . . downwards we hurried fast,
> And enter'd with the road which we had miss'd
> Into a narrow chasm; the brook and road
> Were fellow-travellers in this gloomy Pass,
> And with them did we journey several hours
> At a slow step.   [1805, 6.551–56]

Their hurrying downward is checked; they must submit to the pace of brook and road, their new guides. Losing their former guides, they had "paced the beaten downward way" (l. 568) and had come to a perplexing spot (l. 580) where "After little scruple, and short pause" (1805, l. 507) they had made an error. They had failed to read the perplexing spot correctly—to recognize their new "fellow-travellers"—choosing instead to follow "hopes that pointed to the clouds," a kind of impulse toward origins and ultimates in contrast to the possibility of the stream intercepted in mid course. Their "crossing" of the "unbridged stream" was premature—an unwitting evasion, under the aegis of hope, of the larger crossing (of the Alps) in which they were engaged.

The text that follows has become such a set piece of the sublime that a special effort is required to recover its contextual or experiential dimension. Max Wildi's photographic reconstruction of the fateful hours spent in the Gorge of Gondo makes the travelers' lack of anticipation or forewarning plausible enough.[20] What is less clear is how, with the memory of the spectacular ravine in mind, Wordsworth in 1804 could have approached the Simplon adventure possessed by the "deep and genuine sadness" of his disappointment. There is a genuine problem here, the tip of an iceberg, I think; but even apart from perplexities of sequence the passages offers a difficult grandeur. This is simply not the way Wordsworth writes or thinks, not his kind of greatness:

> The immeasurable height
> Of woods decaying, never to be decayed,
> The stationary blasts of waterfalls,
> And in the narrow rent at every turn
> Winds thwarting winds, bewildered and forlorn,
> The torrents shooting from the clear blue sky,
> The rocks that muttered close upon our ears,
> Black drizzling crags that spake by the way-side
> As if a voice were in them, the sick sight
> And giddy prospect of the raving stream,
> The unfettered clouds and region of the Heavens,
> Tumult and peace, the darkness and the light—
> Were all like workings of one mind, the features
> Of the same face, blossoms upon one tree;
> Characters of the great Apocalypse,
> The types and symbols of Eternity,
> Of first, and last, and midst, and without end.   [6.624–40]

The aspect of Eternity checks and supersedes the evidence of things seen, so that the image of process, change, or motion evokes and indeed signifies its supratemporal contrary. The woods themselves are decaying, but decay itself is eternal: in the aspect of Eternity there is no past or future tense. Water itself falls, but falling itself is "stationary." The elements of nature come and go, passing through the *order* of nature which, abstracted, is Eternity.

The order of Eternity is synchronic, and what Wordsworth earlier calls "the speaking face of earth and heaven" (5.13) participates in that order not substantially, but typologically or symbolically—insofar as, image becoming symbol, phenomena are *read*. At the "level" of perception—at once the human, the imaginative, and the natural domain—things confound themselves ("Winds thwarting winds, bewildered and forlorn"), confusing the perceiver. But this very confusion signifies oneness ("one mind . . . the same face . . . one tree"). Signification here, as always, is not "natural" in the sense that the image participates its meaning: nothing in the self-thwarting winds or in "Tumult and peace, the darkness and the light" conduces perceptionally to oneness. Hence the passage cannot be read phenomenologically, as we nearly always read Wordsworth. We are oddly closer to the Mutability Cantos than to the Snowdon vision. In any case, we are outside the precincts of Imagination, whose conferring, abstracting, and modifying powers—"alternations proceeding from, and governed by, a sublime consciousness of the soul in her own mighty and almost divine powers"[21]—are always transitive operations upon the initially visible, though they may lead to infinitude. The structure of the passage is not immanence but double vision, with the leap of signification between its two terms. This massive sentence pivots rhetorically upon a highly deliberate simile, which itself subverts the metaphoric potentialities of perception.

For the one mind, face, tree, signified in the landscape is not in any meaningful sense human, nor is it here claimed as human possibility. The allusions to the Godhead, biblical and Miltonic, are unusually direct: this is the only occurrence of the word "Apocalypse" in Wordsworth's poetry, and he ends the passage by aligning it conspicuously with Adam and Eve's morning hymn to the Creator, "Him first, him last, him midst, and without end" (PL 5.165). Perhaps an aggressive humanism such as Hegel's could here claim the Godhead as its own archaic aspect, but that is just the claim the poet himself foregoes. In a letter to Dorothy three weeks after his experience of the Gorge, Wordsworth comes in his narrative to the Simplon Pass and remarks that "the impressions of three hours of our walk among the Alps will never be effaced." At the lake of Como, he goes on to say, he felt "complacency of Spirit . . . a thousand dreams of happiness" associated with the "social affections," and it was impossible not to contrast this mood "with the sensations I had experienced two or three days before, in passing the Alps. . . . Among the more awful scenes of the Alps, I had not a thought of man, or a single created being; my whole soul was turned to him who produced the terrible majesty before me."[22] Nothing in The Prelude text suggests that his soul is not still so turned toward the Godhead as he remembers the event and writes some years later.

The passage may strike us as archaic not only in its embrace of traditional ontology but also in its surprising lack of self-consciousness. In the style, for example: the Shakespearean doublets ("the sick sight / And giddy prospect of the raving stream, / The unfettered clouds and region of the Heavens") suggest an amplitude which retards the progress toward climax by detemporalizing it, so that the order of description already subtly leaves the chronicle of experience for the reflective order of Eternity. The climax itself—

Tumult and peace, the darkness and the light—
Were all like . . .

—is not revelation, a lifting of the mask, but the merest sliding over the threshold into interpretation. The mounting rhythm of perception is then discharged in the subsequent phrases and the very variety of alternatives they enlist: "workings . . . features . . . blossoms . . . Characters . . . types and symbols." In a sense, however, the perceptional *gradatio* is illusory, for the interpretative (symbolic) order has already been the aspect of these images: "were all along like" rather than "now suddenly became." In style as well as in thought the "I"—with its characteristic effect of making the progress of the verse the very dramatic progress of a consciousness—has disappeared. Not Wordsworth's kind of greatness.

We wonder, in fact, where the "I" has gone. What kind of experience, after all, is it for the travelers? The strait is "gloomy" (622); in the night to come, "innocent sleep" will "Lie melancholy among weary bones" (6.647–48). De Selincourt finds here an echo of the horror of the regicide Macbeth ("Methought, I heard a voice cry, 'Sleep no more! / Macbeth does murder Sleep,'—the innocent Sleep;"[23]), but that dark suggestion seems to me dubious. Evidently something terrible did happen on that day or night. In 1820, with Dorothy and Mary in tow, Wordsworth revisited the "dreary mansion" where he and Jones had spent that night. Dorothy refers in her journal to the "awful night" of thirty years before and adds mysteriously that the two travelers were "unable to sleep from other causes" than the deafening roar to which *The Prelude* account ascribes their insomnia. She felt a strong desire to know this place, but Wordsworth could not be persuaded to accompany her within. He refused to enter.[24] Wildi concludes that the youth had suffered "some kind of traumatic experience"[25]—which is to say that we don't know and no doubt never will. But the biographical mystery need not distract us from what *may* be its refraction in the blank of soul, the absence of self-consciousness, that the passage about types and symbols exhibits.

It is difficult to see in any case how the three hours spent in the ravine—gloomy, terrifying, and spectacular as we know it to have been—could have slipped Wordsworth's mind in his preoccupation, fourteen years later, with the "dejection," the "deep and genuine sadness," of his disappointment at Simplon. We hear nothing of this disappointment in the contemporary letter to Dorothy, which twice verbally associates the *passing of the Alps* with the sensations and impressions, never to be effaced, of Gondo Gorge. Wildi's reconstruction of the fateful afternoon shows how immediately the gorge follows the actual summit of the pass—a matter of a few minutes, if they hadn't taken the wrong path; the two halves of the total crossing could not have been disjoined in a memory fourteen years later without a powerful secondary motive.

I propose, therefore, that the remembered disappointment—"*that we had crossed the Alps*"—is in fact a screen memory drastically inflated (if not created) in order to block the emergence of the deeper, more terrifying and traumatic memory of Gondo Gorge. The structure of the remembered disappointment and its details—pacing the downward way, crossing the unbridged stream, attempting to translate and interpret the speech of the peasant—suggest that it is a wishful parody of the larger actual crossing, the passing through the gorge itself. Hence the phrase, *that we had crossed the Alps*, with its signal emphasis, fulfills a wish under the mask of a disappointment—the wish to have already passed or crossed the defile looming subliminally before the "eye and progress" of the retrospective song. Probably Wordsworth did meet a peasant and was disappointed, but the experience has been retrospectively augmented and seems to be attracting to itself the emotional valence ("anxious fears") we might have expected to be associated with the gorge. Indeed, if we are prepared to read Wordsworth with the psychological sophistication he invites, we should have to view somewhat sceptically the very matter-of-fact clarity in his memory of getting lost. Not merely the significance of the memory emerged as he was writing in 1804. The memory itself *may* have been formed at this time—to what degree we certainly cannot tell, though we can speculate with more assurance that the affective quality of the event, the deep sadness, came into being retrospectively.

Yet this hypothesis must be cleared of several apparent objections. That the very "impressions" the traveler Wordsworth said would "never be effaced" should much later have been temporarily blocked ought to cause us no difficulty unless we insist absurdly that a man of thirty-four remain consistent to the predictions of his twenty-first year; moreover, those impressions were not in any sense effaced, but displaced and momentarily repressed. (In this connection it is curious that the Ravine of Gondo is conspicuously absent from *Descriptive Sketches* [composed 1791–92], which covers nearly everything else on the Alpine tour: perhaps the "blocking" began thus early.) A second difficulty has a more substantial aspect. In 1845 Wordsworth published the "Characters of the great Apocalypse" passage (6.621–40) under the title "The Simplon Pass," and gave 1799 as the date of its composition.[26] By 1845, however, Wordsworth was notoriously unreliable about dates. De Selincourt was justly sceptical, and Wordsworth's most exact chronologist has since concluded that the passage was probably composed in 1804, in sequence with the rest of book 6.[27] The passage is entirely unlike anything

Wordsworth wrote in 1799, and there is no evidence to corroborate the guess of the poet nearly half a century later.[28] Moreover, if "The Simplon Pass" was composed in 1799, the deep disappointment remembered by the poet as his song approached the pass becomes still harder to explain, and in a sense the hypothesis of a screen memory would be plausible *a fortiori*.

A third objection is indeed substantial, for it has been dramatized by the very course of our analysis. We found in the "Characters" passage a notable absence of self-consciousness, a soul turned wholly toward the original Maker and the terrible majesty of his signifying creation. Yet we have argued that the poet's actual impressions of Gondo Gorge were traumatic enough to have caused their threatened emergence to be blocked by a memory of disappointment. Can these two readings possibly be reconciled? We should have to suppose that for Wordsworth the greatest threat was the experience which denied him the possibility of self-consciousness.

We have already come to such a supposition following the path of theory through the negative sublime. We may recall that the sensible imagination (here the mental eye of retrospection) is checked in an experience of exhaustion or terror as it attempts to comprehend the relative infinity of phenomena. An "identification" with the higher power—ultimately with the Godhead—is required in order to cross the threshold into the domain of the supersensible, and this identification requires the suppression or turning against the narcissistic self-consciousness associated with perception. Hence the sensible imagination is depressed; it feels a sacrifice or deprivation of its "hopes that pointed to the clouds." Such, at any rate, was Kant's theory, and it helped us to locate the terror precisely at the threshold of the supersensible—*sublimen*, as the etymology oddly (and no doubt fortuitously) confirms: the ego is terrified into annihilating its sensible portion. In Burke and elsewhere we found the structure of the negative sublime converging with the drama of poetic influence, which finds its archetype in the relation of the human imagination to the "Omnific Word," the absolute originality, of the Godhead. In the light of this theory, here too roughly reprised, we can speculate about the grounds of Wordsworth's terror. To reenter Gondo Gorge in memory would have exposed him to the extinction of the self-consciousness with which he identified imagination and originality. To remember a disappointment, however, enabled this threat to be usurped and displaced and had as well the advantage, as we must now proceed to appreciate, of confirming his consciousness of self.

Yet the objection still points to two readings of the event, and still carries force. It has merely been reformulated, not answered. For evidently, Wordsworth was *not* halted at the threshold of the symbolic order, even by his own screen memory. He did cross the passage through the types and symbols of eternity. It is no longer possible to suppress what may be the most important element of the whole sequence, the astonishing intervention between *"that we had cross'd the Alps"* (1805, 6.524) and "The dull and heavy slackening that ensued / Upon those tidings by the Peasant given / Was soon dislog'd" (1805, 6.549–51). As he remembers and writes in 1804 Wordsworth is suddenly interrupted:

> Imagination! lifting up itself
> Before the eye and progress of my Song
> Like an unfather'd vapour; here that Power,
> In all the might of its endowments, came
> Athwart me; I was lost as in a cloud,
> Halted, without a struggle to break through.
> And now recovering, to my Soul I say
> I recognise thy glory. . . .   [1805, 6.525–32]

The "eye and progress" of the song is nothing more or less than the mental journey of retrospection which we know is just on the verge of coming to Gondo Gorge. The Imagination rises athwart this progress: this can only be a moment, how long we do not know, of amnesia. The memory of the next steps, the fateful hours in Gondo Gorge, is blocked again, more directly and violently. It is as if the screen memory of disappointment were not enough, as if it did not work: the Imagination operates first *through* memory, and then, this failing, *against* memory, and with such intensity as to occlude sight. The Imagination rises in flight from the Word; or (in another metaphor) in resistance to the showing forth of the Word. We have seen the pattern before, in the spots of time passages and in particular in the boy's flight from the "Characters . . . fresh and visible" (12.245) which signified a death and a sacrifice.

What then is this "awful Power" which Wordsworth names "Imagination"? In the late version, Wordsworth will tell us that the power is "so called / Through sad incompetence of human speech" (6.592–93), but the name is of course entirely right, for the power of sight does rise in intensity from memory through salience to the occlusion of the visible. The Imagination may be structurally defined as a power of resistance to the Word, and in this sense it coincides exactly with the psychological necessity of originality. But a structural definition merely locates an experience; as an experience or moment the Imagination is an extreme consciousness of self mounting in dialectical recoil from the extinguishing of the self which an imminent identification with the symbolic order enjoins. Hence the Imagination rises "Like an unfather'd vapour": it is at once the ego's need and its attempt to be *unfathered*, to originate itself and thereby refuse acknowledgment to a superior power. The Imagination is not an evasion of the oedipus complex but a rejection of it. From a certain perspective (such perspective, for example, as is implied by the history of poetic influence) that rejection is purely illusory, a fiction. To reject the oedipus complex is not, after all, to dispel it. But the fiction is a necessary and saving one; it founds the self and secures the possibility—the chance for a self-conviction—of originality. And so Wordsworth can turn to his "conscious soul" (1850) and say, "I recognise thy glory."

We might speculate along lines suggested by Harold Bloom in *The Anxiety of Influence* that something like the distortion evident in the construction of a screen memory characterizes the poet's first line of defense against the identification which would absorb him into his precursor. But the Imagination as it is defined dramatically in the Simplon sequence is the poet's ultimate defense, the final foundation of his individuality. Hence it is the expression of a wish deeper than anxiety, an answer, therefore, to terror. Wordsworth was "Halted, without a struggle to break through" (1805, 6.530): he made no "effort" (1850) to break through because the usurpation answered a need deeper than the rhythm of his retrospective progress; such defenses are final. In life, it is our defenses that enable us to exist and therefore to create; so in poetry, the fiction of originality founds a poet. That the critic must be aware of the dialectical, "negative" structure of originality is precisely what separates his perspective from the poet's. For the critic the fiction of originality can never be a final term, but this situation does not render the power of the founding fiction any the less efficacious.

The Imagination's usurpation issues for Wordsworth in triumphant self-recognition and self-vindication: "to my Soul I say / I recognise thy glory." The lines which follow spill over from this climatic moment, and they are justly celebrated. But they need to be read as a response not only to the remembered disappointment but also to the anxiety of self-effacement associated with the memory of Gondo Gorge, the memory the Imagination rose to occlude. We need to recover the "negativity" of these lines, the presence in them of what is being magnificently denied:

> . . . in such strength
> Of usurpation, when the light of sense
> Goes out, but with a flash that has revealed
> The invisible world, doth greatness make abode,

> There harbours; whether we be young or old,
> Our destiny, our being's heart and home,
> Is with infinitude, and only there;
> With hope it is, hope that can never die,
> Effort, and expectation, and desire,
> And something evermore about to be.
> Under such banners militant, the soul
> Seeks for no trophies, struggles for no spoils
> That may attest her prowess, blest in thoughts
> That are their own perfection and reward,
> Strong in herself and in beatitude
> That hides her, like the mighty flood of Nile
> Poured from his fount of Abyssinian clouds
> To fertilise the whole Egyptian plain.   [6.599–616]

Where the usurpation is strong, there "greatness" lies; not in the "invisible world" itself, but this side of the supersensible threshold, in a domain properly human. Yet the movement here, from the "light of sense" through the blinding usurpation of Imagination to infinitude, somehow evades or leaps over the mediating signs or characters which abide at the threshold. This is the unmediated path of imagination, from sight to the invisible without the necessity of a signifier. Phenomena can drop away without first becoming signs: Eternity without types and symbols, apocalypse without the characters. Following this path the soul has no anxiety of originality, it "Seeks for no trophies, struggles for no spoils / That may attest her prowess," because it is "Strong in herself" and because the affective exaltation of the self, its beatitude" or "access of joy" (1805) "hides" the soul. "Hides" hints ever so slightly at the necessity of a fiction sustained by joy, without which the soul would lie like a barren plain.[29]

But we cannot expect a poet to subvert his own most fortunate and saving illusion, and the passage is overwhelmingly positive in its claims and its tone. Hence it is that Wordsworth's amnesia is dispelled, and he could go on to Gondo Gorge. The terror of that defile has been answered; with such assurance behind him he could confront and momentarily disappear before the awful characters. In a way the "types and symbols" passage returns to answer and deny the great claims born of Imagination, as it had itself been answered by the Imagination. No moment of consciousness unites the two passages, or the two kinds of greatness they imply. They remain dialectically confronted, side by side in the center of Wordsworth's greatest poem, the positive and negative poles of the Romantic sublime.

Notes

1. Approaching the Romantic Sublime

1. The *Peri Hypsous* is quoted from the translation of W. Rhys Roberts, *Longinus on the Sublime*, 2d ed. (Cambridge, 1907); all reference is to this edition. There are several contemporary translations, such as that by D. A. Russell (Oxford, 1964) and G. M. A. Grube's version, *On Great Writing* (Indianapolis, 1957); the latter is usefully prosaic where Roberts is grandiloquent.

2. Friedrich von Schiller, "On the Sublime," in *Naive and Sentimental Poetry and On the Sublime: Two Essays*, trans. Julius A. Elias (New York, 1966), p. 210.

3. For a clear exposition of Longinus' mimesis and of the philosophical matrix of the *Peri Hypsous*, see Charles P. Segal, "ΥΨΟΣ and the Problem of Cultural Decline in the *De Sublimitate*," *Harvard Studies in Classical Philology*, 64 (1959), 121–46.

4. Neil Hertz, "Lecture de Longin," *Poetique: revue de théorie et d'analyse littéraires*, 15 (1973), 303.

5. S. H. Monk, *The Sublime: A Study of Critical Theories in Eighteenth-Century England* (New York, 1935). For a valuable, concentrated reading of the sublime and the poetry it directly inspired, see Martin Price, "The Sublime Poem: Pictures and Powers," *Yale Review*, 58 (1969), 194–213.

6. Among many studies see especially Ernest Tuveson, "Space Deity, and the 'Natural Sublime'," *Modern Language Quarterly*, 12 (1951), 20–38; Marjorie Nicolson, *Mountain Gloom and Mountain Glory: The Development of the Aesthetics of the Infinite* (Ithaca, N.Y., 1959); and David B. Morris, *The Religious Sublime: Christian Poetry and Critical Tradition in Eighteenth-Century England* (Lexington, Ky., 1972).

7. See Nicholas Taylor, "The Awful Sublimity of the Victorian City: The Aesthetic and Architectural Origins," in *The Victorian City: Images and Realities*, ed. H. J. Dyos and Michael Wolff, 2 vols. (Boston, 1973), II, 431–47 and illustrations nos. 296–337. Taylor correlates architectural effects with Burke's theory of the sublime. This architecture, still so much a part of our cities, seems to me to institutionalize the alienation which is the source of the "political" sublime.

8. Friedrich Nietzsche, *Beyond Good and Evil: Prelude to a Philosophy of the Future*, trans. Walter Kaufmann (New York, 1966), p. 42.

9. Geoffery Chaucer, *Troilus and Criseide*, 5.1815–16.

10. *The Journals and Miscellaneous Notebooks of Ralph Waldo Emerson*, vol. VII, ed. A. W. Plumstead and Harrison Hayford (Cambridge, Mass., 1969), 303.

11. See *Milton* 1.10:6–11, in *The Poetry and Prose of William Blake*, ed. David V. Erdman (Garden City, N.Y., 1965); Blake's writings are quoted subsequently from this edition, cited hereafter as E.

12. "Analytic of the Sublime," in *Kant's Critique of Aesthetic Judgement*, trans. J. C. Meredith (Oxford, 1911), p. 128.

13. W. Jackson Bate, *The Burden of the Past and the English Poet* (Cambridge, Mass., 1970; rpt. New York, 1972); Harold Bloom, *The Anxiety of Influence: A Theory of Poetry* (New York, 1973); many of the studies in Geoffrey Hartman's *Beyond Formalism: Literary Essays, 1958–1970* (New Haven, 1970) are concerned with the poet's struggle with tradition; see also Thomas McFarland, "The Originality Paradox," *New Literary History*, 5 (Spring 1974), 447–76.

14. Morris provides a full reading of Dennis and an argument for his importance in *The Religious Sublime*, pp. 47–78.

15. Edmund Burke, *A Philosophical Enquiry into the Origin of Our Ideas of the Sublime and Beautiful*, ed. James T. Boulton (London, 1958), p. 54. This edition is

used for all subsequent quotation from Burke; Boulton's extensive introduction ranks with Monk's account as a history of the idea of the sublime.

16. As Byron says in the "Dedication" to *Don Juan*, time made "the word 'Miltonic' mean *'sublime'* " (st. 10), and Milton's presence in the eighteenth century has been studied in dozens of books, the most basic of which is still Raymond D. Havens' *The Influence of Milton on English Poetry* (Cambridge, Mass., 1922); see Morris, *The Religious Sublime*, pp. 66–71 and passim, and of the older studies, Arthur Barker," '. . . And on his crest sat Horror': Eighteenth-Century Interpretations of Milton's Sublimity and His Satan," *University of Toronto Quarterly*, 11 (1942), 421–36.

17. Bloom, *The Anxiety of Influence*, pp. 19–24 and passim.

18. Milton's poems are quoted from the Longmans edition, *The Poems of John Milton*, ed. John Carey and Alastair Fowler (London, 1968); *Paradise Lost* is abbreviated *PL*.

19. Bate, *The Burden of the Past*, p. 129.

20. Burke, *Of the Sublime and Beautiful*, pp. 50–51.

21. The relation between terror (and the somewhat different horror) and the supernatural has been fully studied by Patricia Meyer Spacks, *The Insistence of Horror: Aspects of the Supernatural in Eighteenth-Century Poetry* (Cambridge, Mass., 1962); this study is especially good on the change from a religious to an affective rationale for the aesthetic of terror.

22. R. S. Crane, *Philological Quarterly*, 15 (1936), 165–67.

23. *The Spectator*, ed. Donald F. Bond, 5 vols. (Oxford, 1965), III, esp. p. 539 (no. 411).

24. Kant, "Analytic of the Sublime," p. 91.

25. See Tuveson, "Space, Deity, and the 'Natural Sublime'," and *The Imagination as a Means of Grace: Locke and the Aesthetics of Romanticism* (Berkeley and Los Angeles, 1960).

26. In *Mountain Gloom and Mountain Glory*, Nicolson incorporated Tuveson's early work and argued that the natural sublime preceded the introduction of the rhetorical sublime and was religious in origin (pp. 29 n., 30, 143).

27. John Baillie, *Essay on the Sublime* (London, 1747), pp. 6–7, quoted in Monk, *The Sublime*, p. 74.

28. John Locke *An Essay concerning Human Understanding*, ed. A. C. Fraser, 2 vols. (Oxford, 1894; rpt. New York, 1959), II, 140.

29. Ibid., pp. 162–64.

30. For an analysis of the adjectival diction of sublimity, see Josephine Miles, "The Sublime Poem," in *Eras and Modes in English Poetry* (Berkeley and Los Angeles, 1957), pp. 48–77.

31. Burke, *Of the Sublime and Beautiful*, p. 173.

32. Ibid., pp. 60–62.

33. Monk, *The Sublime*, p. 75.

34. Subsequent quotation from Fraser's edition of Locke, *Essay concerning Human Understanding*, I, 332–40 (book 2, chap. 21, secs. 31–41).

35. For the revisions in Locke's fourth edition which anticipate the modern notion of the unconscious, see Tuveson, "Locke and the 'Dissolution of the Ego'," *Modern Philology*, 52, no. 3 (1955), 159–74.

36. Burke, *Of the Sublime and Beautiful*, p. 31.

37. *Peri Bathous: or, Of the Art of Sinking in Poetry* (1727), in *Alexander Pope: Selected Poetry and Prose*, ed. W. K. Wimsatt, 2d ed. (New York, 1972), p. 382.

38. Ibid., p. 381.

39. On the rhetorical underpinnings and strategy of *The Dunciad*, see Aubrey L. Williams, *Pope's Dunciad: A Study of Its Meaning* (1955, rpt. Hamden, Conn., 1968), chap. 5.

40. Samuel Taylor Coleridge, *Biographia Literaria*, ed. J. Shawcross, 2 vols. (Ox-

ford, 1907), II, 109–10. Of Wordsworth's fault, incidentally, "none but a man of genius is capable."

41. "I Wandered Lonely as a Cloud," ll. 17–18, *The Poetical Works of William Wordsworth*, ed. Ernest De Selincourt and Helen Darbishire, 5 vols. (Oxford, 1940–49), II, 216. Wordsworth's poems are quoted from this edition, cited hereafter as *PWW*.

42. Paul Goodman, *The Structure of Literature* (Chicago, 1954), pp. 253–54, 276.

43. Prussian Academy edition of *Kant's gesammelte Schriften*, 22 vols. (Berlin, 1900–1942), V, 268.

44. Kant, "Analytic of the Sublime," p. 91.

45. Ibid., p. 120.

46. Northrop Frye, "The Romantic Myth," in *A Study of English Romanticism* (New York, 1968), pp. 3–49.

47. Kant, "Analytic of the Sublime," pp. 94, 107.

48. Semiotics has many sources in classical thought—and in Locke—but was first postulated as a general science of signs by Ferdinand de Saussure in 1916. It is rapidly becoming a technical and somewhat imperialistic discipline, to which a recent survey in the *Times Literary Supplement* (October 5 and 12, 1973) attests. The terms used here are elementary and derived mainly from Saussure, *Course in General Linguistics*, ed. Charles Bally and Albert Sechehaye, trans. Wade Baskin (New York, 1959), and Roland Barthes, *Elements of Semiology*, trans. Annette Lavers and Colin Smith (Boston, 1970).

49. Burke, *Of the Sublime and Beautiful*, p. 82.

50. Northrop Frye, *Anatomy of Criticism: Four Essays* (Princeton, 1957), p. 124. Frye is discussing the anagogic aspect of meaning, the "radical form" of metaphor.

51. Geoffrey Hartman, *Wordsworth's Poetry, 1787–1814* (New Haven, 1964), p. 122 and passim.

52. Quotations from *The Prelude* 14.58; the Isabella Fenwick note to the "Intimations" Ode (*PWW*, IV, 463); *Prelude* 3.167. Wordsworth's *Prelude*, cited hereafter as *P*, will be quoted from the 1850 version in the edition of Ernest De Selincourt, rev. Helen Darbishire (Oxford, 1959), unless otherwise indicated.

53. See Barthes, *Elements of Semiology*, p. 77.

54. Bloom, *The Anxiety of Influence*, chap. 4.

55. Barthes, *Elements of Semiology*, p. 92.

56. Burke, *Of the Sublime and Beautiful*, p. 143.

57. Goodman, *The Structure of Literature*, p. 254.

58. "Tintern Abbey," ll. 93–102 (*PWW*, II, 261–62).

59. Roman Jakobson, "Two Aspects of Language and Two Types of Aphasic Disturbances," in Jakobson and Morris Halle, *Fundamentals of Language* (The Hague, 1956), pp. 55–82.

60. Ibid., p. 69, quoting Kurt Goldstein, *Language and Language Disturbances* (New York, 1948), p. 270.

61. The best brief discussion of sublimation is the article in the invaluable vocabulary of psychoanalysis by J. Laplanche and J.-B. Pontalis (Paris, 1967), recently translated by Donald Nicholson-Smith as *The Language of Psycho-analysis* (London, 1973), pp. 431–34. After reviewing scattered and inconclusive passages in Freud, the authors conclude that "the lack of a coherent theory of sublimation remains one of the lacunae in psycho-analytic thought." For earlier attempts at an overview, see Ernest Jones, "The Theory of Symbolism," in *Papers on Psychoanalysis*, 4th ed. (London, 1938), pp. 129–86; Edward Glover, "Sublimation, Substitution, and Social Anxiety" (1931), in *On the Early Development of Mind* (New York, 1956), pp. 130–59; and J. C. Flugel, "Sublimation: Its Nature and Conditions," in *Studies in Feeling and Desire* (London, 1955), pp. 1–48.

62. *PWW*, II, 239.

2. The Ethos of Alienation: Two Versions of Transcendence

1. Friedrich von Schiller, "On the Sublime," *Naive and Sentimental Poetry and On the Sublime: Two Essays*, trans. Julius A. Elias (New York, 1966), pp. 204–8.

2. Ruskin to Rev. Walter Brown (1843), in *The Literary Criticism of John Ruskin*, ed. Harold Bloom (Garden City, N.Y., 1965), p. 1.

3. S. H. Monk, *The Sublime: A Study of Critical Theories in Eighteenth-Century England* (New York, 1935), p. 6.

4. *Conversations of Goethe with Eckermann and Soret*, trans. John Oxenford (London, 1882), p. 242.

5. References within the text are to Meredith's translation of the Analytic and, where useful, to the Prussian Academy edition, *Kant's gesammelte Schriften*, 22 vols. (Berlin, 1900–1942); the "Analytik des Erhabenen" is in vol. V, 244–78. I have occasionally altered Meredith's version (e.g., "power" instead of "might" for *Macht*).

6. Friedrich von Schiller, *On the Aesthetic Education of Man*, trans. Reginald Snell (New York, 1965), p. 94.

7. Richard Payne Knight, *An Analytical Inquiry into the Principles of Taste* (London, 1805), pp. 374–75.

8. For the mainline Protestant tradition of hope, see Jürgen Moltmann, *Theology of Hope: On the Ground and Implications of a Christian Eschatology*, trans. J. W. Leitch (New York, 1967).

9. Lucien Goldmann, *Immanuel Kant*, trans. Robert Black (London, 1971); first published as *Mensche, Gemeinschaft, und Welt in der Philosophie Immanuel Kants* (Zurich, 1945). Goldmann's dissertation is heavily influenced by the idealist Marxism of George Lukacs and is somewhat tendentious, but it is a useful recovery of Kant as a whole from the emphases of the neo-Kantians.

10. Goldmann, *Immanuel Kant*, p. 192.

11. *PWW*, V, 3–6. The fragment, probably composed in the early spring of 1798, was first published at the end of the preface to the *Excursion* in 1814. For the three extant manuscripts, see M. H. Abrams, *Natural Supernaturalism: Tradition and Revolution in Romantic Literature* (New York, 1971), pp. 470–79.

12. "Annotations to Wordsworth's Preface to The Excursion . . . ," E, 655–56.

13. Marcuse holds that the effort to reduce or close the gap between art and reality is doomed to failure. The art which rebells against art "remains artistic without the negating power of art. To the degree to which it makes itself part of real life, it loses the transcendence which opposes art to the established order—it remains *immanent* in this order, one-dimensional, and thus succumbs to this order. Precisely its immediate 'life-quality' is the undoing of this anti-art, and of its appeal. It *moves* (literally and figuratively) here and now, within the existing universe, and it terminates in the frustrated outcry for its abrogation." Classical and Romantic art inspire "a profound uneasiness" because they belong to the past and seem to have lost their meaning. "Is it because this art is too sublime, because it substitutes for the real, living soul an 'intellectual,' metaphysical soul, and is therefore repressive? Or could it be *the other way around?*" See "Art and Revolution," in *Counterrevolution and Revolt* (Boston, 1972), pp. 101–2.

14. Schiller, "On the Sublime," pp. 208–11.

15. Keats to Richard Woodhouse, 27 October 1818, *The Letters of John Keats, 1814–1821*, ed. Hyder Edward Rollins, 2 vols. (Cambridge, Mass., 1958), I, 387.

16. Keats's poems are quoted from the Longmans edition, *The Poems of John Keats*, ed. Miriam Allott (London, 1970).

17. *Letters of John Keats*, I, 386–87.

18. Quotations from *The Collected Poems of Wallace Stevens* (New York, 1968), pp. 403–5.

19. "I Wandered Lonely as a Cloud," ll. 17–18 (*PWW*, II, 216).

20. Hegel's commentary on the sublime may be found in the *Vorlesungen über die Aesthetik*, ed. D. H. G. Hotho, Second Part, Subsection I, esp. chap. 2, in *Werke:*

Vollständige Ausgabe, 18 vols. [actually 21] (Berlin, 1832–45), XI, 391–547, esp. pp. 465–85; English translation by F. P. B. Osmaston, *The Philosophy of Fine Art,* 4 vols. (London, 1920), II, 7–168, esp. pp. 85–105.

21. Hegel, *Werke,* XI, 478; Osmaston, *The Philosophy of Fine Art,* II, 97.

22. Albert Wlecke, *Wordsworth and the Sublime* (Berkeley and Los Angeles, 1973), pp. 15–19.

23. "The Circus Animals' Desertion," *The Collected Poems of W. B. Yeats,* 3d. ed. (New York, 1956), p. 336.

24. *Karl Marx: Early Writings,* trans. T. B. Bottomore (New York, 1964), p. 115.

25. "Frost at Midnight," *Coleridge: Poetical Works,* Oxford Standard Authors, ed. E. H. Coleridge (London, 1912), pp. 240–42.

26. "Preface to *Poems* (1815)," in *Literary Criticism of William Wordsworth,* ed. Paul M. Zall (Lincoln, Nebr., 1966), pp. 149, 152.

27. See Stillinger's Riverside edition of Wordsworth, *Selected Poems and Prefaces* (Boston, 1965), p. 530.

28. Wordsworth, "Preface to *Poems* (1815)," pp. 148–49.

29. Ibid., p. 149.

3. Darkning Man: Blake's Critique of Transcendence

1. *The Collected Poems of Wallace Stevens* (New York, 1968), pp. 405–6.

2. *Essays by Ralph Waldo Emerson,* intro. Irwin Edman (New York, 1926), pp. 214, 216.

3. Emerson, *Essays,* p. 212.

4. The contradiction between Blake's aggressive preference for determinate outline and his rejection of Urizenic closure is the subject of a useful recent study by Anne Kostelanetz Mellor, *Blake's Human Form Divine* (Berkeley and Los Angeles, 1974).

5. For a suggestive but somewhat inconclusive survey of Blake's changing relations to Urizen and its bearing on the critical seventh Night of the *Four Zoas,* see John Sutherland, "Blake and Urizen," in *Blake's Visionary Forms Dramatic,* ed. David V. Erdman and John E. Grant (Princeton, 1970), pp. 244–62.

6. "Analytic of the Sublime," in *Kant's Critique of Aesthetic Judgment,* trans. J. C. Meredith (Oxford, 1911), p. 120.

7. Hegel, *Werke: Vollständige Ausgabe,* ed. D. H. G. Hotho, 18 vols. [actually 21] (Berlin, 1832–45), XI, 483–84; F. P. B. Osmaston, *The Philosophy of Fine Art,* 4 vols. (London, 1920), II, 102–3.

8. See Northrop Frye, "Blake's Reading of the Book of Job," in *William Blake: Essays for S. Foster Damon,* ed. Alvin H. Rosenfeld (Providence, 1969), pp. 221–34.

9. Kant, "Analytic of the Sublime," pp. 113–14.

10. Edmund Burke, *A Philosophical Enquiry into the Origin of Our Ideas of the Sublime and Beautiful,* ed. James T. Boulton (London, 1958), p. 63. Cf. Job 4:13–17.

11. Cf. the view of S. Foster Damon (*Blake's "Job": William Blake's "Illustrations of the Book of Job"* [1966; rpt. New York, 1969], p. 28): "His arms are concealed: he is obliged to reward or punish according to the deserts of mankind."

4. The Logic of Terror

1. For this argument see R. W. Bretall, "Kant's Theory of the Sublime," in *The Heritage of Kant,* ed. George Tapley Whitney and David F. Bowers (Princeton, 1939; rpt. New York, 1962), pp. 379–402.

2. Edmund Burke, *A Philosophical Enquiry into the Origin of Our Ideas of the Sublime and Beautiful,* ed. James T. Boulton (London, 1958), pp. 45, 46. Page references in the text are to this edition.

3. See Boulton's introduction, Burke, *Of the Sublime and Beautiful*, pp. xcix–ciii; Albert Wlecke, *Wordsworth and the Sublime*, (Berkeley and Los Angeles, 1973), pp. 148–49; W. J. B. Owen, "The Sublime and the Beautiful in *The Prelude*," *The Wordsworth Circle*, 4 (Spring 1973), 67–86, and *Wordsworth as Critic* (Toronto, 1969), pp. 203–10 (a report on Wordsworth's unpublished essay on the sublime, designed to preface the *Guide to the Lakes*). The foregoing are among the important additions to S. H. Monk's account of Burke's influence (*The Sublime: A Study of Critical Theories in Eighteenth-Century England* [New York, 1935], pp. 98 ff., 134–63, 204, 228–32).

4. E. R. Dodds, *The Greeks and the Irrational* (Berkeley and Los Angeles, 1951), p. 5; see p. 19, n. 17 for the reading of *Iliad*, 24.480; the whole of chap. 1 is relevant.

5. Pope, *Iliad*, 24.584–603; text from the Twickenham edition of *The Poems of Alexander Pope*, vol. VIII, ed. Maynard Mack (New Haven, 1967), pp. 561–62.

6. Ibid., pp. 561–62.

7. Dodds, *The Greeks and the Irrational*, pp. 28 ff.

8. See Otto Fenichel, *The Psychoanalytic Theory of Neurosis* (New York, 1945), pp. 147–48.

9. "The Economic Problem of Masochism," *The Standard Edition of the Complete Psychological Works of Sigmund Freud*, ed. James Strachy et al., 23 vols. (London, 1953–66), XIX, 169 [with some rephrasing].

10. Friedrich von Schiller, "On the Sublime," in *"Naive and Sentimental Poetry" and "On the Sublime": Two Essays*, trans. Julius A. Elias (New York, 1966), p. 208.

11. Freud, "The Ego and the Id," *Standard Edition*, XIX, 54–55.

12. Fenichel, *Psychoanalytic Theory of Neurosis*, pp. 387–406. See Freud, "Mourning and Melancholia," *Standard Edition*, XIV, 243–58.

13. In the preface (p. 1), however, Longinus is mentioned, and Burke twice uses his examples (pp. 64 and 143).

14. "The Ego and the Id," *Standard Edition*, XIX, 34.

15. "Tintern Abbey," ll. 122–23 (*PWW*, II, 262).

16. See Fenichel, *Psychoanalytic Theory of Neurosis*, pp. 62–63.

5. The Sublime as Romance: Two Texts from Collins

1. *Lives of the English Poets*, Everyman edition, 2 vols. (London, 1925), II, 314–15.

2. Coleridge to John Thelwall, 17 December 1796, *Collected Letters of Samuel Taylor Coleridge*, ed. Earl Leslie Griggs, 4 vols. (Oxford, 1956–1959), I, letter 169, p. 277.

3. See especially Northrop Frye, *Fearful Symmetry: A Study of William Blake* (Princeton, 1947), pp. 169–70; and Harold Bloom, *The Visionary Company: A Reading of English Romantic Poetry*, rev. ed. (Ithaca, N.Y., 1971), pp. 11–14. Earlier identifiers of the youth as the poet include Garrod (1928), Blunden (1929), and Ainsworth (1937).

4. Earl Wasserman, "Collins' 'Ode on the Poetical Character'," *ELH*, 34 (1967), 92–115.

5. A. S. P. Woodhouse, "The Poetry of Collins Reconsidered," in *From Sensibility to Romanticism: Essays Presented to Frederick A. Pottle*, ed. Frederick W. Hilles and Harold Bloom (New York, 1965), pp. 93–137; quotation from Woodhouse's earlier essay, "Collins and the Creative Imagination," in *Studies in English by Members of University College, Toronto*, ed. M. W. Wallace (Toronto, 1931), p. 60.

6. *Letters to Gilbert White of Selborne . . . from Rev. John Mulso* (1907), p. 14; for the episode see Oliver Sigworth, *William Collins* (New York, 1965), pp. 42–43.

7. *Poetics* 11.2, trans. S. H. Butcher, in Butcher, *Aristotle's Theory of Poetry and Fine Art*, 4th ed. (London, 1911), p. 41.

8. Quotations from Collins are from the superb Longmans edition, *The Poems of Thomas Gray, William Collins, Oliver Goldsmith*, ed. Roger Lonsdale (London, 1969). I am indebted to Lonsdale's copious annotation.

9. Otto Fenichel, *The Psychoanalytic Theory of Neurosis* (New York, 1945), p. 215.

10. See Freud, "Introductory Lectures," *The Standard Edition of the Complete Psychological Works of Sigmund Freud*, ed. James Strachey et al., 23 vols. (London, 1953–66), XVI, 369–71; "From the History of an Infantile Neurosis," sect. 4, *Standard Edition*, XVII, 29–47.

11. Fenichel, *Psychoanalytic Theory of Neurosis*, p. 214.

12. Norman Holland, *The Dynamics of Literary Response* (New York, 1968), p. 46.

13. Horace, *Odes* 1.2.2–3; Dryden, *Aeneid* 6. 800–801; Pope, *Odyssey* 12.456; 24.623. See editor's note in Lonsdale, ed., *The Poems of Thomas Gray . . .* , p. 419.

14. "Medusa's Head," *Standard Edition*, XVIII, 273–74.

15. *Oedipus Coloneus*, ll. 1620–28, trans. Robert Fitzgerald, in *The Complete Greek Tragedies: Sophocles I*, ed. D. Grene and R. Lattimore (Chicago, 1954), p. 149.

16. Harry Slochower, *Mythopoesis: Mythic Patterns in the Literary Classics* (Detroit, 1970), pp. 89–90. Slochower is synthesizing the views of Freud, Fromm, Rank, and others.

17. Trans. W. Rhys Roberts, in *The Basic Works of Aristotle*, ed. Richard McKeon (New York, 1941).

18. See the discussion in Butcher, *Aristotle's Theory of Poetry and Fine Art*, chap. 6, esp. pp. 255 ff.

19. Bertrand Bronson, "The Pre-Romantic or Post-Augustan Mode," in *Facets of the Enlightenment: Studies in English Literature and Its Contexts* (Berkeley and Los Angeles, 1968), p. 164.

20. "I Thought of Chatterton, the marvellous Boy, / The sleepless Soul that perished in his pride"; "Resolution and Independence," ll. 43–44 (*PWW*, II, 236).

21. Quotations from Gray, "The Bard: A Pindaric Ode," ll. 19–20; Blake, "To Summer," ll. 6, 13; Coleridge, "Kubla Khan," ll. 49–50; Stevens, "Mrs. Alfred Uruguay" (*Collected Poems*, p. 249).

22. "Remembrance of Collins," ll. 15–16 (*PWW*, I, 41).

23. *PWW*, I, 92–94.

24. *Lives of the English Poets*, II. 314–15.

25. *The Spectator*, ed. Donald F. Bond, 5 vols. (Oxford, 1965), III, 570–71 (no. 419).

26. See Freud, "Family Romances," *Standard Edition*, IX, 237–41.

27. On the subtle opportunities of "belief" in the old romances in the context of Enlightenment sophistication, see Geoffrey Hartman, "False Themes and Gentle Minds," in *Beyond Formalism: Literary Essays, 1958–1970* (New Haven, 1970), pp. 283–97. I am in general indebted to Hartman's subtle formulations, here and throughout *Beyond Formalism*, of the problem of romance.

28. See *The Faerie Queene*, 4.5. 1–20, for the main allusion, but also 4.2. 25–26 and 4.4. 15–16 for the background of the competition, and 5.2. 27–28 for the girdle's ultimate award to the true Florimel, even though it had fit Amoret.

29. Angus Fletcher, *Allegory: The Theory of a Symbolic Mode* (Ithaca, N.Y., 1964), chap. 2, esp. pp. 108–20.

30. William Browne, *Britannia's Pastorals*, 2.1. 984–85, cited by Lonsdale, ed., *The Poems of Thomas Gray . . .* , p. 431.

31. Frye, *Fearful Symmetry*, pp. 169–70; Harold Bloom, *The Visionary Company: A Reading of English Romantic Poetry*, rev. ed. (Ithaca, N.Y., 1971), pp. 11–14; cf. Woodhouse, "The Poetry of Collins Reconsidered" (p. 101); Wasserman, "Collins' 'Ode on the Poetical Character' " (p. 98); and Lonsdale's summary in *The Poems of Thomas Gray . . .* , (p. 432), for the view that only the sun may be found in these lines.

32. Wasserman, "Collins' 'Ode on the Poetical Character'," p. 95 n.

33. *Collected Letters of Samuel Taylor Coleridge*, I, letter 164, p. 279.

34. Wasserman points germanely to the tradition of scriptural commentary in which chastity and the spiritual virtues of the priest-prophet are "the two recurrent categories" which dominate interpretation of the biblical girdle (p. 104).

35. C. S. Lewis, *A Preface to Paradise Lost*, (New York, 1961), p. 49.

36. *Faerie Queene*, 2.8. 5; see also 1.5. 2 for another source of Collins' youth: "And *Phoebus* fresh, as bridegrome to his mate, / came dancing forth, shaking his deawie haire."

6. Absence and Identity in the Egotistical Sublime

1. Hegel, *Werke: Vollstände Ausgabe*, ed. D. H. G. Hotho, 18 vols. [actually 21] (Berlin, 1832–45), XI, 466–85.

2. James Thomson, *The Castle of Indolence*, canto 1, st. 63. Wordsworth composed "Resolution and Independence" on May 4, 7, and 9 (morning), and "Stanzas Written in my Pocket-Copy of Thomson's 'Castle of Indolence'" on May 9 (after tea) and May 11, See *PWW*, II, 470 and 510.

3. Geoffrey Hartman, *The Unmediated Vision: An Interpretation of Wordsworth, Hopkins, Rilke, and Valéry* (New Haven, 1954; rpt. New York, 1966) p. 33.

4. See Richard Onorato, *The Character of the Poet: Wordsworth in "The Prelude,"* (Princeton, 1971).

5. *PWW*, II, 261–62.

6. "Preface" to *Alastor*, in *Shelley: Poetical Works*, ed. Thomas Hutchinson, Oxford Standard Authors (London, 1905; rpt. London, 1967), pp. 14–15. All quotations are from this edition.

7. Freud *Civilization and its Discontents*, *The Standard Edition of the Complete Psychological Works of Sigmund Freud*, ed. James Strachey et al., 23 vols. (London, 1953–66), XXI, 118.

8. Preface to *Alastor*, pp. 14–15.

9. See Anthony Wilden, "Lacan and the Discourse of the Other," in Jacques Lacan, *The Language of the Self: The Function of Language in Psychoanalysis*, trans. Anthony Wilden (Baltimore, 1968), pp. 159–77, and the article on "Mirror Phase" in Laplanche and Pontalis, *The Language of Psycho-analysis*, trans. Donald Nicholson-Smith (London, 1973), pp. 250–52; the basic text in Lacan is "Le Stade du miroir comme formateur de la fonction du Je," in *Ecrits* (Paris, 1966), pp. 93–100.

10. "Meditation II," *The Philosophical Works of Descartes*, trans. Elizabeth Haldane and G. R. T. Ross, 2 vols. (Cambridge, 1911; rpt. 1970), I, 151–52.

11. "Discourse on the Method," in ibid., I, 101.

12. *The Prelude*, p. 633; for MS JJ see pp. xxvi, 633–42 (see chap. 1, n. 52).

13. "Ode: Intimations of Immortality, . . ." ll. 6, 9 (*PWW*, IV, 279).

14. "To Wordsworth," l. 5; *Shelley: Poetical Works*, p. 522.

15. Coleridge, *Biographia Literaria*, ed. J. Shawcross, 2 vols. (Oxford, 1907), I, 202.

16. *Standard Edition*, XIV, 85.

17. J. H. Van den Berg, *The Changing Nature of Man: Introduction to a Historical Psychology (Metabletica)*, trans. H. F. Croes (New York, 1961), p. 235.

18. Harold Bloom, "The Internalization of Quest Romance," in *The Ringers in the Tower: Studies in the Romantic Tradition* (Chicago and London, 1971), p. 18.

19. Van den Berg, *The Changing Nature of Man*, p. 235.

20. *The Problem of Anxiety*, sect. 8, *Standard Edition*, XX, 132–43.

21. "On Narcissism," *Standard Edition*, XIV, 96; cf. pp. 92–102.

22. *Biographia Literaria*, II, 12.

23. Laplanche and Pontalis, *The Language of Psycho-analysis*, p. 257.

7. Wordsworth and the Defile of the Word

1. MS. V, *The Prelude*, p. 39.
2. *The Prelude*, p. 445, *app. crit.*
3. "Screen Memories," *The Standard Edition of the Complete Psychological Works of Sigmund Freud*, ed. James Strachey et al., 23 vols. (London, 1953–66), III, 322.
4. *The Fall of Hyperion*, 1.13–15.
5. Geoffrey Hartman, *Wordsworth's Poetry, 1787–1814* (New Haven, 1964), p. 65.
6. *The Prelude*, p. 163.
7. MS. V, *The Prelude*, p. 447.
8. See M. H. Abrams, "The Correspondent Breeze: A Romantic Metaphor," in *English Romantic Poets: Modern Essays in Criticism*, ed. M. H. Abrams (New York, 1960), pp. 37–54, esp. 40–42.
9. *Hamlet*, 1.4.43–44.
10. See Mary Moorman, *William Wordsworth, a Biography: The Early Years, 1770–1803* (Oxford, 1957), pp. 67–70, esp. 68 n.
11. *PWW*, I, 270–83.
12. *The Prelude*, p. 452.
13. "Repression," *Standard Edition*, XIV, 146–58.
14. See Dorothy's journal entry for Tuesday, February 2, 1802, in *Journals of Dorothy Wordsworth*, ed. Mary Moorman (Oxford, 1972), p. 84: "After tea I read aloud the 11th Book of Paradise Lost. We were much impressed and also melted into tears. The papers came in soon after I had laid aside the Book—a good thing for my William." The theme is finely explored by Neil Hertz, "Wordsworth and the Tears of Adam," *Studies in Romanticism*, 7 (1967), 15–33; reprinted in *Wordsworth: A Collection of Critical Essays*, ed. M. H. Abrams (Englewood Cliffs, N.J., 1972), pp. 107–22.
15. *The Letters of John Keats, 1814–1821*, ed. Hyder Edward Rollins, 2 vols. (Cambridge, Mass., 1958), I, 281.
16. Quotations from *The Fall of Hyperion* 1.78, 287–88.
17. See *PL* 7.163 ff.
18. *PWW*, I, 270.
19. The Simplon sequence is an inevitable occasion in the many discussions of the Wordsworthian imagination and the sublime. The preeminence of Hartman's reading (in *Wordsworth's Poetry*, pp. 39–69) has not in my view been seriously touched by the attempts of subsequent commentators to elide the significance of the Imagination's usurpation at 6.592 ff. My reading is intended to complement Hartman's definition of the Imagination as *"consciousness of self raised to apocalyptic pitch"* (p. 17) by uncovering the dialectical status of that consciousness not only with respect to Nature but also with respect to the symbolic order of Eternity. In one sense this makes Imagination a middle term—for the critic, not for the poet. In another sense the Imagination is the final term of this dialectic, for it follows and responds to an intuition—strangely "traumatic" in Wordsworth—of the Word. At all events, the Imagination must certainly be considered in its dialectical "negativity" if we would attend to what Wordsworth does and what happens to him as well as what he says. Hartman brilliantly and persuasively redefines *apocalyptic* "to characterize any strong desire to cast out nature and to achieve an unmediated contact with the principle of things" (p. x). In the following reading I emphasize the mediating Characters of the great Apocalypse (6.638), which appear to threaten or signify the extinction of self-consciousness as the cost of its identification with the synchronic "principle of things." I therefore neglect the relation of the Imagination to Nature, as I have no fresh light to shed on the problem and no basic objection to Hartman's formulation of it.
20. Max Wildi, "Wordsworth and the Simplon Pass," *English Studies*, 40 (1959), 224–32; see also Wildi's interpretative sequel under the same title, *English Studies*, 43 (1962), 359–77.

21. "Preface to *Poems* (1815)," in *Literary Criticism of William Wordsworth*, ed. Paul M. Zall (Lincoln, Nebr., 1966), p. 149.

22. *The Letters of William and Dorothy Wordsworth*, ed. Ernest De Selincourt, 2d ed., *The Early Years, 1787–1805*, rev. Chester L. Shaver (Oxford, 1967), pp. 33–34.

23. *Macbeth* 2.2.34–36.

24. *Journals of Dorothy Wordsworth*, ed. Ernest De Selincourt, 2 vols. (New York, 1941), II, 258.

25. Wildi, "Wordsworth and the Simplon Pass," p. 232.

26. *PWW*, II, 212. De Selincourt prints "(?1804)" next to the earlier date.

27. Mark L. Reed, *Wordsworth: The Chronology of the Early Years, 1770–1799* (Cambridge, Mass., 1967), pp. 31, 261; see also a reading of the sequence by the same author, "The Speaker of *The Prelude*," in *Bicentenary Wordsworth Studies in Memory of John Alban Finch*, ed. Jonathan Wordsworth (Ithaca, N.Y., 1970), pp. 281–87, esp. p. 286 n. 13.

28. It should be remembered that Wordsworth determined to expand his auto-biographical poem and treat of the Alpine tour only in March, 1804, i.e., about a month before the sequence was written.

29. For Coleridge's tentative and interesting objection to the line (616), see *The Prelude*, p. 559.

Index

The Johns Hopkins University Press

This book was composed in Linotype Palatino text
and foundry Palatino display type by the Maryland
Linotype Composition Co., Inc., from a design
by Susan Bishop. It was printed on 50-lb. Cream
White Bookmark and bound in Joanna Arrestox cloth
by Thomson-Shore, Inc.

Library of Congress Cataloging in Publication Data

Weiskel, Thomas
  The romantic sublime.

  Includes bibliographical references and index.
  1. Sublime, The.   2. Transcendence (Philosophy) I. Title.

BH301.S7W44   128'.3   75-36932
ISBN 0-8018-1770-6